MANAGING
ECONOMIC CRISIS
IN SOUTHEAST ASIA

The **Saw Centre for Quantitative Finance** was established at the National University of Singapore on 1 December 2003. The Centre is named after a distinguished NUS alumnus Professor Saw Swee-Hock, whose generous endowed gift has enabled the founding of this Centre. The Saw Centre is situated within the vibrant community of the renowned NUS Business School.

The Saw Centre's purpose is to conduct quality research, educational activities and training programmes related to the financial services industry in the Asia Pacific region. With the resources of the university and active contribution from industry professionals, it is a resource centre that will benefit both academics and practitioners.

The **Institute of Southeast Asian Studies (ISEAS)** was established as an autonomous organization in 1968. It is a regional centre dedicated to the study of socio-political, security and economic trends and developments in Southeast Asia and its wider geostrategic and economic environment. The Institute's research programmes are the Regional Economic Studies (RES, including ASEAN and APEC), Regional Strategic and Political Studies (RSPS), and Regional Social and Cultural Studies (RSCS).

ISEAS Publishing, an established academic press, has issued more than 2,000 books and journals. It is the largest scholarly publisher of research about Southeast Asia from within the region. ISEAS Publishing works with many other academic and trade publishers and distributors to disseminate important research and analyses from and about Southeast Asia to the rest of the world.

MANAGING
ECONOMIC CRISIS
IN SOUTHEAST ASIA

Edited by
SAW SWEE-HOCK

Saw Centre
for
Quantitative Finance

ISEAS
Institute of Southeast Asian Studies
Singapore

First published in Singapore in 2011 by ISEAS Publishing
Institute of Southeast Asian Studies
30 Heng Mui Keng Terrace
Pasir Panjang
Singapore 119614
E-mail: publish@iseas.edu.sg
Website: http://bookshop.iseas edu.sg

jointly with
Saw Centre for Quantitative Finance
NUS Business School
National University of Singapore
BIZ 2 Building, #04-01
1 Business Link
Singapore 117592

ISEAS Library Cataloguing-in-Publication Data

Managing economic crisis in Southeast Asia / edited by Saw Swee Hock.
    Papers originally presented at a Conference on Managing Economic Crisis in Southeast Asia, 29 January 2010, Singapore, organized by the National University of Singapore, Saw Centre for Quantitative Finance and Institute of Southeast Asian Studies.
    1.   Global Financial Crisis, 2008-2009—Congresses.
    2.   Financial crises—Southeast Asia—Congresses.
    3.   Southeast Asia—Economic conditions—21st century—Congresses.
    I.   Saw, Swee-Hock, 1931–
    II. National University of Singapore.
    III. Saw Centre for Quantitative Finance.
    IV. Institute of Southeast Asian Studies.
    V.   Conference on Managing Economic Crisis in Southeast Asia (2010 : Singapore)
HB3812 C74   2011

ISBN 978-981-4311-23-6 (soft cover)
ISBN 978-981-4311-79-3 (hard cover)
ISBN 978-981-4311-24-3 (e-book PDF)

Typeset by Superskill Graphics Pte Ltd
Printed in Singapore by Seng Lee Press Pte Ltd

Contents

List of Tables

List of Figures

Preface

In January 2010, the Institute of Southeast Asian Studies (ISEAS) and the Saw Centre for Quantitative Finance, NUS Business School, jointly organized the International Conference on Managing Economic Crisis in Southeast Asia. The seven papers included in this book consist of a selection of the papers presented in the conference, and subsequently revised for publication. Chapter 1 was specifically written by the volume editor to highlight the more salient features of the similar as well as different approaches adopted by the countries to combat the global financial crisis that impacted the region.

I would like to thank the chapter writers for their excellent cooperation for presenting the papers in the conference and, more importantly, for revising the papers for publication. My thanks also go to Mrs Triena Ong of ISEAS Publications Unit for overseeing the expeditious publication of the book.

Saw Swee-Hock

The Contributors

Muhammad Chatib Basri is a Senior Lecturer in the Faculty of Economics and Research Associate at the Institute of Economic and Social Research, University of Indonesia. He also serves as a special advisor to the Minister for Finance of the Republic of Indonesia. His research interests are in international trade, macroeconomics, and political economy. He is co-editor of *Indonesia Business in Indonesia: New Challenges and Old Problems*. He received his Ph.D. in economics from the Australian National University.

Suthiphand Chirathivat is Associate Professor of Economics at the Faculty of Economics, Chulalongkorn University. He was former Dean of the Faculty of Economics as well as Chairman of the Economic Research Centre. He is Advisor to the Ministry of Foreign Affairs and is a Member of the Thailand's Committee on International Economic Policy. He is co-editor of *East Asian's Monetary Future: Integration in the Global Economy*. He received his Ph.D. in economics from Université de Paris 1 Panthéon-Sorbonne.

K. K. Foong is a Senior Research Fellow at the Malaysian Institute of Economic Research. His research interests include the evolution of the financial sector, economic growth, and econometrics. He has previously worked at the Central Bank of Malaysia. He has served as a consultant to many international organizations. He obtained his Ph.D. in finance and economics from the University of Melbourne.

Srinivasa Madhur is Senior Director in the Office of Regional Economic Integration at the Asian Development Bank. He has served as Economic Advisor to several ministries in the Government of India. He also served as a Member of the Economic Advisory Council to the Indian Prime Minister. He was a Fulbright Fellow at the Department of Economics, Yale University. He obtained his Ph.D. in economics from the Delhi School of Economics.

Ruperto P. Majuca is a Senior Research Fellow at the Philippine Institute for Development Studies. His research interests are in the areas of macroeconomics, monetary economics, and applied time series. He was a Fulbright Scholar at the University of Illinois at Urbana-Champaign where he obtained his Ph.D. in economics.

Sothitorn Mallikamas is in the Faculty of Economics at Chulalongkorn University. He was the Dean of the Faculty of Economics from 2005 to 2008. His research interests are in economic and financial liberalization and regional economic integration. He received his Ph.D. in economics from the University of Wisconsin-Madison.

Nguyen Anh Duong is a Researcher at the Department for Macroeconomic Policy and Integration Studies, Central Institute for Economic Management. His research interests are in econometric forecasts, trade policy, and monetary policy. He has a M.A. degree in economics from the Australian National University.

Saw Swee-Hock is Professorial Fellow at the Institute of Southeast Asian Studies and President's Honorary Professor of Statistics at the National University of Singapore. He is also an Honorary Fellow of the London School of Economics and Honorary Professor at the University of Hong Kong and Xiamen University. He is a Member of the Board of Trustees of the National University of Singapore. His publications are mainly on statistics, demography and finance. Among his major publications are *Investment Management* (Fifth Edition), *Sovereign Wealth Funds* (co-author), *Introduction to Islamic Finance* (co-author), *ASEAN-China Economic Relations* (editor) and *Managing Economic Crisis in East Asia* (co-editor). He received his Ph.D. in statistics from the London School of Economics.

Tan Chwee Huat is Professorial Fellow at the Department of Management and Organization, NUS Business School, National University of Singapore. His research interests include human capital management and employment relations. His main publications are *Personal Finance in Singapore, Financing for Entrepreneurs and Business, Financial Services in Singapore, Financial Markets and Institutions, Singapore and Hong Kong as Competing Financial Centres* (co-author) and *Managing Financial Crisis in Singapore*. He obtained his Ph.D. from the University of Wisconsin-Madison.

Vo Tri Thanh is Vice-President of the Central Institute for Economic Management. His research interests are in trade and international economic integration policies, monetary policy and fiscal policy. He has published *Vietnam's Export to EU: An Overview and Assessment Using CMS-based*

Approach. He obtained his Ph.D. in economics from the Australian National University.

Joseph Yap is President of the Philippine Institute for Development Studies. He is also the regional coordinator of the East Asian Development Network. His research interests are in the areas of macroeconomic policy, applied econometrics, and regional economic integration in East Asia. He is co-author of *The Philippine Economy: East Asia's Stray Cat? Structure, Finance and Adjustment.* He received his Ph.D. in economics from the University of the Philippines.

1
The Global Financial Crisis: Impact and Response in Southeast Asia

Saw Swee-Hock

Introduction

The global financial crisis, started in the summer of 2007 in the United States, triggered the greatest post-World War II economic recession that spread rapidly to all parts of the world. The ensuing shocks to the international financial system severely disrupted credit plans and dislocated economic activity everywhere. Though the financial sector in Southeast Asia was spared the more serious repercussions of the sub-prime crisis, the resultant economic recession was experienced in the region as exports of raw materials and manufactured products took a sharp downturn as external demand shrank. The countries in the region had experienced considerable damage during the Asian financial crisis in 2008–09, and have implemented many important and necessary reforms which have placed the countries in a good position to overcome the latest global economic crisis.

Economic growth had been moving on a satisfactory path throughout the region in recent years, but was severely disrupted by the economic recession. Some countries experienced a marked slowdown in their economic growth in 2008 and 2009, while the others even recorded a contraction as the impact of the recession became more serious. Businesses were affected by shrinking demand and unemployment rose to record levels in most countries. The governments in the region acted swiftly by putting in place significant stimulus packages designed to prop up the damaged sectors and to stem the rise in unemployment. By and large, the bold policy responses have enabled the countries to prevent the economic downturn from worsening and to permit the normal trajectory of economic growth to resume expeditiously. With the economic recovery well on track, the countries might have to move on to the next stage of how and when to start unwinding the stimulus packages.

Origin of Financial Crisis

The root of the financial crisis that started in the United States can be traced to the method of mortgage loans offered by financial institutions to home buyers. The normal procedure is for the lenders to go through a standard process of due diligence by verifying the status of the borrowers' income and assets to ensure that they are in a good position to pay the regular mortgage payments. During the period of housing boom engendered by prolonged low interest rates and easily-available loans, the lenders became extremely lenient in extending loans even to borrowers who did not satisfy the prime credit requirements. Some mortgage loans were recklessly provided to so-called "NINJA" borrowers known to have no job, no income, and no asset at all. More importantly, the explosion of sub-prime loans due to lax lending occurred at a time when the U.S. Government, for mainly political reasons, was actively encouraging home ownership.

The beginning of the sub-prime crisis seemed to have emerged sometime in 2006 when the Federal Reserve Bank (the Fed) began to up interest rates to combat the growing inflationary pressure. This rising cost of servicing mortgage loans led to many home owners encountering great difficulty in making their regular mortgage payments. When home value appreciates due to rising prices, the borrowers could circumvent the unfriendly interest rate environment by refinancing the original loans on more favourable terms. On the other hand, when the home value started to tumble during the market slump, refinancing was almost impossible. This led to increased defaults in mortgage payments, and eventually to foreclosures becoming rather common. In fact, 1.3 million homes were foreclosed in 2007 in the United States as compared to about 0.65 million during the period 2001–05.

There was another phenomenon that had contributed to the emergence of the sub-prime crisis, and this refers to the common practice of securitization of the mortgage loans. To make more funds available to home buyers, the banks bundled the loans together and repackaged them as new securities known as Collaterized Debt Obligations (CDOs). These derivative products based on mortgage-backed loans were then sold to investors, mostly investment banks, at very attractive terms. The investors were attracted by the better returns of the securitized CDOs and the relatively higher ratings accorded by rating agencies. There is also the perception that the CDOs were quite safe since they were secured by properties pledged as collateral by the borrowers. The additional funds raised from the sale of CDOs enabled the banks to provide more mortgage loans to primarily sub-prime borrowers.

When the sub-prime borrowers could not make their regular mortgage payments, banks had no choice but to foreclose the properties at values much lower than at the time of purchase by the borrowers. The losses incurred by the borrowers and the lenders contributed to a further downward spiral in the housing market. The value of the CDOs collaterized on the mortgage loans tumbled swiftly, or even became worthless, and the investors ceased to receive payment from the banks. In fact, it was the sub-prime mortgages that eventually led to the massive losses incurred by the holders of CDOs, and even to bankruptcy in cases where the investment banks have devoted an enormous proportion of their business to CDOs.

The final step in the sequence of events starting with the original sub-prime loans refers to the practice of Credit Default Swap (CDS). The investment banks were not unaware of the risk involved in buying CDOs upon which they used to issue derivative bonds. To deal with the possibility of these bonds defaulting, the investment banks bought insurance cover from insurance companies by making fixed periodic payments or premiums. Under this Credit Default Swap (CDS) arrangement, the insurance companies would guarantee to reimburse the investment banks any losses when the bond issuer defaulted. There are instances when the insurance companies were unable to make good these losses because they had insufficient funds to defray the huge losses arising from their massive holding of CDSs. To these insurance companies, bankruptcy became a real option.

Impact on Financial Institutions

The sub-prime problem has weighed heavily on the U.S. financial markets, resulting in permanent declines in valuation across many asset classes amidst rapid deterioration of the financial environment. Among the insurance companies that suffered massive loans by participating in the CDS arrangement was the giant American International Group (AIG). While the core insurance business of AIG was essentially sound and profitable, the same cannot be said of one of its subsidiaries which had been issuing voluminous amounts of CDSs to offer protection against losses from CDOs based on mortgage loans.

The rapid fall in home values resulting from a collapse of the property market had triggered a chain reaction that inflicted huge losses on AIG. In the last quarter of 2008 alone, it suffered a loss of US$62 billion, the biggest quarterly loss in U.S. corporate history. To limit the potential damage to the financial system, the U.S. Government came to the rescue with an infusion of US$30 billion into AIG, aside from the earlier bailout funds of US$150 billion, to prevent the company from going bankrupt. In the end, the U.S. Government was left owning some 79.9 per cent of the company's equity. Undoubtedly, the global insurance industry would have faced a great catastrophe if AIG were to be allowed to go bust. This is a good example of too big to be allowed to fail.

It was inevitable for the sub-prime mortgages to exert such a great impact on Freddie Mac and Fannie Mae, the government-sponsored enterprises entrusted with providing the much-needed finance to home buyers. They bought the mortgage loans from lenders and repackaged the mortgages and sold them as mortgage-backed loans to investors. The sharp rise in loan defaults by home owners during the property slum led to enormous losses and imminent bankruptcy. To restore some semblance of financial stability and confidence in the market, the U.S. Government nationalized these two companies. About US$1 million preferred shares in each company was acquired by the U.S. Treasury. In addition, more stringent controls were introduced governing capital requirements, portfolio holdings, and acquisition of exotic loan products. In an attempt to provide more businesses to these two ailing companies, they were permitted to extend loans to buyers of more expensive houses and to hold less cash in treasury.

The sub-prime housing bubble had inflicted tremendous strain on investment banks, particularly those which had been purchasing vast amount of CDOs and CDSs. One of them was Bear Stearns which was holding a large quantity of these financial products. As expected, it posted big losses, and by March 2008 did not have sufficient funds to open for business. It had to approach J.P. Morgan for a big loan, and it was eventually agreed that the latter would undertake to guarantee US$29 billion for potential losses. The U.S. Government was also forced to come in with an exposure limited to US$29 billion. With the infusion of new capital, Bear Stearns was able to resume normal business.

The other venerable investment bank, Lehman Brothers, was not so lucky when it suffered massive losses during the sub-prime crisis. Without the injection of additional working capital from other financial institutions and/or the U.S. Government, it came as no surprise that Lehman Brothers should file for bankruptcy on 15 September 2008. The collapse of such an important institution disrupted the smooth functioning of the entire financial market in the United States and other countries where Lehman Brothers had a significant presence. For sure, the financial environment in Singapore was rocked by the collapse of Lehman Brothers, with the Lehman Minibond Notes and other structured products becoming worthless to many individual investors.

A somewhat different path was undertaken by the two investment banks, Morgan Stanley and Goldman Sachs, which have taken a serious beating by the sub-prime crisis. In an attempt to save themselves, they have chosen to convert into commercial banks to enable them to accept deposits to boost their capitalization. In adopting this survival strategy, the two newly converted banks had to accept the prohibition of dealing in unfamiliar derivative products and credit instruments that caused them to get into trouble in the first place. Like other commercial banks, they were subjected to stricter level of control and surveillance and by a lower leverage ratio of assets-to-borrowing.

Aside from insurance companies and investment banks, some commercial banks were exposed to the financial disruption, with smaller unknown banks declaring bankruptcy. The big banks, exerting a pre-eminent influence in the U.S. economy, were just not allowed to go bust, and even encouraged to receive financial aid from the U.S. Government. Among the nineteen banks that secured government aid was the Bank of America which received US$25 billiion in late 2008 and a further US$20 billion in the following year. The infusion of capital came from the U.S. Government bailout fund known as Troubled Asset Relief Program (TARP).

TARP was a special plan established by the U.S. Government to curb the financial turmoil by taking over troubled mortgages held by financial institutions. Armed with an initial sum of US$250 billion, the U.S. Treasury was authorized to buy and sell the mortgages, and to use the profits to purchase more assets. This enabled the initial function to be enlarged to US$350 billion. Financial institutions that took advantage of the facilities offered by TARP were able to lower their debt-to-capital ratio, and were therefore more willing to resume lending to consumers, businesses, and other banks. This rescue plan succeeded in injecting greater liquidity into the financial system, although the government loans were expected to be paid back in due course. What has also happened is that the U.S. Government has become a major shareholder of the participating institutions.

Not surprisingly, the negative impact of the sub-prime loans was quickly felt in Europe because of the close links among the major financial institutions across the Atlantic. Many financial institutions in Europe had to be bailed out by their respective governments, while others had to file for bankruptcy. In Britain, Northern Rock was the first to suffer a bank run in the autumn of 2007 when some £1 billion, or 5 per cent of its deposits, was withdrawn in one day on 14 September. The Bank of England stepped in to provide an emergency funding of about £26 billion, which in reality meant that the bank was being nationalized by the British Government. This was followed by a comprehensive bailout plan designed to provide extra capital, greater deposit insurance, more loan guarantees, and repurchase of securities. The British plan, with some modifications, was adopted by many European countries to weather the financial tsunami that was deepening and spreading relentlessly. Clearly, the governments would have to continue to improve and streamline their regulatory and supervisory regimes.

Economic Recession in Southeast Asia

The turmoil engendered by the sub-prime loans was felt in almost every sector of the economy, and swiftly developed into the worst global economic recession since the Great Depression in the 1930s. In the United States, particularly affected were the housing market, the car industry, manufacturing and retail trade, resulting in a drastic reduction in demand for imported goods. As the U.S. economy deteriorated and shrank, unemployment rose to unprecedented level. In an interdependent globalized world, the economic recession originating in the United States quickly spilled over into almost every part of the world. Countries that have built their economic system with great emphasis on export-orientated activities have been affected more severely as the demand for their products in the West collapsed.

Although Southeast Asia escaped the initial shock as its financial institutions did not hold much toxic assets, the region was pummelled by the sharp drop in external demand from the developed countries. Suddenly, the economies of some countries grew at a slower rate, while the others even contracted as the global demand for their raw materials and/or manufactured goods fell dramatically. Many businesses barely survived and others went into receivership. Unemployment rose sharply as workers lost their jobs when companies began to downsize their workforce or went bankrupt. New jobs were of course scarce during recessionary period. As expected, there was considerable differences in the severity of the economic recession among the ten countries in the region.

At the height of the recession in 2009, negative growth was indeed experienced by Thailand (–2.2 per cent), Cambodia (–2.0 per cent), Malaysia (–1.7 per cent), Singapore (–1.3 per cent) and Brunei (–1.2 per cent). The prolonged political unrest in Thailand, accompanied by a steep decline in tourist arrivals, has undoubtedly contributed to the worst recession recorded in the region. As for the oil-state of Brunei, the economic contraction can be attributed mainly to the fall in the value of exports due to the drop in the price of oil. The economies of the other five countries managed to expand in 2009, but at a much reduced pace. Fortunately, for the region, the Indonesian economy, anchored essentially by domestic demand, fared quite well with 4.5 per cent growth. So did the relatively closed economy of Myanmar with 4.4 per cent, and Vietnam with 5.3 per cent. Due to the sharp reduction in remittances from its overseas workers, the Philippines did not do so well, registering only a small growth of 0.9 per cent.

The immediate response to the economic recession from the countries in the region took the form of significant monetary and fiscal stimulus aimed at supporting domestic demand and paving the way for an early recovery. Fortunately, the past reforms undertaken during the Asian financial crisis of 1997–98 have provided many ASEAN nations the monetary and fiscal space to ease liquidity and pump-prime the local economy. The various stimulus programmes could therefore be more effective in allowing the economy to weather the recession and to perform better than one can possibly expect in 2009. The continuation of the economic expansion in early 2010 seems to suggest that a V-shaped recovery is a distinct possibility, with however some variation in the exact timing of the recovery among the countries in the region.

One should not forget that the economic recovery was, to some extent, made possible by the improving external environment in the developed countries most affected by the sub-prime loans. Indeed, the various stimulus measures implemented in the developed countries have stabilized the financial markets, and thus permitting the recovery to be sustained and widespread. China and Japan, the region's biggest trading partners, have registered satisfactory growth in the last quarter of 2009, and poised for stronger growth in 2010. The brighter outlook for the global economy, coupled with the effective local stimulus, will see all the countries in ASEAN experiencing better growth in 2010 and beyond, albeit at a slower pace as compared to the pre-crisis period.

In examining the experience of the individual countries in the region, we have decided to focus on those important countries more influenced by the global financial crisis. These countries have responded decisively by implementing diverse but significant stimulus packages to revive their battered economies. The more important objectives of the stimulus were to help the suffering businessmen, reduce unemployment, and minimising individual hardships among citizens most affected by the economic slump. The countries that are not covered in this book are Myanmar, Cambodia and Laos, which are the least developed economies primary dependent on domestic demand. Also excluded is the tiny nation of Brunei whose economy is dominated by the oil industry.

Country Experience

We will begin with the city-state of Singapore which has the most open economy with a significant financial sector and a high-end manufacturing industry churning out products for the world market. Against the backdrop of the global economic recession, the economy of Singapore started to contract in late 2008 on account of its manufacturing, transport, logistic and external trade closely linked to global and regional trade flows. It is not surprising that the impact of the crisis on the real economy proved to be quite damaging culminating in a slow growth of 1.8 per cent in 2008 and a negative growth of 1.3 per cent in 2009.

The collapse of Lehman Brothers devalued all the Lehman related structured products marketed in Singapore, with huge losses incurred by retail investors. There is apparently some mis-selling of these products such as Lehman Minibond Notes, DBS High Notes, Jubilee Notes and Pinnacle Notes. The Monetary Authority of Singapore (MAS) intervened and investigated the sale of these products by ten financial institutions. The outcome was a ban imposed on the sale of the products by the institutions for periods ranging from six to twenty-four months, the length of which depended on the extent of mis-selling. Furthermore, the institutions were encouraged to compensate their clients saddled with troubled loans, and investors were given the opportunity to channel their grievances to the newly-established Financial Industry Dispute Resolution Centre.

As for the wider issue of tackling the economic recession, the Singapore Government responded swiftly by implementing a wide range of stimulus measures. By far the most significant programme was the S$20.5 billion Resilience Package presented in the 2009 Budget in February of the year. The key aims of the stimulus were to assist badly damaged companies to stay afloat and to save jobs in the midst of deteriorating employment condition. On the whole, the stimulus has succeeded in preventing a further worsening of recession and in engendering a quick and robust recovery. The financial crisis in Singapore, as in other countries, was influenced not only by the sub-prime mortgages, but also by the failure of some proper supervision and regulation of the financial system. In this respect, some remedial measures were introduced in Singapore.

The chapter on Malaysia presents a detailed account of the performance of the economy during the period 2007–09. The Malaysian economy expanded by a healthy 6.2 per cent in 2007, but by a lower pace of 4.6 per cent in 2008. In fact, the quarterly figures for the latter year has already pointed to a clear downturn of the economy, progressive lower rates of 7.4, 6.6, 4.8 and 0.1 per cent in the respective four quarters. This downtrend continued into 2009 when the economic recession first emerged with the economy contracting by 6.2 per cent in the first quarter. This was followed by better figures of −3.9 per cent and −1.2 per cent in the next two quarters. Other aspects of the economy such as industrial production, tourism, international trade, domestic and foreign investments, inflation and external reserves were also examined in the chapter.

The quick response of the Malaysian Government to the economic recession took the form of monetary and fiscal stimulus programmes. A RM700 million stimulus package was implemented to create some 163,000 training and job placement opportunities in the public and private sectors. One component of the package was a RM50 million worth of modular training for workers wishing to upgrade their skills. All these measures served as a useful buffer to the depressed labour market.

Another component of the stimulus package was the liberalization of twenty-seven services sub-sectors in April 2009 for foreign investors to make up the shortage of local capital and expertise. Among the sub-sectors opened up were computer and related services, health services, tourism, transport and shipping. To reinforce this measure, the 30 per cent Bumiputra equity requirement for newly-listed companies was abolished with effect from June 2009 to create a less oppressive environment for investors. In regard to taxation, the personal income tax was reduced from 27.0 per cent to 26.0 per cent in 2010. Individual relief and deduction were also increased for the same year.

The financial sector of Thailand has escaped the more serious negative impact of the sub-prime loans. This is because the Asian financial crisis of 1997–98 has forced the Thai Government to introduce many important reforms.

Consequently, the Thai banks have adopted a conservative strategy by not exposing themselves to risky foreign assets and non-performing loans. Their capitalization and liquidity remained essentially intact during the current global financial crisis. However, the real economy could not escape being damaged by the economic recession that inflicted the whole world. In the first place, the steep fall in external demand led to a massive contraction of total trade, by 19.7 per cent in 2009. The detailed quarterly figures for the year revealed a steep decline of 28.7, 29.7 and 22.9 per cent in the first three quarters respectively, with a small rise of 6.1 per cent in the fourth quarter. Mainly because of this unfavourable trend, the economy contracted by 2.3 per cent in 2009 as compared with a positive growth of 2.5 per cent in the previous year. Unlike the other countries in the region, there was the extensive political unrest that inflicted considerable damage to the Thai economy.

Two stimulus packages were implemented by the Thai Government. Stimulus Package I, amounting to 117 billion baht, was introduced in March 2009 to encourage more consumption and to mitigate the hardships of the people. They, especially the low income earners and senior citizens, were given special allowances, free utilities, and free travel on bus and train. With the aim of assisting home buyers, real estate developers, building material producers, and construction workers, the income tax deduction for home buyers was raised from 100,000 billion baht to 300,000 billion baht and the tax rate on property transfer and registration was also lowered. Pump-primary infrastructure projects such as road building, canal development and water projects were started, particularly in the rural areas.

In mid-2009, the Abhisit Vejjajiva Government decided to introduce Stimulus Package 2 with the specific objective of promoting long-term economic development. This second package consisted of a 1.43 trillion baht for the three-year period 2010–12 to be utilized to fund important infrastructure projects. The total sum was divided into 1.11 trillion baht meant for government projects and 321 trillion baht for state-owned enterprise investment projects. In a way, the objective of the second package was intended to remedy the inadequate funding for infrastructure development in the past. The lack of good infrastructures has been a major bottleneck in the economic development of the country.

Vietnam did not dip into recession during the current global economic crisis. What happened was that its predominantly agricultural economy continued to expand, though at a slower rate. The annual growth rate was lowered from 8.5 per cent in 2007 to 6.2 per cent in 2008 and 5.3 per cent in 2009. In the main, the growth of the economy has been driven by domestic consumption rather than external demand. In responding to the economic slowdown, the Vietnamese Government has therefore placed greater emphasis on encouraging domestic activities and consumption. First, there was the easing of the monetary policy. The required reserve ratio was lowered significantly from 10 per cent to 3 per cent in March 2009. The base interest rate was slashed from 13 per cent to 7 per cent in February 2009, remaining unchanged until November 2009 when it was raised to 8 per cent. The exchange rate policy was implemented in a more flexible manner. Consequently, the official interbank exchange rate was gradually adjusted upward, and the band for exchange rate was widened from

2 per cent to 3 per cent in November 2008, and eventually to 5 per cent in March 2009.

A stimulus package worth some VND145.6 billion, about US$8 billion, was implemented by the Vietnamese Government. The four main components in the package are interest rate subsidy for current capital loans, state development investments, exemption, reduction and deferral of taxes, and other expenditures to strengthen social safety. The positive outcome of the government anti-recession programmes is reflected in the continuous improvement in the quarterly GNP figures for 2009. The quarterly growth registered an improvement from 2.1 per cent in the first quarter to 4.5 in the second quarter, 5.8 in the third and 7.8 in the fourth.

As in the case of Vietnam, the Philippines did not experience a recession but suffered a greater slowdown in economic growth. The relatively small financial sector was little affected by the sub-prime mortgages, but the real economy was subjected to a reduction in exports as external demand shrank and a drop in remittances from its overseas workers. In the Philippines, remittances constitute an extremely high proportion of GDP, about 10 per cent. The quarterly figures for GDP show a clear downward movement, being reduced from 4.6 per cent in the third quarter of 2008 to 2.9 per cent in the last quarter. Further deterioration was witnessed in 2009, moving to the low of 0.4 per cent in the third quarter. For the whole year, the Philippines economy just managed to expand by 0.9 per cent.

In January 2009, the Philippine Government launched a P330 billion fiscal stimulus programme known as the Economic Policy Plan. Under this plan, there were the community-level infrastructure and social welfare, large infrastructure projects, tax cuts for individuals and companies, and additional social welfare benefits. The Philippine Central Bank cut interest rate six times, and the reserve requirement was slashed by 2 percentage points to maintain liquidity. Other measures meant to help the more vulnerable sectors were implemented, 50 per cent reduction in wharfage fees for exporters, introduction of flexible work arrangement, rapid assistance to laid-off workers, and expansion of the social protection programme.

The last chapter on Indonesia highlights the major differences in the 1997–98 Asian financial crisis and the recent 2008–09 financial crisis in so far as the local economy is concerned. In the first crisis, monetary policy was rather tight with very high interest rates, a fixed exchange rate regime, and a weak banking system. Financial reforms instituted since then meant that in the latest crisis the easing of monetary policy was possible, with interest rate lowered, a flexible exchange rate system, a healthy banking, and more importantly, an expansionary fiscal policy. Consequently, the country was better poised to withstand the onslaught of the global economic crisis. Another factor working in favour of Indonesia was the relatively low value of export to GDP, and its share of the intra-ASEAN trade has always been rather small.

The huge domestic demand was able to insulate the economy from the ravages of the global recession. Over the years, Indonesia has in fact increased its share of domestic demand in GDP to the high of 97 per cent in 2008 from 88 per cent in 2000. Unlike the other governments in Southeast Asia, the Indonesian Government did not face the necessity of implementing massive stimulus packages. Even so, the economy continued to expand at a fairly healthy pace, chalking up a reasonable growth rate of 4.5 per cent in 2009, just a slight dip from the 6.0 per cent in the previous year. This can be considered as a good sign for the whole region since Indonesia is the largest and most important country in Southeast Asia.

Road to Economic Recovery

The authors were required to submit their chapters for publication by March 2010, and were in a way handicapped by the paucity of more up-to-date data to comment on the possibility and nature of the economic recovery in their own country. This chapter was completed in early July 2010, and the writer had more time to look at the latest available information to reflect on the main features of the economic recovery in the region. The most up-to-date statistics seem to suggest that the economies that went into a deep recession have bottomed out, and a clear recovery has started in late 2009 in some countries, or, at the latest, in early 2010 in the other countries. In 2010, the first quarter growth reached 16.9 per cent in Singapore, 12.0 per cent in Thailand, 10.1 per cent in Malaysia, 7.3 per cent in the Philippines and 5.7 per cent in Indonesia. The economic outlook for the region in 2010 will be very bright.

These countries have indeed rebounded very strongly with green shoots pointing to a V-shaped or, at worst, a U-shaped recovery. This development can be attributed to two sets of factors: the first was the immediate and significant stimulus programmes adopted by the countries and the second was the marked improvement in the international economic environment brought about by the decisive steps undertaken by the developed countries. Southeast Asia has also benefitted by the resilience of the Chinese economy which has performed remarkably well during the global recession, achieving even a high of 10.5 per cent growth in 2009. For the same reasons, the other countries in the region that did not dip into recession began to experience faster growth again. A double-dip recession is quite unlikely to occur in any of the countries in the region, though in the United States and Britain, there has been increasing talk about the possibility of such an event taking place.

The global economic crisis that hit all the countries in Southeast Asia has underlined the problem of having an economy too dependent on external demand that is beyond their control. The countries have to pay greater attention on the necessity to boost local and regional demand to continue to drive their economies in the years ahead. The task is made more urgent by the increasing emphasis on greater savings and less consumption in the United States and Europe, leading to less imports from the developing economies. What it means is that the countries can no longer depend primarily or solely on the old export-oriented development strategy to drive their economic growth.

The region should therefore redouble its efforts to pursue mutually-beneficial free trade agreements and other areas of regional cooperation to stimulate demand and promote economic development. In this respect, lies the significance of the Chiang-Mai Initiative launched towards the end of 2009 to strengthen regional cooperation. Indeed, the integration of the economies in the ASEAN region has become more significant and urgent in light of the recent economic recession. Southeast Asia has emerged somewhat stronger from the economic crisis, and, with greater economic integration, sustained rapid growth will be possible in the years ahead.

REFERENCES

Bamber, Bill and Andrew Spencer. *Bear Trap: The Fall of Bear Sterns and the Panic of 2008*. New York: Brick Tower Press, 2008.

Bonner, William and Addison Wiggin. *Financial Reckoning Day Fallout*. New Jersey: John Wiley, 2009.

Brummer, Alex. *The Crunch: How Great and Incompetence Sparked the Credit Crisis*. London: Random House, 2009.

Carney, Richard, ed. *Lessons from the Asian Financial Crisis*. New York: Routledge, 2008.

Cooper, George. *The Origin of Financial Crisis*. New York: Vintage Book, 2008.

Eichengreen, Barry. *Capital Flows and Crisis*. Cambridge: MIT Press, 2003.

Faber, David. *And Then the Roof Caved In: How Wall Street's Greed and Stupidity Brought Capitalism to Its Knees*. Hoboken: John Wiley, 2009.

Foster, John Bellomy and Fred Magdoff. *The Regulatory Responses to the Financial Crisis: Causes and Consequences*. New York: Monthly Review Press, 2009.

Goodhart, Charles A.E. *The Regulatory Response to the Financial Crisis*. Cheltenbam: Edward Elgar, 2009.

Kelly, Fate. *Street Fighters: The Last TZ House of Bear Stern*. New York: Penguin Group, 2009.

Kindleberger, Charles P. *Manias, Panics and Crashes: A History of Financial Crisis*. New York: Wiley, 2000.

Lim Mah Hui and Lim Chin. *Nowhere To Hide: The Great Financial Crisis and Challenges for Asia.* Singapore: Institute of Southeast Asian Studies, 2010.

Muolo, Paul. *$700 Billion Bailout: The Emergency Economic Stabilization Act.* New Jersey: John Wiley, 2009.

O'Brien, J. *Engineering A Financial Bloodbath: How Subprime Securitization Destroyed the Legitimacy of Financial Capitalism.* London: Imperial College Press, 2009.

Png, Ivan, ed. *Financial Crisis 2008.* Singapore: Saw Centre for Financial Studies, NUS, 2008.

Posner, Richard A. *A Failure of Capitalism: The Crisis of 2008 and the Descent into Depression.* Cambridge: Harvard University Press, 2009.

Ritholtz, Barry. *Bailout Nation: How Greed and Easy Money Corrupted Wall Street and Shook the World Economy.* Hoboken: John Wiley, 2009.

Roberts, Lawrence. *The Great Housing Bubble: Why Did House Prices Fall?* Las Vegas: Monetary Cypress Publishing, 2008.

Saw Swee-Hock and John Wong, eds. *Managing Economic Crisis in East Asia.* Singapore: Institute of Southeast Asian Studies, 2010.

Shiller, Robert. *The Subprime Solution: How Today's Global Financial Crisis Happened and What to Do About It.* Princeton: Princeton University Press, 2008.

2
Global Crisis and ASEAN: Impact, Outlook and Policy Priorities

Srinivasa Madhur

Introduction

The 2008/09 global financial and economic crisis severely affected the Association of Southeast Asian Nations (ASEAN). Although the region was spared much of the initial shock — as it held little of the "toxic" assets that spawned the financial turmoil — it suffered as the real economic effects pummelled the region. External demand, which drives a good portion of the region's substantial raw material and manufacturing exports, tumbled dramatically. Firms scrambled to adapt, and the result was major layoffs and disruption of the region's supply chains and production networks — the hallmark of the ASEAN's rapid growth since the recovery from the 1997/98 Asian financial crisis.

The region responded swiftly with significant monetary and fiscal stimulus supporting domestic demand and paving the way for an early recovery. The reforms following the

1997/98 crisis allowed most ASEAN countries the monetary and fiscal space required to ease liquidity and pump prime economic activity. This combined stimulus allowed ASEAN to weather the global downturn and perform better than expected in 2009. And it bodes well for a V-shaped recovery into 2010, although with significant variance across the region's ten economies.

Coupled with an improving external environment, the swift policy response has added substantial traction to the region's recovery. Over the last few months, recovery in advanced economies has broadened and global financial markets have stabilized. ASEAN's two biggest trading partners, Japan and China, grew strongly in the final quarter of 2009 and the first quarter of 2010. External demand is poised to return as recovery in advanced economies gather pace. The improved outlook for the global economy combined with aggressive policy rate cuts and prompt fiscal stimulus have clearly benefited ASEAN economies.

This chapter explores the impact of the crisis on ASEAN, the region's growth prospects, and policy issues — both short- and long-term — that can make the recovery both sustainable and more inclusive. First, we discuss the external environment facing the region and second, the prospects over the short term. Third, we examine ASEAN's integration imperative — why it is so important for ASEAN to integrate. And finally, we look into the longer-term issues that need to be addressed now: the importance of the ASEAN Economic Community (AEC), bridging development gaps between members, and escaping the middle income trap that has affected many developing middle income countries.

External Environment

Advanced economies are beginning to emerge from the worst recession since World War II. Global financial markets have stabilized, credit has eased, and public confidence in the financial system is gradually returning. G3 economies have turned the corner (see Figure 2.1). For example, there are indications that the decline in imports in advanced economies has bottomed out and world trade, which contracted in

FIGURE 2.1
GDP Growth — Eurozone[1], Japan, and
United States, 2007–10
(quarter-on quarter, saar[2], %)

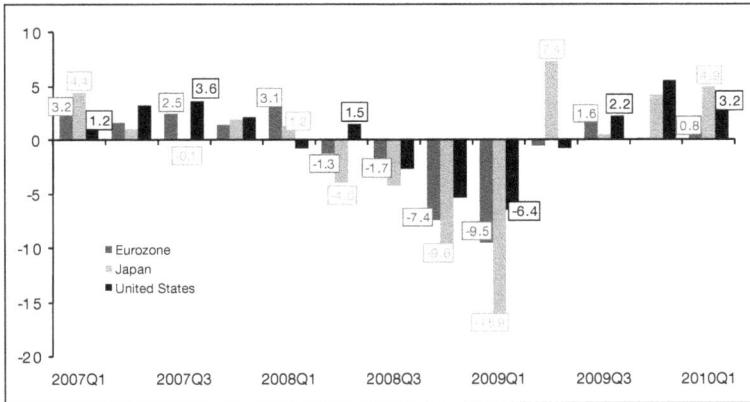

GDP = gross domestic product.
Notes: Eurozone refers to Euro area sixteen countries.
    1. Refers to Euro and 16 countries.
    2. Saar = seasonally adjusted annualized rate.
Sources: Eurostat (Eurozone); Bureau of Economic Analysis (United States); and CEIC database.

2009 for the first time in twenty-seven years, will begin to recover in 2010 (see Figure 2.2). With the global recession seemingly ended, demand for exports should recover — a welcome boost to ASEAN's export-oriented economies. But with the need for consumers in advanced economies, particularly the United States, to boost savings and reduce debt, a return to pre-crisis external demand for ASEAN products will be gradual at best.

Leading indicators suggest the U.S. economy will continue its recovery into 2010. The U.S. economy grew by 3.2 per cent (q-o-q, seasonally adjusted annualized rate)

FIGURE 2.2
Imports — Advanced Economies; Emerging and Developing Economies, 2006–10

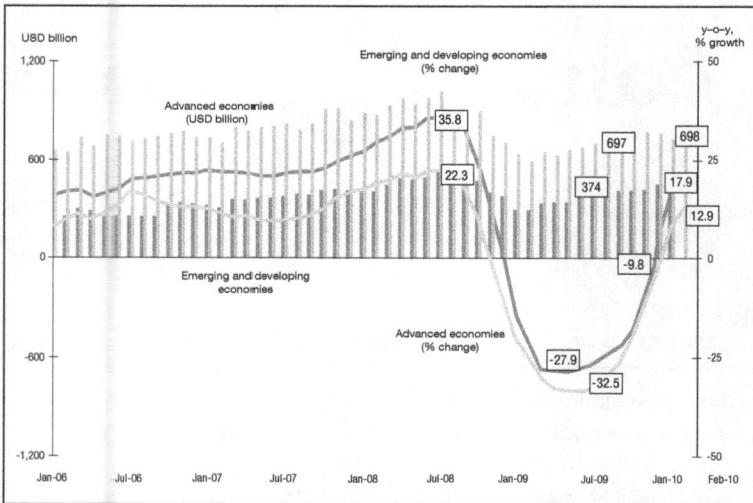

Note: Year-on-year (y-o-y) growth rates of three-month moving averages.
Source: *International Financial Statistics*, International Monetary Fund.

in the first quarter of 2010, 2.5 per cent higher than the first quarter of 2009. The quarterly growth of 5.7 per cent in the last quarter of 2009 marked the end to four consecutive quarters of negative growth. The recovery, partly attributed to the aggressive fiscal and monetary policies taken to stimulate the economy, will get an additional boost as the weaker U.S. dollar helps increase exports. The U.S. economy is forecast to grow by 2.4 per cent in 2010 (see Table 2.1). There is fear, however, that the continued loss of jobs could pose a threat to recovery as the lack of job creation suggests that consumer spending power will remain weak. Although the economic outlook for the United States is far more upbeat, indicators suggest the recovery will be fragile, as substantial concerns remain over the size of the fiscal deficit and health of the financial system.

The Eurozone is slowly entering a recovery phase with exports rising and consumer sentiment improving, although the sovereign debt crisis originated in Greece has added significant uncertainties to the recovery process. The Eurozone has begun its recovery in the third quarter of 2009 when GDP grew 1.6 per cent (q-o-q, seasonally adjusted annualized rate). However, the recovery is slow and fragile, with GDP growing 0.8 per cent (q-o-q, seasonally adjusted annualized rate) in the first quarter of 2010, much slower than in the United States and Japan. The smaller fiscal stimulus in Europe meant that government consumption did not contribute as much to growth as in the U.S. The recent sovereign debt crisis is expected to slow the recovery further as some member countries are forced to consolidate fiscal positions and to repair their balance sheets. However, the depreciation of the euro against the U.S. dollar may stimulate demand for Europe's exports in the months ahead. Other leading indicators suggest that the economy may be on the path toward recovery. As a result, growth is expected to return to Eurozone economies in 2010, but the recovery is expected to be anemic with GDP growth expected to rise by 1.1 per cent.

TABLE 2.1
GDP Growth of Major Trading Partners (% y-o-y), 2007–10

	ASEAN Trade Share,[1] % 2008	*GDP Growth,[2] %*			
		2007	*2008*	*2009*	*2010*
NIE-3[3]	16.0	5.5	1.9	−0.7	5.1
Japan	14.4	2.4	−1.2	−5.2	1.3
People's Republic of China	13.9	14.2	9.6	8.7	9.6
United States	13.1	2.1	0.4	−2.4	2.4
Eurozone[4]	11.1	2.8	0.6	−4.1	1.1
India	3.6	9.2	6.7	7.2	8.2
Weighted growth of major trading partners		5.7	2.5	−0.2	4.3

Notes: 1. Share of country or area to total ASEAN trade.
     2. Aggregate weighted by the share of country or area to total ASEAN trade. Figures for 2010 refer to forecast values.
     3. Newly industrialized economies, which include Hong Kong, China; Republic of Korea; and Taipei, China.
     4. Eurozone refers to Austria, Belgium, Finland, France, Germany, Greece, Ireland, Italy, Luxembourg, Netherlands, Portugal, Slovenia, and Spain.
Sources: Direction of Trade Statistics, International Monetary Fund; Asian Development Bank; Eurostat website; Bureau of Economic Analysis (United States); and CEIC.

After a steep downturn, the Japanese economy is expected to post a modest recovery in 2010. The Japanese economy expanded by 4.9 per cent (q-o-q, seasonally adjusted annualized rate) in the first quarter of 2010, up from 4.2 per cent (q-o-q, seasonally adjusted annualized rate) growth in the fourth quarter of 2009. Growth in consumption and net exports contributed to growth. While an improvement in exports is welcome, its sustainability is uncertain as the strengthening Japanese yen may hurt the competitiveness of Japanese exports. Private investment has started to grow and is likely to strengthen as corporate profits are rising and business sentiment improving in the past few months. The economy is forecast to grow 1.3 per cent in 2010.

The early return to pre-crisis growth rates in the PRC and India — and the faster-than-expected recovery in the newly industrialized economies (Hong Kong, China, Republic of Korea and Taipei, China) — should help reignite intra-regional demand, trade, and investment between ASEAN and its regional partners. The solid rebound from the global crisis in the PRC and India will help boost demand for ASEAN products. The PRC-ASEAN Free Trade Agreement came into force on 1 January 2010, which should increase trade between the two for commodities and manufactured goods (the PRC accounts for about 14 per cent of total ASEAN trade). Nearly 4 per cent of ASEAN's total trade is with India, and 16 per cent with the three NIEs of Hong Kong, China; Republic of Korea; and Taipei, China. A strong recovery in these economies should be a significant boost in demand for ASEAN products.

The PRC will likely continue its strong economic momentum in 2010. The PRC economy returned to double-digit growth in the fourth quarter of 2009 and first quarter of 2010, 11.9 per cent (y-o-y) and 10.7 per cent, respectively. Its massive fiscal stimulus and monetary easing should continue to help economic growth accelerate to 9.6 per cent in 2010. While fiscal stimulus has boosted both public and private investment, private investors remain cautious, waiting to see if external demand recovers. The global trade slump badly affected exports, but it has started to grow again since mid-2009. Industrial production continues to rise, suggesting the recovery has gained significant traction. It is clear that fiscal stimulus succeeded in restoring domestic demand and in keeping economic growth strong. The stimulus was accompanied by a very aggressive monetary stance, flooding the banking system with liquidity. Broad money (M2) rose more than 30 per cent in 2009. Authorities say they will continue fiscal stimulus and maintain an "appropriately" accommodative monetary stance into 2010, which are expected to contribute to the PRC's robust growth.

India's economy also performed better than expected. GDP grew 8.6 per cent in the first quarter of 2010, led by rapid growth in manufacturing. This was a sharp acceleration from the last quarter of 2009's 6.1 per cent growth. Managing the rise in inflation is becoming a challenge, however, and coordination between monetary and fiscal policy is extremely important to moderate inflationary expectations while sustaining growth momentum. While wholesale price inflation remains low due to the base effect (high inflation the previous year), rapid rises in wholesale food prices (20 per cent in December 2009 y-o-y) are worrisome. Despite these challenges, India is now expected to grow 8.2 per cent in 2010, a full percentage point higher than its growth in 2009.

The newly industrialized economies (Hong Kong, China; Korea; and Taipei, China) — badly battered by plummeting global demand — are expected to recover quickly in 2010. The NIEs, after being badly battered by plummeting global demand in early 2009, turned the corner in the fourth quarter of 2009. The precipitous export decline was over for the NIEs with exports picking up across the board. Exports for the NIEs are recovering rapidly with growth turning positive towards the end of 2009. The trend continued into 2010, with exports in Korea and Singapore surging 30.5 per cent (y-o-y) and 28.1 per cent (y-o-y) in February 2010, respectively. Other leading indicators such as industrial production have moved back into positive growth and retail sales are improving. In aggregate, the NIEs are forecast to move from a 0.7 per cent contraction in 2009 to 5.1 per cent GDP growth in 2010.

ASEAN's 2010 Outlook, Risks, and Policy Issues

The improved external environment and ASEAN's swift policy responses show the region amid a V-shaped recovery, with economic growth in 2010 expected to be above 2008 levels. Leading indicators, such as purchasing managers' indexes, indicate strong activity in the coming months. The inventory cycle has started to reverse and is expected to contribute to GDP growth in the coming quarters, after subtracting from it for most of 2009. Given the improving external environment, particularly the strong growth in the PRC, India, and the NIEs, aggregate GDP growth in ASEAN is forecast to rebound strongly to 5.1 per cent in 2010 from 1.3 per cent in 2009 (see Table 2.2, Figures 2.3 and 2.4).

TABLE 2.2
Annual GDP Growth Rates (% y-o-y), 2000–10

	2000–07 Average	2004	2005	2006	2007	2008	2009	2010Q1	ADB Forecast[8] 2010
ASEAN[1,2]	5.5	6.5	5.7	6.1	6.6	4.4	1.3	—	5.1
Brunei Darussalam	2.2	0.5	0.4	4.4	0.2	-1.9	-1.2e	—	1.1
Cambodia	9.5	10.3	13.3	10.8	10.2	6.7	-2.0e	—	4.5
Indonesia[3]	5.1	5.0	5.7	5.5	6.3	6.0	4.5	5.7	5.5
Lao PDR	6.7	7.0	6.8	8.7	7.8	7.2	6.5e	—	7.0
Malaysia[4]	5.6	6.8	5.3	5.8	6.5	4.7	-1.7	10.1	5.3
Myanmar[e]	9.1	5.0	4.5	7.0	5.5	3.6	4.4	—	5.2
Philippines[5]	5.1	6.4	5.0	5.3	7.1	3.8	0.9	—	3.8
Singapore	6.3	9.2	7.4	8.6	8.5	1.8	-1.3	15.5	6.3
Thailand	5.1	6.3	4.6	5.1	4.9	2.5	-2.2	12.0	4.0
Vietnam	7.6	7.8	8.5	8.2	8.4	6.2	5.3	5.8	6.5

e = ADB estimates, GDP = gross domestic product, Lao PDR = Lao People's Democratic Republic, U.S. = United States, y-o-y= year-on-year, — = not available

Notes: 1. Includes Brunei Darussalam; Cambodia; Indonesia; Lao People's Democratic Republic; Malaysia; Philippines; Singapore; Thailand; and Vietnam. Myanmar is not included for all years as weights are unavailable.
2. Aggregates are weighted according to gross national income levels (atlas method, current $) from World Development Indicators, World Bank.
3. GDP growth rates from 1999–2000 are based on 1993 prices, growth rates from 2001 onwards are based on 2000 prices.
4. Growth rates from 1999–2000 are based on 1987 prices, growth rates from 2001 onwards are based on 2000 prices.
5. There is a break in the series starting in 2003: figures for 2004–06 are not linked to the GDP figures prior to 2003 due to National Statistics Office revisions of sectoral estimates.

Sources: Asian Development Outlook 2010, Asian Development Bank; Eurostat website (eurozone); Economic and Social Research Institute (Japan); Bureau of Economic Analysis (United States); and CEIC.

FIGURE 2.3
Quarterly Real GDP Growth — ASEAN-6
(% y-o-y), 2006–09

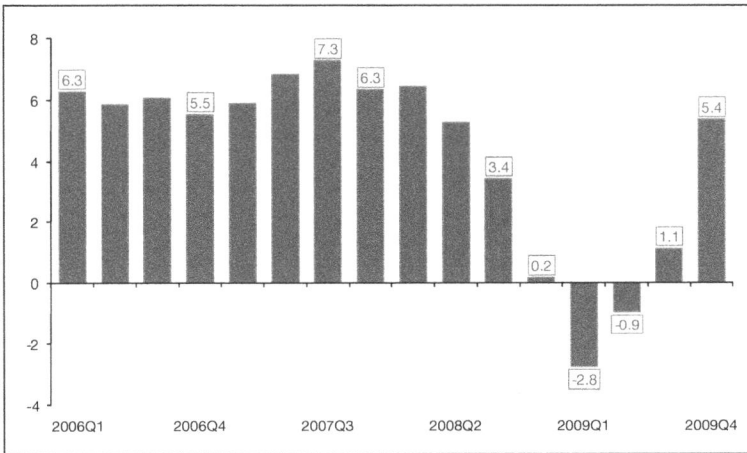

GDP = gross domestic product, y-o-y = year-on-year
Note: ASEAN-6 includes Indonesia, Malaysia, Philippines, Singapore, Thailand, and Vietnam. Does not include Brunei Darussalam, Cambodia, Lao People's Democratic Republic, and Myanmar for which quarterly data unavailable. Weighted by gross national income (atlas method).
Source: Staff calculations based on data from CEIC and World Development Indicators, World Bank.

ASEAN economies were hurt to varying degrees, but most seem poised for recovery in 2010. In terms of overall economic impact, Thailand and Malaysia were hurt the most. With the global economy slowly recovering, both economies are expected to return to growth in 2010, with Malaysia's GDP growing 5.3 per cent and Thailand's up 4.0 per cent. Indonesia and the Philippines — less reliant on exports — fared better in 2009. Indonesia's robust growth is expected to continue in 2010, with GDP growth rising to 5.5 per cent. Healthy remittances and government spending should help the Philippine economy grow 3.8 per cent this year. Singapore is expected to recover in 2010, growing 6.3 per cent, supported by the global upturn and

FIGURE 2.4
Gross Domestic Product — ASEAN[1,2]
(% y-o-y growth), 2000–10

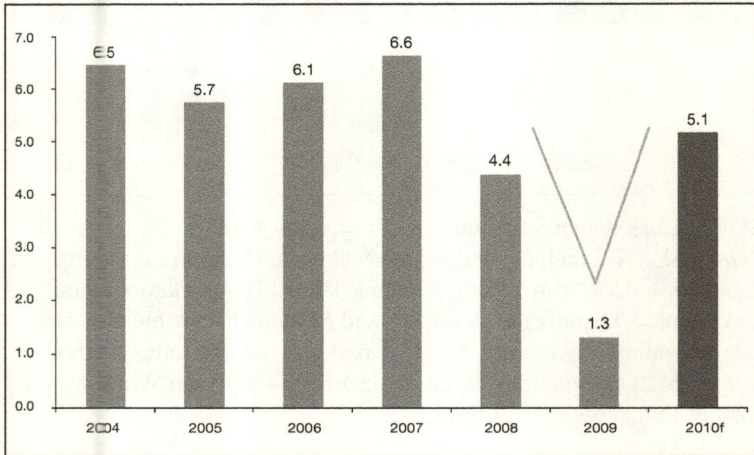

f = forecast from Asian Development Outlook 2010

Notes: 1. Includes Brunei Darussalam; Cambodia; Indonesia; Lao People's Democratic Republic; Malaysia; Philippines; Singapore; Thailand; and Vietnam. Myanmar is not included for all years as weights are unavailable.

2. Aggregates are weighted according to gross national income levels (atlas method, current $) from World Development Indicators, World Bank.

Sources: *Asian Development Outlook 2010*, Asian Development Bank; Eurostat website (Eurozone); Economic and Social Research Institute (Japan); Bureau of Economic Analysis (United States); and CEIC.

domestic fiscal stimulus. The remaining ASEAN countries should also see economic growth return to 2008 levels as the global economic environment improves and export demand rises.

Due to the robust recovery, inflation is slowly rising, but should remain manageable, particularly where excess

FIGURE 2.5
Inflation Rate — ASEAN (% y-o-y), 2004–11

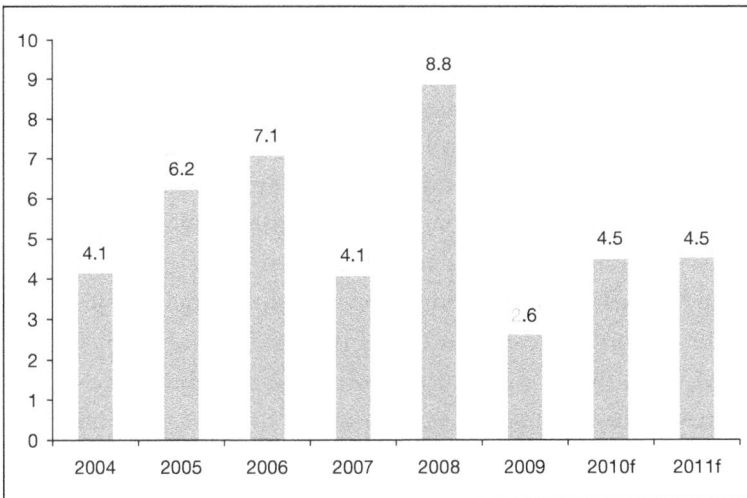

y-o-y = year-on-year, f = forecast
Note: ASEAN includes Brunei Darussalam, Cambodia, Indonesia, Malaysia, Lao People's Democratic Republic, Philippines, Singapore, Thailand, and Vietnam. Weighed by gross national income (atlas method). Excludes Myanmar for all years as weights are unavailable.
Sources: Staff calculations based on data from various issues of *Asian Development Outlook* (ADO), Asian Development Bank; CEIC; and World Development Indicators, World Bank. Forecasts are from *ADO 2010*.

productive capacity exists. Inflationary pressures start to emerge, but should remain subdued in the short term due to a negative output gap. Inflation appears to be well under control for the moment. While recently showing small increases, inflation is still expected to remain benign as economies operate with excess capacity. In the medium term, inflation could pick up in line with the general global economic recovery and higher commodity prices (see Figure 2.5). Several countries will need to keep an eye on inflationary pressures as they build exit strategies for their stimulus packages.

Risk appetite for ASEAN asset markets has returned adding appreciation pressures on most of the region's currencies. After the massive capital outflows during the second half of 2008 and early 2009, financial account balances, which narrowed in 2009, are likely to remain strong in 2010 as investors' risk appetite grows and capital inflows intensify. Equity markets have risen significantly, while the inflows have added appreciation pressures to most of the region's currencies (see Figures 2.6 and 2.7).

Major downside risks to the outlook include (i) a reversal in growth in advanced economies; (ii) a loss of economic momentum in the PRC; and (iii) destabilizing capital inflows. ASEAN now faces the challenge of converting economic rebound to sustained recovery. Stimulus, both monetary and fiscal, has helped the region's economies weather the global downturn. But much needs to be done to ensure the recovery is solid. External demand is likely to be fragile at least in the initial stages of recovery in advanced economies. And it may not return to pre-crisis levels over the short- to medium-term — as G3 consumers, particularly in the United

FIGURE 2.6
Stock Price Indexes (% change), 2 January 2009
to 25 May 2010

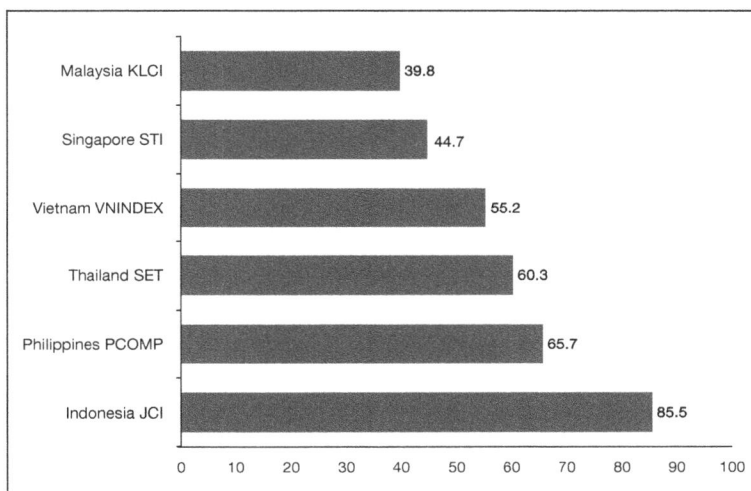

Note: Latest closing as of 25 May 2010.
Source: OREI staff calculations based on data from Reuters.

States, attempt to readjust their balance sheets. The European sovereign debt crisis has added uncertainties to its recovery. If the recovery in advanced economies is derailed, reduced external demand could once again jeopardize ASEAN's growth prospects. As one of the region's biggest trading partners, any disruption in the PRC's economic momentum could hurt ASEAN's growth prospects. Large or destabilizing capital flows will complicate macroeconomic management, adding uncertainty to the growth forecast.

The recovery in ASEAN has been uneven, suggesting that exit strategies from policy stimulus will naturally

FIGURE 2.7
Regional Currencies (% change), 2 January 2009
to 25 May 2010

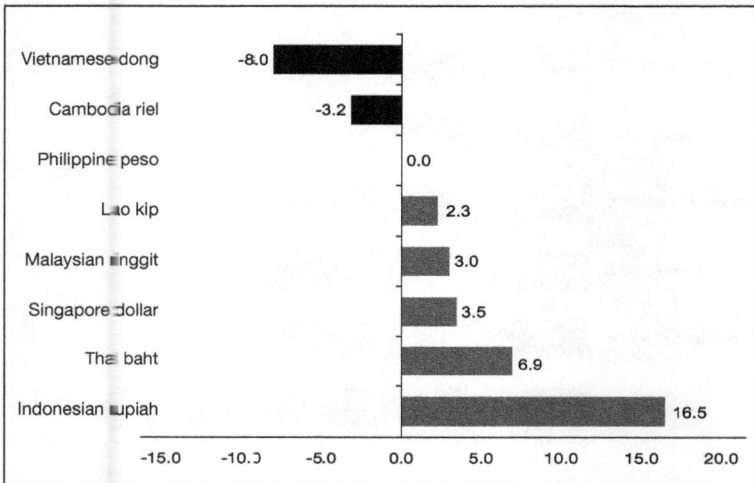

Note: Latest closing as of 25 May 2010, based on the local currency value of the U.S. dollar. Negative values indicate depreciation of local currency.
Source: OREI staff calculations based on Reuters data.

differ among countries — both in timing and policy mix. In economies such as Vietnam, where recovery is strong and inflationary pressures are emerging, it is time to begin "normalizing" macroeconomic policies. Economies where recovery is firming and inflation pressures are subdued need to prepare for exiting from policy stimulus; Malaysia, and Thailand may fall into this category. Malaysia was the first ASEAN member to raise policy rates (50 basis points in total) in the first half of 2010, and also listed fiscal consolidation as a priority for 2010. For other ASEAN economies where macroeconomic conditions are improving, yet recovery remains somewhat fragile, policies could remain accommodative for some time. With inflation low, these economies can rationalize maintaining a loose policy stance (see Figure 2.8). It is also crucial that fiscal deficits

FIGURE 2.8
Decline in Policy Rates[1] (in basis points), 4Q08[2] to 25 May 2010

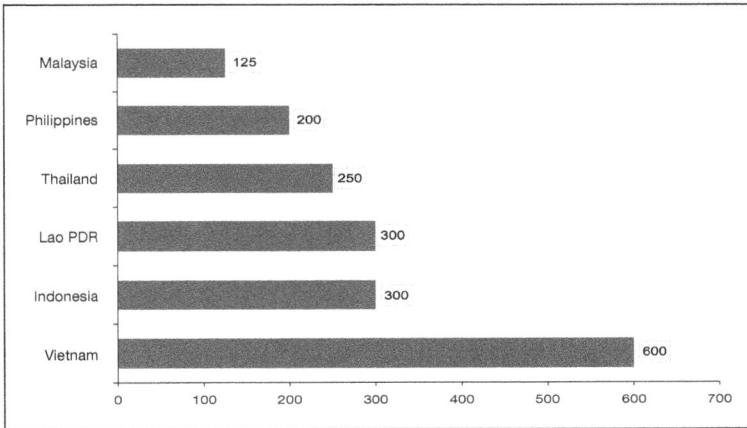

Notes: 1. Policy rates for each economy are as follows: Bank Indonesia rate (Indonesia); overnight policy rate (Malaysia); reverse repurchase (repo) rate (Philippines); one-day repo rate (Thailand); prime rate (Vietnam); Bank of Lao lending interest rate — less than one week (Lao People's Democratic Republic). Malaysia raised its rate by 25 bps on 4 March 2010 after being unchanged since February 2009. State Bank of Vietnam raised its rate by one percentage point effective 1 December 2009.

2. 2008Q4 refers to October for Vietnam and Lao People's Democratic Republic; November for Malaysia; and December for Indonesia, Philippines, and Thailand.

Source: OREI staff calculations using data from Bloomberg, DataStream and Bank of the Lao PDR website.

need to be sustainable during the rebound and beyond. Policy-makers should be prepared to pull back on large government intervention to avoid policy distortions and keep a lid on inflationary pressures. Deficits will remain large in the near term (see Figure 2.9). But they need to be carefully managed to avoid impeding recovery.

FIGURE 2.9
Change in Fiscal Balance (percentage points), 2007–09

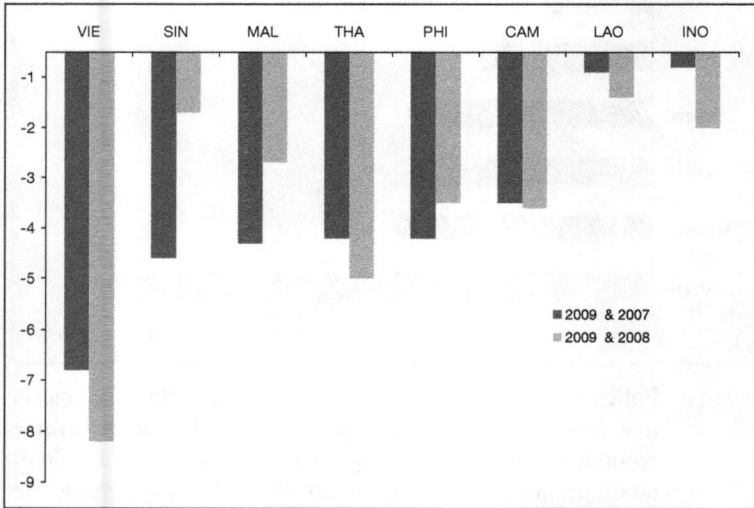

CAM = Cambodia; INO = Indonesia; LAO = Lao People's Democratic Republic; MAL = Malaysia; PHI = Philippines; SIN = Singapore; THA = Thailand; and VIE = Vietnam. Data not available for Myanmar, while 2009 data not available for Brunei Darussalam.

Note: Refers to fiscal balance of central government (as per cent of GDP).

Source: *Asian Development Outlook*, Asian Development Bank, March 2010.

Within each country, coordination between fiscal and monetary authorities — and perhaps financial regulators as well — is key to implementing effective exit strategies. Monetary and fiscal institutions must closely coordinate to craft coherent policy stimulus exit strategies — to ensure economic recovery is sustained. If there is limited fiscal space and inflation remains low, it may be more prudent to exit fiscal stimulus first before normalizing monetary policy. If inflation and asset prices threaten, then normalizing monetary policy makes better sense — first to anchor inflationary expectations and cool asset prices. In short, monetary and fiscal authorities should work closely to avoid doing too little too late, as well as doing too much too soon. Moreover, they should coordinate with financial regulators to ensure financial stability. Regulatory coordination could also form part of the exit strategy to prevent any financial excess stemming from the extraordinary monetary and fiscal stimulus.

Managing capital flows must be done judiciously to ensure external volatility does not disrupt domestic financial markets. There is no magic solution to effectively manage capital flows or excessive jumps in asset prices. Every policy option has its merits and shortcomings. An appropriate policy mix includes currency flexibility, a clear and stable monetary and fiscal policy, and enhanced regulatory and supervisory efforts to prevent asset bubbles. Each country will have its own optimum policy mix. Specifically, better policy coordination on exchange rates should be explored. Aside from contributing to better macroeconomic management, coordination would bolster intra-regional trade and lessen the fear of losing export competitiveness between neighbours.

Beyond Recovery — Long-Term Priorities for ASEAN

Despite the 2008/09 global economic crisis, ASEAN must ensure it stays the course towards building an ASEAN Economic Community (AEC) by 2015. Amid the rise of the PRC and India, it is critical that ASEAN ensures that it follows the roadmap to an ASEAN Economic Community by 2015. In its early days, integration was more of a luxury. Now it is an imperative. A single market and production base can make ASEAN a highly competitive global economic region. As an integrated entity, ASEAN would be the tenth largest economy in the world and the third most populous country. In trade, it would the fifth largest trading power, after the United States, Germany, the PRC, and Japan. An integrated ASEAN carries numerous benefits. A functioning AEC would reduce transaction costs and enhance the investment climate. Today, businesses and investors treat ASEAN as a collection of ten different countries rather than a single economic entity. Deeper integration with standardized business parameters, improved trade facilitation, and easing of capital flows would significantly improve competitiveness of the region as a whole. The free flow of goods and services — and the removal of non-tariff barriers and "behind the border" restrictions — helps allow ASEAN to move beyond basic production integration that has developed over the years.

A functioning AEC is crucial for future Asian integration; ASEAN needs to deepen its own integration to be an effective "driving force" for Asian regionalism. Aside from the benefits integration accrues to ASEAN members individually, it also gives it the opportunity to be the "hub" of regional integration. ASEAN is at the centre of a wide and growing range formal and informal institutions or arrangements (see Figure 2.10). Whether the expanded ASEAN+3 — with its established dialogue process, formal reserve pooling arrangement (the Chiang Mai Initiative Multilateralization), or cooperation in deepening finance (the Asia Bond Markets Initiative) — or the East Asia Summit (EAS) process, or the wider umbrella of Asia-Pacific Economic Cooperation (APEC), an integrated ASEAN gives each member a larger, more effective voice. It is time for ASEAN to take regional cooperation to the next level, in trade, finance, and economic surveillance. ASEAN should maintain its "open regionalism" approach — aim for a regionally integrated, yet globally connected ASEAN.

FIGURE 2.10
Regional and Transregional Forums

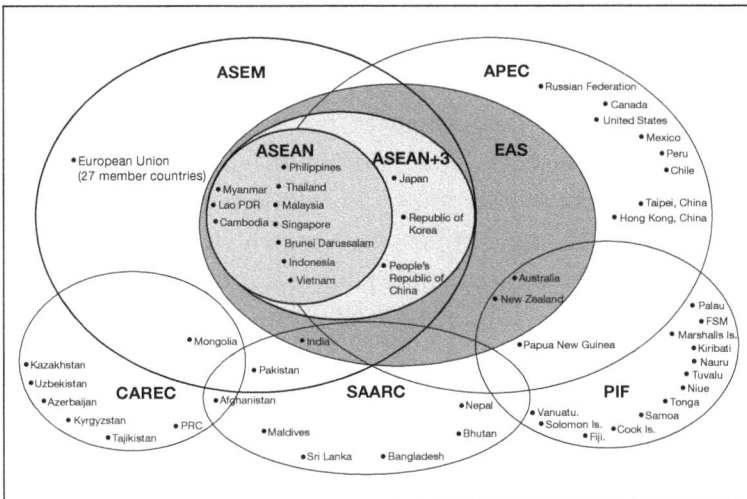

The ASEAN Economic Community (AEC) aims for a single market and production base by 2015 that can become a highly competitive economic region globally. The AEC is intended to be an open, outward looking, inclusive, and market-driven economic community that adheres to international best practices and rules-based systems to ensure economic commitments are met. Several agreements provide a set of rules and monitoring mechanisms to make the ambitious 2015 target attainable. Infrastructure agreements and coordinating measures on intellectual property rights, consumer protection, taxation and e-commerce, among others, are also part of the plan. But much needs to be done to ensure the AEC does not appear from the minimalist standpoint of simply a "customs union plus".

A functioning AEC will inevitably reduce transaction costs, enhance the investment climate, and better align "doing business" parameters to build investment demand, both domestic and foreign. Businesses and investors have tended to key in on specific countries rather than treat the region as a whole. For example, decisions on FDI tend to focus on comparative advantages and cost effectiveness pertaining to individual countries, not to ASEAN as a unified community or market. One measure of the diversity among ASEAN members relevant to investment decisions is the World Bank's Doing Business Survey, which ranks countries according to the ease of setting up and running a business, along with the legal certitude of protecting a company's interests (see Table 2.3). The huge disparity in rankings illustrates the difficulties ASEAN faces in constructing an AEC with a level playing field for all investors.

Improving trade facilitation is critical to deepening ASEAN integration. Intra-regional trade within ASEAN

TABLE 2.3
Doing Business in ASEAN — Ease
of Doing Business Ranking

Country	Rank
Singapore	1
Thailand	12
Malaysia	23
Vietnam	93
Brunei Darussalam	96
Indonesia	122
Philippines	144
Cambodia	145
Lao People's Democratic	167

Source: World Bank Doing Business Survey 2010.

has grown to become a major component of its total trade. It has more than doubled since 2003 — from U$113 billion in 2003 to U$251 billion in 2008 (though it fell to U$204 billion in 2009 due to the global crisis). Its consumer base continues to grow in both quantity and quality — as poverty is reduced and the middle class rapidly expands. Major multinationals have long built supply chains, production networks, and distribution systems within ASEAN to build and tap that consumer demand. More and more, however, it is domestic firms and corporations that are becoming ASEAN multinationals and/or outsourcing component manufacturing throughout the region. And while there is currently wide income disparity across ASEAN economies, the steady economic growth — from the largest ASEAN member, Indonesia, to the smaller ASEAN members — means per-capita incomes will continue to rise over time. Free trade lowers costs and boosts intra-ASEAN demand, as well as helps remove over-reliance on those markets in advanced economies that have reduced demand during the current crisis.

Intra-Asian trade — particularly with the PRC and India — is an extremely important growth channel for ASEAN. The PRC is already a significant export destination for ASEAN, with imports of ASEAN intermediate goods and raw materials rising fivefold in the past decade. Even with its rapid economic growth, however, many of PRC final products remain bound for advanced economies like the United States. So the tie with external demand remains a critical issue. Nonetheless, the ASEAN-China Free Trade Agreement, which came into force at the start of 2010, should allow for a significant increase in trade across a variety of product types, though it is unclear how rapid this rise will be. India's trade with ASEAN has been rising rapidly as well. India also signed its long-awaited Free Trade Agreement with ASEAN in August 2009, which will see tariff reductions on over 90 per cent of products traded between the two regions.

ASEAN needs to move forward in helping the private sector compete. There is increasing recognition of the benefits derived from having a working competition law and policy. This is particularly true as (i) trade regimes are further liberalized in the context of globalization, as (ii) domestic manufacturing competes to provide components for supply chains and production networks, and as (iii) small and medium enterprises (SMEs) are promoted to make economic growth more inclusive. Currently, each ASEAN member has a diverse set of competitions-related regulations or legislation — from Singapore's wide-ranging 2004 Competition Act (replete with a Competition Commission) to Malaysia, which takes a more sectoral approach with no national competition law. In many countries, the culture for competition has yet to fully evolve from the cronyism or favouritism that existed under former authoritarian regimes. From the regional perspective, should ASEAN move towards creating a central competition authority to ensure a level playing field across industries and sectors?

ASEAN needs to build greater institutional strength. The ASEAN Charter is an important step forward, but it remains to be seen how far its more rules-based structure accelerates formation of the AEC and ASEAN cooperation generally. The new ASEAN Charter, which came into force in December 2008, gives ASEAN a legal basis and shifts the group towards a more rules-based system rather than one relying entirely on consensus. But many still see the Charter as insufficient to truly bind such a diverse region together. One of the challenges ASEAN has always faced is the perception from both from within the region — and especially outside the region — that the priorities and development requirements of individual members are too diverse to forge a truly integrated union. The ASEAN Secretariat remains small relative to the task, and although it has grown as an institution in both size and in its capacity to manage ASEAN issues, it is minuscule compared with the manpower and institutional capability of, for example, the European Union (the ASEAN Secretariat has a staff of 270 while the EU has 14,000).

ASEAN also needs to focus on bridging the development gap among its members to ensure that a two-tier ASEAN does not derail its integration process. As ASEAN integrates, it must be careful not to exacerbate the development gaps between its larger, original members and its smaller, newer, and less developed members, known as the CLMV countries (Cambodia, Lao PDR, Myanmar, and Vietnam). Several initiatives were begun in the early 2000s to tackle this problem, particularly the Initiative for ASEAN Integration (IAI) and the 2004 Vientiane Action Programme, the latter also concerned with development gaps that exist internally within the larger ASEAN economies. The worry is that development gaps may actually widen given the differing pace of growth among members and within the larger ASEAN economies. One way to help meld the two- or even three-tier ASEAN (Singapore, middle income ASEAN-4, and the CMLV members) is to exploit complementarities within ASEAN.[1] One way would be to focus on developing integration programmes targeted specifically at bringing less developed ASEAN members in closer alignment with their more prosperous neighbours. The Greater Mekong Subregion Program — linking Cambodia, Lao PDR, and Vietnam with Thailand and the PRC's Yunnan Province — is one such example.

The development of small and medium enterprises (SMEs) is key to making economic development in the region more inclusive. The second work plan for the IAI (2009–15) specifically aims to narrow the development gap prior to establishing the AEC. The plan hopes to enhance the competitiveness of SMEs, which are the backbone of domestic business expansion throughout ASEAN. Since the Asia financial crisis, private investment has lagged pre-crisis levels. And although previous levels may have created an investment overhang, it is SMEs that represent a qualitative change towards more inclusive economic growth.

The longer term rebalancing towards domestic demand will partly depend on making SMEs in the region more dynamic. There are two sets of issues that need to be addressed: (i) designing and implementing effective policies and programmes to improve SME access to finance; and (ii) assisting SMEs adopt new technologies and access new markets — both domestic and regional, as well as outside the G3 economies. Introducing rigorous policy and programme evaluations to assist SMEs will be crucial for improving their effectiveness. Enhancing government-private sector collaboration in designing policies and programmes is also critical, particularly in promoting SME support services such as skills, trade, entrepreneurship, and other business development services.

The other great challenge facing many ASEAN countries is how to avoid the "middle income trap". A middle income trap occurs when rapidly growing economies exit lower income levels only to become trapped — unable to compete with low income, low wage economies in manufactured exports and unable to compete with advanced economies in high skill innovation. In emerging markets throughout the world, while many countries have been able to graduate from low to middle income status, relatively few have carried on to high income. To do so requires a move up the value chain — from assembly to manufacturing, followed by a shift to knowledge- and innovation-based products and services. Increased specialization in sectors with large economies of scale with little transfer of technology required has worked in economies such as Korea. Most advanced economies are in fact technological innovators.

Investing in human capital through the enhancement of social services is critical to increasing productivity and income. Many studies of economic growth confirm the importance of human capital investment as a major source of growth. Rapid accumulation of physical capital in many ASEAN countries merely accents the need for developing human capital. Activities that improve human capabilities typically include health facilities and services, education, on-the-job training and adult study programmes. As economies move up the value chain and growth accelerates, the demand for skilled labour is even higher, with social and private returns to education and skills upgrading increasing. To satisfy this demand and to improve the quantity and quality of skilled labour, it is more urgent to improve educational systems — such as providing incentives, encouraging competition, better recruitment, curriculum development, as well as teacher training.

Allowing the free movement of labour within ASEAN members and across countries in the region will also increase productivity and cut production costs. By directing scarce labour resources to their productive use, free labour movement generates a wide variety of benefits — improving resource allocation within a country or ASEAN as a whole. Labour migration also reduces significant wage differences for the same type of qualified workers in richer and poorer countries in the region. This suggests that the gains from increased regional labour mobility would be enormous. With a combined population of more than half a billion (third after the PRC and India), ASEAN has the potential to reap huge gains from easier labour migration. Labour flows in the region are rapidly growing, given the diversity in levels of economic development, employment opportunities, wage levels, and the existence of labour surplus and deficit countries. Further cooperation among ASEAN members is needed.

ASEAN should continue to reform, deepen, and integrate financial markets. Further progress on ASEAN financial integration will need to address fundamental causes — weaknesses in national financial systems, differences in national financial regulations, and the complexity of open markets and capital-market liberalization. There is a growing consensus that much can — and should — be done about these issues on a regional level, both to improve the efficiency of markets and to avoid or delay the effects of financial shocks. At the regional level, the priorities are strengthening regional dialogue and financial market surveillance; promoting internationally accepted standards and codes of practice and the mutual recognition of minimum standards; fostering the growth of regional bond markets; and building market infrastructure such as regional clearing houses, payment and settlement systems, credit rating agencies, research and training facilities, and databases.

Singapore has made the jump to advanced status; but the four middle income ASEAN members vary widely within the middle income range, though in specific industries they have made progress. Many things are needed to have growth momentum translate into higher income per GDP. The skill level of labour must be raised, safety nets need to be secured, financial systems require a level of sophistication, legal consistency is needed for confidence, technological innovation must flourish, and industrial specialization must have both comparative advantage and economies of scale.

Conclusion

The Great Recession of 2008/09 hit ASEAN hard; but the response was swift and the rebound quick — with the key challenge to convert recovery to sustained growth. The global crisis had an immediate impact on ASEAN, initially through the trade channel, but later struck the overall economy as well. Countries with larger populations or less connected globally tended to fare better as domestic demand remained more intact. Nonetheless, accommodative monetary and fiscal policies were used to help fill the demand gap — and will continue to be used to drive economic activity until private sector demand can take over and exit strategies implemented. Managing capital flows judiciously can avoid the deleterious effects that volatility can have on domestic markets.

ASEAN integration is an imperative; no longer a luxury. As ASEAN moves toward an ASEAN Economic Community in 2015, it is essential it expedites economic integration in trade, money, finance, and in fostering greater cross-border connectivity, whether in infrastructure or labour mobility. With the speed of development in the huge economies of the PRC and India, ASEAN must deepen integration if it is to be the "driving force" for a wider Asian regionalism.

ASEAN must bridge the development gap and avoid the middle income trap. Building on complementarities between individual ASEAN members can help make development more inclusive and help make ASEAN better integrated. By helping the private sector compete nationally, regionally, and globally, it can more easily construct deeper supply chains and production networks to increase regional integration, while remaining connected globally. This, along with investments in human resources, increasing labour mobility, enhancing the investment climate, and deepening financial market integration, can help ASEAN attain its goal of a true ASEAN Economic Community by 2015.

NOTE

1. For example Lao PDR hydropower plants provide Thailand with needed electricity. But how does it finance the huge infrastructure expense? One way being tried is revenue-backed bonds that use future royalties from hydropower — which sell electricity to Thailand — to cover bond payments. Issued on the Thai capital market, the bonds can provide better terms and conditions to the Lao PDR than commercial borrowing, while providing Thai investors — mostly pension funds and other institutional investors — steady returns.

3
Managing Financial Crisis in Singapore

Tan Chwee Huat

Introduction

This chapter begins with a brief discussion on the housing bubble in the United States and how the sub-prime crisis caused the collapse of major financial institutions such as Lehman Brothers and AIG. Their collapse severely devalued Lehman-related structured products sold in Singapore and diminished the savings of many retail investors. The crisis also had serious spillover effect on the exports of Singapore. Workers lost their jobs when companies cut costs to remain competitive. The Singapore Government introduced a Resilience Package to save jobs and to minimize the negative impact caused by the crisis. The chapter then discusses the effectiveness of these rescue measures and the lessons to be learnt from the crisis.

Many books, articles and reports have been written by economists, financial analysts, journalists and political observers about the financial crisis caused by the sub-prime housing bubble in the United States.[1]

Beginning around 2000, the demand in the U.S. property market began to rise as house buyers took advantage of the low interest rates. Some banks even offered incentives such as interest only adjustable rate mortgage (IO-ARM) loans. Borrowers only had to pay interest during the initial period. Without the normal due diligence, loans were even offered to sub-prime or "NINJA" borrowers (people with No Income, No Job or Asset). As a result, the share of sub-prime mortgages to total originations increased from 5 per cent (US$35 billion in 1994) to 20 per cent (US$600 billion in 2006) (Tilson and Tongue 2009).

The crisis started in 2006 when there were signs of inflation. When the Federal Reserve Board increased interest rates to combat inflationary pressures, many Americans were unable to make their mortgage payments. Defaults and foreclosure increased sharply. In 2007, nearly 1.3 million homes were foreclosed, up by 80 per cent from 2006. In comparison, between 2001 and 2005, there were only 650,000 foreclosures (Leong 2008).

The sub-prime housing bubble affected many major U.S. institutions such as Bear Stearns, Lehman, AIG, Bank of America, Fannie Mae and Freddie Mac. On 15 September 2008, Lehman Brothers filed for bankruptcy and its collapse affected the entire financial market in the United States and many other countries.

Global Impact of the AIG Collapse

In March 2009, U.S. insurance giant American International Group (AIG) reported a loss of US$62 billion for the last quarter of 2008, the biggest quarterly loss in U.S. corporate history. To prevent another rumble in the equity markets, the U.S. Government injected US$30 billion into AIG, on top of the US$150 billion in bailout funds first meted out to it at the end of 2008. AIG's global reach is so extensive that there is literally no single bond insurance in the world that does not have some affiliation to the insurance group. The global insurance industry would face catastrophe if AIG were to go bust, leaving millions of underwritten insurance policies exposed (Wong 2009). What caused the collapse of AIG was not its core insurance business but its subsidiary which issued Credit Default Swap (CDS) to offer buyer protection against losses from Collateralized Debt Obligations (CDOs) based on mortgage loans.

At first, it seemed that the crisis was confined to the United States. Shortly after, the contagion spread to Asia and other parts of the world. In Singapore, export sales declined and workers were retrenched. Other people, including many retirees, were affected as they had invested in structured products like Lehman Minibond Notes which were sold through local financial institutions. These investments became worthless and their life savings vanished overnight. As the financial crisis unfolded, it became clear that its direct impact on retail investors was mainly caused by the mis-selling of structured products, particularly those that were linked to Lehman Brothers. However, the slowdown of the U.S. economy has caused wider impact on businesses in Singapore.[2] The MAS has stepped in to investigate the mis-selling of structured products. At the macro level, the government took steps to deal with broader issues such as job loss and lack of credit for businesses.

Offering Structured Products

During the past decade, many structured products were introduced by financial institutions in Singapore. By using persistent selling tactics, these institutions persuaded customers to switch from their regular fixed deposits to structured products with the promise of higher returns. Some were marketed as "capital guaranteed" or "capital protected". Examples of these structured products included the Lehman Minibonds, Merrill Lynch Jubilee Series 3 Link Earner Notes, DBS High Notes, Morgan Stanley Pinnacle Notes and others.

The higher returns from the structured deposits are accompanied by higher risks. There is also the possibility of receiving lower or no returns at all. One of the conditions is that investors are not allowed to withdraw structured deposits before maturity unless they pay an early-withdrawal penalty. Withdrawal before maturity may also lead to capital loss. This loss depends on the market value of the underlying financial products that the structured product is linked to. During the financial crisis, many of the underlying investments suffered great losses as a result of "credit events" that affected institutions in the United States. Examples of these "credit events" were the collapse of Lehman Brothers and AIG. Several of the structured deposits sold to Singapore retail investors were linked to Lehman Brothers, Merrill Lynch, Morgan Stanley and others.

Mis-selling by the Banks

After the collapse of Lehman Brothers, all its derivative products became worthless. In Singapore, many retail investors claimed that they were misled into buying these products and were victims of ignorance. Some were retirees or housewives who belonged to the unsophisticated group of investors who did not have sufficient financial knowledge on such investments.

The issue was more complicated than it seemed. Who should be responsible for their loss? Fingers were pointed at the banks for mis-selling products which were inappropriate for unsophisticated customers. The MAS was criticized for acting too slowly and not responding to earlier signals of public disquiet. These products were introduced several years ago and retail investors had complained about the hard sell tactics of the banks. The banks were partly liable as their sales people were not adequately trained to explain the risks involved in structured products. These sales people were provided with incentives for pushing these products. Investors were liable for not seeking clarification with regards to the products. Attracted by the higher returns, many of them signed the contract without fully understanding the risks involved.

Lehman Minibond Notes

Series 1, 2, 3, 5, 6, 7, 8, 9 and 10 of the Minibond Notes were issued by Minibond Limited and arranged by Lehman Brothers Inc. (for series 1, 2, 3, 5 and 6) and Lehman Brothers Singapore Pte. Ltd. (for series 7, 8, 9 and 10). They were offered from 3 April 2006 to 25 July 2008. The total issue size of Minibond Notes programme was S$508 million, with S$373 million sold to about 7,800 retail investors through financial institutions.[3]

Was there misrepresentation in the sales? In the first place, the Lehman bankers who designed this product were not only smart in finance, they were also geniuses in marketing. They gave the name "Minibond Limited" to the special purpose vehicle that issued the notes. So the shorthand name for the credit-linked notes issued by Minibond Limited was simply "Minibond". But the notes were not bonds at all (Png 2008).

In the Minibond series, sales pitch was presented in such a way that investors could benefit from the creditworthiness of several well-known "reference entities" such as Deutsche Bank, Barclays and CitiGroup. The perception developed by the names, position and words used in the promotional material was that the "bond" was issued by these "reference entities". Lehman, the "arranger" was deemed to be an intermediary only. It did state that if any one of the "reference entities" were to experience a "credit event", the whole deal was off and that it was acting as the "swap counterparty". Lehman would be exposed to the risk of a default by any one of the underlying "reference entities". Thus, it passed the risk to the investing public via a complex structure involving swaps (Sivanithy 2008).

MAS Scope of Investigation

In September and October 2008, Lehman Brothers Holdings Inc. and Lehman Brothers Special Financing Inc. respectively filed for bankruptcy protection in the United States. This resulted in the default or early redemption of Lehman-related credit-linked structured notes sold in Singapore. They included: (a) Minibond Notes, (b) DBS

High Notes, (c) Jubilee Notes, (d) Pinnacle Notes. Retail investors suffered great losses as a result of the Lehman collapse. Many complained that they had been misled by distributors in buying these notes.

In early 2009, the MAS investigated ten financial institutions that distributed these structured notes. It also investigated ten licensed financial advisers who were appointed by two of the distributors. The investigation covered the following areas:[4]

1. Due diligence conducted by the financial institutions.
2. The procedures at the point of sale of these notes.
3. How the notes were sold to clients whose investment objectives and risk tolerance matched the risk profile of the notes.
4. The training and supervision of representatives involved in the sale of these notes.

Observations by MAS on the Sale and Marketing Practices[5]

Sale on "Advisory Basis"
The MAS noted that most of the financial institutions sold the Notes on an "advisory basis". The process usually involved a representative of the distributor offering to conduct a fact-find and needs analysis of the client's circumstances. The representative would advise the client about an investment product according to the client's assessed risk appetite and investment objectives.

Policies and Procedures Were in Place
The MAS found that the distributors had proper policies, procedures and controls for the approval, sale and marketing of the Notes.

Non-compliance with Guidelines and Notices

The MAS noted various forms of non-compliance by the distributors with regards to MAS Notices and Guidelines on the marketing and sale of investment products. For example, the product briefing materials disseminated to their representatives did not highlight the fact that the performance of the Underlying Securities was a source of risk to the performance of the Minibond Notes.

Observations by MAS on Redress for Individual Investors.[6]

In the context of redress for individual investors, the MAS noted the following:

Under Section 64 of the Financial Advisers Act (FAA), the failure of any financial institution to comply with Guidelines under this Act may be relied upon to establish liability against this institution in any criminal or civil proceedings. However, any such failure does not by itself render the institution liable to any individual client.

Under Section 27 of the FAA, to make a claim for damages, the client must show that in his decision to purchase, he has relied on the recommendation from the adviser. There is a need to produce oral and documentary evidence to support the claim.

Investors were asked to sign document containing risk warning and disclaimer of liability of the seller. Some clients were even required by the distributors to sign acceptance form which stated that (i) the Notes were not fixed deposits and not principal guaranteed, (ii) there were product risks.

To the distributors, the documents signed by a client meant that they did not have any legal liability to the client. Nevertheless, they agreed to adopt MAS recommendation not to take an overly legalistic approach in resolving client complaints.

In handling the complaints, the distributors considered numerous factors such as: (i) the client's investment experience, (ii) the degree of reliance on the advice from the distributor, (iii) the client's ability to understand the product and the documents signed.

Clients were offered either no or partial redress, depending on the distributor's view of their level of responsibility. All offers of settlement were made on a voluntary basis without any admission of liability.

Appointment of Independent Persons

The MAS also required the distributors to appoint Independent Persons (IPs) to oversee their complaint handling and resolution process. It worked closely with these IPs to ensure that the distributor's processes were consistent and impartial. Each distributor was also required to have an assessment framework to offer fair financial settlement. The MAS also required that the assessment of complaints should be made by an internal review panel chaired by the distributor's chief executive officer in accordance with the framework agreed with the IP.[7]

The outcomes of settlement by the respective institutions are summarized in Tables 3.1 and 3.2.

After the investigation, the MAS banned the sale of structured notes by ten financial institutions which had sold Lehman-linked structured notes. The ban ranged from six months to two years.[10]

TABLE 3.1
Settlement Outcomes for Minibond Notes, HN5 and Pinnacle Notes by Banks and Finance Company as of 31 May 2009[8]

	ABN	*DBS*	*MBB*	*HLF*	*Total*
Number of investors	870	1,083	2,456	2,781	7,190
Cases received	637	873	1,757	2,284	5,551
Cases decided[1]	**637**	**866**	**1,704**	**2,145**	**5,352**
Settlement outcomes for cases decided (% of cases decided)					
- full or partial	**262** **(41.1%)**	**197** **(22.8%)**	**1,100** **(64.6%)**	**2,048** **(95.5%)**	**3,607** **(67.4%)**
- full	91 (14.3%)	64 (7.4%)	325 (19.1%)	893 (41.6%)	1,373 (25.7%)
- partial (50% and above)	123 (19.3%)	71 (8.2%)	172 (10.1%)	958 (44.7%)	1,324 (24.7%)
- partial (below 50%)	48 (7.5%)	62 (7.2%)	603 (35.4%)	197 (9.2%)	910 (17%)
- nil	**375** **(58.9%)**	**669** **(77.2%)**	**604** **(35.4%)**	**97** **(4.5%)**	**1,745** **(32.6%)**
Amount invested for cases decided	S$71.9m	S$84.1m	S$82.4m	S$86.1m	S$324.5m
Value of settlement offers (% of amount invested for cases decided)	**S$14.1m** **(19.6%)**	**S$7.6m** **(9%)**	**S$25.3m** **(30.7%)**	**S$57.6m** **(66.9%)**	**S$104.6m** **(32.2%)**

Notes: ABN: ABN AMRO Bank
DBS: DBS Bank
MBB: Malayan Banking Berhad
HLF: Hong Leong Finance

Tan Chwee Huat

TABLE 3.2
Settlement Outcomes for Minibond Notes, Jubilee Notes and Pinnacle Notes by Stockbroking Firms as of 31 May 2009[9]

	CIMB	DMG	KESPL	OSPL	PSPL	UOBKH	TOTAL
Number of investors	217	63	208	1,204	712	315	2,719
Cases received	91	16	49	404	242	150	952
Cases decided[1]	**88**	**15**	**49**	**377**	**213**	**147**	**889**
Settlement outcomes for cases decided (% of cases decided)							
- full or partial	**53** (**60.2%**)	**1** (**6.7%**)	**21** (**42.9%**)	**128** (**34%**)	**86** (**40.4%**)	**8** (**5.5%**)	**297** (**33.4%**)
- full	3 (3.4%)	1 (6.7%)	2 (4.1%)	0 (0%)	3 (1.4%)	2 (1.4%)	11 (1.2%)
- partial (50% and above)	6 (6.8%)	0 (0%)	10 (20.4%)	18 (4.8%)	1 (0.5%)	2 (1.4%)	37 (4.2%)
- partial (below 50%)	44 (50%)	0 (0%)	9 (18.4%)	110 (29.2%)	82 (38.5%)	4 (2.7%)	249 (28%)
- nil	**35** (**39.8%**	**14** (**93.3%**)	**28** (**57.1%**)	**249** (**66%**)	**127** (**59.6%**)	**139** (**94.5%**)	**592** (**66.6%**)
Amount invested for cases decided	S$4.6m	S$0.5m	S$2.9m	S$23.1m	S$9.2m	S$8.9m	S$49.2m
Value of settlement offers (% of amount invested for cases decided)	**S$0.49m** (**10.7%**)	**S$0.02m** (**4%**)	**S$0.31m** (**10.7%**)	**S$1.22m** (**5.3%**)	**S$0.61m** (**6.6%**)	**S$0.09m** (**1%**)	**S$2.74m** (**5.6%**)

Notes: CIME: CIMB-GK Securities
DMG: DMG & Partners Securities
KESPL: Kim Eng Securities
OSPL: OCBC Securities
PSPL: Phillip Securities
UOBKH: UOB Kay Hian

Advice by MAS on How to Resolve Complaints[11]

Earlier in February 2009, the MAS issued specific advice for retail customers who invested in Lehman Minibond Notes, DBS High Notes 5, or Merrill Lynch Jubilee Series 3 LinkEarner Notes. The advice was for those who felt that they were mis-sold these products. The objective was to help these investors to resolve their complaint with their financial institutions (FIs). Meanwhile, the MAS had also asked these FIs to give priority to reviewing those cases involving vulnerable customers where the products were clearly inappropriate for them. Regardless of the circumstances, the MAS had also required the FIs to have a rigorous process to look into every complaint of mis-spelling and to resolve them fairly. If customers were not satisfied with that decision, they could refer the case to the Financial Industry Dispute Resolution Centre (FIDReC). If they did so, the information that they had earlier provided to the FI would be given to the FIDReC under a fast-track process arranged by the MAS with FIDReC. The decision of FIDReC would be binding on the FI but not on the customers. Those who were not satisfied could consider other options including legal action.

As at 22 November 2009, 1,760 cases had been lodged at the FIDReC. They included those shown in Table 3.3.

By the end of November 2009, about 72 per cent of the cases that were received by FIDReC were resolved. These figures did not include cases that were awaiting the outcome of court action and further instructions from the customers (Robin Chan 2009).

TABLE 3.3
Cases Lodged at FIDReC

Cases Lodged (as at 22 November 2009)	Number of Cases	Per Cent of Total
DBS High Notes 5	333	18.9
Lehman Minibond Notes	1,263	71.8
Merrill Lynch Jubilee Series 3 Linmearner Notes	375	4.2
Morgan Stanley Pinnacle Series (1, 9, 10) Notes	89	5.1

Source: Robin Chan, "Steady progress in resolving cases", *Straits Times*, 1 December 2009, p. B18.

Payout for Minibond Note Holders

In early February 2010, PricewaterhouseCoopers (PwC), the receivers for Minibond Notes announced that holders of these notes would get back part of their investments. Payments would vary according to the types of notes as indicated in Table 3.4. The value of the different series depended on several factors including the underlying collateral such as bonds, how long they have to maturity and the currency in which the notes were denominated. The payout was in addition to any compensation the investors might have received from the financial institutions that sold them the investments (Lorna Tan 2010).

Deposit Insurance Scheme

In Singapore, the Singapore Deposit Insurance Corporation (SDIC) executes the Deposit Insurance Scheme which

TABLE 3.4
Payout for Minibond Note Holders

Minibond Series	Payout (per cent)
2B	70.8
3B	64.0
B	63.1
2A	62.4
10	62.4
7	59.5
9	57.7
3A	55.9
3C	47.3
6	40.0
5	29.8
1B	24.0
1A	21.5

Source: PwC (as quoted in *Straits Times*,
4 February 2010).

safeguards the depositors in the case of the collapse of a financial institution. The types of deposits covered under Deposit Insurance Scheme include savings accounts, fixed deposit accounts, current accounts and CPF Investment Scheme. Individuals and charities with insured deposits in full banks and finance institutions in Singapore will be insured by SDIC. The government has also declared the guarantee for all Singapore dollar and foreign currency deposits in financial institutions licensed by the MAS. The guarantee is for all bank deposits until 31 December 2010 under a special ruling made in October in response to the increasing number of worried investors.

Guidelines on Fair Dealing

On 3 April 2009, under the Financial Advisers Act, the MAS issued Guidelines on Fair Dealing — Board and Senior Management Responsibilities for Delivering Fair Dealing Outcomes to Customers (Guidelines No. FAA-G11).[12] The guidelines focus on the responsibilities of the Board and Senior Management to deal fairly with their customers. The Guidelines apply to the selection, marketing and distribution of investment products and the provision of advice for the products The accountability for after-sales services and complaints handling are also included.

Guidelines on Structured Deposits

Under the Financial Advisers Act, the Guidelines on Structured Deposits (FAA-G09) were first issued on 7 October 2004 and revised on 4 May 2006. The purpose of the Guidelines is to establish a standard code of conduct for licensed and exempt financial advisers and their representatives during the advice on structured products.

Financial advisers must present a good reason for recommending any structured deposit to their customers. Screening should be conducted especially for customers who wish to withdraw before maturity so that they are fully aware of the operation of the relevant financial instruments before investing. Financial advisers must know structured deposits well especially the complex ones in order to offer a more reasonable advice. There is a need to separate structured deposits from traditional fixed deposits. This is to prevent customers from being misled into believing that both of these deposits contain similar returns and risks.

Strengthen the Financial System

After reviewing how banks and insurance companies manage their risks, the MAS introduced several measures to strengthen Singapore's financial system.[13] For example, it has broadened the range of debt securities that banks can use as collateral when borrowing from the MAS facility. To prevent failed Singapore Government Securities (SGS) auctions that could undermine confidence in government debt securities, MAS now has the flexibility to adjust the size of an SGS issue or vary the amount it buys, to stabilize an auction. Previously, the issuance amount would be fixed when an upcoming auction was announced. MAS may now cancel an SGS auction if needed.

Discussion in Parliament

The issue of mis-selling of structured products was discussed in Parliament. On 20 July 2009, MAS Deputy Chairman Lim Hng Kiang (who is also Minister for Trade and Industry) said that it was not the central bank's role to judge the merits of products being sold. Its task was to ensure that the financial institutions properly disclosed the features and risks of the products, and did not publish false or misleading statements. The financial institutions had adopted the MAS's recommendation not to take an overly legalistic approach in resolving customer complaints. They paid the refund even though they were not legally liable as some clients had signed documents acknowledging that they were aware of the risks of the products and the role of the distributors (U-Wen Lee 2009).

Assessing Retail Investor's Knowledge

In January 2010, the MAS issued a consultation paper about its proposal to safeguard retail investors on a wide range of investment products. Under the proposal, the MAS would impose a new obligation on financial advisers and brokers to formally assess a retail customer's investment knowledge or experience before selling investment products to the customer. Customers with no knowledge or experience in specific unlisted investment products must be given advice. The proposal would also require intermediaries to conduct a customer account review on retail customers before approving their accounts to trade listed non-excluded products. Exempted from these measures are established products such as shares, rights, warrants, real estate investment trusts (REITs) and money market instruments (Siow 2010).

Additional proposals included the following:[14]

a) Expand the scope of the Capital Markets Financial Advisory Services (CMFAS) examination module that was planned for the three classes of unlisted "complex investment products" to cover other non-excluded investment products.
b) Require issuers of debentures which are asset-backed securities and structured notes, collective investment schemes and sub-funds of investment-linked life insurance policies to prepare Product Highlight Sheets.

Great Eastern Offers Redemption

In August 2009, Great Eastern Life (GE) offered to return money to clients who bought its single premium investment-linked insurance product sold as "GreatLink Choice" (GLC). This product was sold in five tranches between 2005 and 2007, totalling $594 million. The product was linked to a class of complex financial instruments whose value was badly hit by the financial crisis. Its value plummeted between 40 per cent to 80 per cent. As a gesture of goodwill and to retain the trust of its policyholders, GE volunteered to redeem these investments in full to policyholders without any admission of liability. The 18,000 GLC policyholders could cancel their units and receive a sum equal to the original purchase price of $1 per unit, less the total annual payouts they have received (Lorna Tan 2009).

UOB Redeems Prudential Funds

On 20 October 2009, the UOB offered to redeem at full value $150 million worth of structured investment products that were sold to retailer investors in 2005. The market value of the Prudential Yield 15 and Yield 20 funds, both of which mature in June 2010, fell to less than half their starting price in March 2009. Instead of accepting the offer, investors had the choice of holding their units until maturity on 10 June 2010. They may have a chance of receiving not just the full principal of $1 or US$1 for each unit, but also the final yearly coupon payment as well. As of 25 November 2009, more than half of the 4,000 odd customers took up the offer to redeem their units.[15]

Budget 2009 and the Resilience Package

As a result of this financial crisis, the Singapore economy went into a recession. Export businesses were affected by the slow-down in the U.S. market and began to retrench workers. The government introduced a S$20.5 billion "resilience package" in the 2009 Budget. The main objectives were to help viable companies to stay afloat and to save jobs.[16] The following sections highlight some of the major schemes.

Special Risk-Sharing Initiative, Tax Rebate, Jobs Credit Scheme

The Special Risk-Sharing Initiative (SRI) was introduced to encourage lending by banks. The government would bear 80 per cent of the risk of bank loans to local businesses. As of December 2009, about $6.7 billion worth of government-backed loans were given to more than 12,000 local businesses, many of which were SMEs.[17] Corporate tax was reduced from 18 per cent to 17 per cent. There was a 40 per cent tax rebate on industrial and commercial properties.

In order to encourage employers to retain their workers, the government introduced a new Jobs Credit Scheme to subsidize the cost of hiring workers. Companies would get a cash grant of 12 per cent on the first S$2,500 of the wages of each employee on their Central Provident Fund (CPF) payroll. By October 2009, there was indication that the scheme has served its purpose well. It has helped to keep retrenchment and unemployment numbers down. In order to sustain its success, the scheme has been extended for another six months before it is phased out.

New Job Opening and Fund for Innovation

The government opened up 18,000 new public sector jobs in various ministries and statutory boards. The Skills

Programme for Upgrading and Resilience (SPUR) was increased to cater for 230,000 people in more than 800 courses covering 24 industries. In order to help professionals, managers, executives and technicians (PMETs), the Workforce Development Agency (WDA) doubled the number of professional conversion programme. Workers whose pay were reduced during the recession would get a temporary top-up to their Workfare Income Supplement (WIS). To encourage creation and test-bedding of new ideas, the Economic Development Board offered a $200 million Test-Bedding Fund for companies and individuals to nurture new ideas, test innovative solutions and develop future global businesses. The government has also set up a Core Innovation Fund to help private companies to collaborate with government agencies to develop innovative solutions for public services.

SPUR and Skill Upgrading

SPUR was introduced in December 2008. It was developed by WDA in consultation with tripartite partners including the Ministry of Manpower (MOM), National Trades Union Congress (NTUC) and Singapore National Employers Federation (SNEF). Under the scheme, companies that were affected by declining business were encouraged to retain workers by sending them for training. They would receive course fee support of 90 per cent for rank-and-file employees as well as professionals, managers, executives and technicians. Other benefits included absentee payroll. Training courses could be modified to suit the needs of individual employers and workers. SPUR also supported customized industry-wide plans such as those for service companies to improve their service quality. It also encouraged retrenched workers in the manufacturing sector to attend short redeployment courses such as the Certified Service Professional (CSP) programme to prepare them for jobs in the services industry.[18]

Action by SPRING

In May 2009, SPRING Singapore introduced the Professional Skills Programme Traineeships (PSPT) scheme to help fresh graduates and retrenched professionals to find advisory jobs with SMEs. About 230 SMEs put up more than 800 trainee positions under the Executive Training Programme (ETP) which was launched jointly with Nanyang Technological University (NTU), National University of Singapore (NUS) and Singapore Management University (SMU). Fresh graduates were placed in twelve-month traineeship with SMEs. Under the Business Advisers Programme, about sixty PMETs were attached to SMEs to work on areas such as strategic planning, financial management and market expansion (Chay 2009).

Recommendation by NWC

The National Wages Council (NWC) is a good example of how tripartism has worked in Singapore, especially during a crisis. It was formed in 1972 to monitor wage trends. Since then, it has issued annual guidelines on wage practices. In 2009, the tripartite partners (MOM, NTUC and SNEF) discussed the impact of the financial crisis on the Singapore economy. The Council then issued guidelines on how to cut costs, save jobs and enhance competitiveness. It urged companies with excess manpower to implement measures such as shorter work week, temporary layoffs, no-pay leave and other work arrangements as alternatives to retrenchment. Workers should cooperate with employers to implement these measures so as to cut costs and save jobs. In freezing or cutting wages, management should lead by example.[19]

Cut and Restore Pay by Some Companies

As one of the most successful Singapore companies, Singapore Airlines (SIA) took the lead in cutting wages. As agreed between management and the Air Line Pilots Association (Alpa-S), the pilots took one day of no-pay leave each month and a cut of 65 per cent of one day's pay a month. From July 2009, management staff took a pay cut of at least 10 per cent while the pay of the chief executive and board members were reduced by 20 per cent. Employees may volunteer for no-pay leave for two years (Yang 2009).

In December 2008, another major company Singapore Press Holdings (SPH) also introduced some cost-cutting measures to keep jobs for its 3,500 employees. It reduced the basic monthly salary of staff who earned more than $2,000. The reduction ranged from 2 per cent to 10 per cent. When the company did well in 2009, it restored half of the cut from January 2010. The media group gave a special one-off amount to staff to thank them for the sacrifice they made in cutting operating costs.[20]

Post-crisis Performance of the Singapore Economy

As a small open economy, Singapore has not been immune to the financial turmoil but has also benefitted from the global recovery. After hitting a trough in March 2009, the domestic equity market has mounted a sharp rebound, in tandem with global and regional equity markets. The Singapore economy contracted in Q4 of 2008 and Q1 of 2009, but has since posted two quarters of strong sequential growth. For the whole of 2009, GDP growth is projected at between –2.5 per cent and –2 per cent, a much less adverse outcome than expected early this year. The corporate and household sectors have thus far weathered the economic slowdown relatively well on the back of strong balance sheets and government policies such as the Special Risk-Sharing Initiative and the Jobs Credit Scheme.[21]

According to the MAS Financial Stability Review released in November 2009, based on the balance sheets, Singapore households have weathered the financial crisis relatively well. Household assets were six times more than household debts. Household net wealth stood at all time high, at about $1,001 billion in Q3 of 2009, after hitting a low of $895 billion in Q1 of 2009 (see Figure 3.1).

The GDP figures released by the Ministry of Trade and Industry (MTI) on 19 November 2009 confirmed the end of recession in Singapore. The growth rate of 14.2 per cent q-o-q for Q3 of 2009 saw the second consecutive quarter of sequential expansion and the first positive rate of 0.6 per cent y-o-y growth in four quarters. The MTI has forecast a cautious but realistic GDP growth rate of 3–5 per cent for 2010 (see Figure 3.2).

FIGURE 3.1
Household Net Wealth, 1997–2009

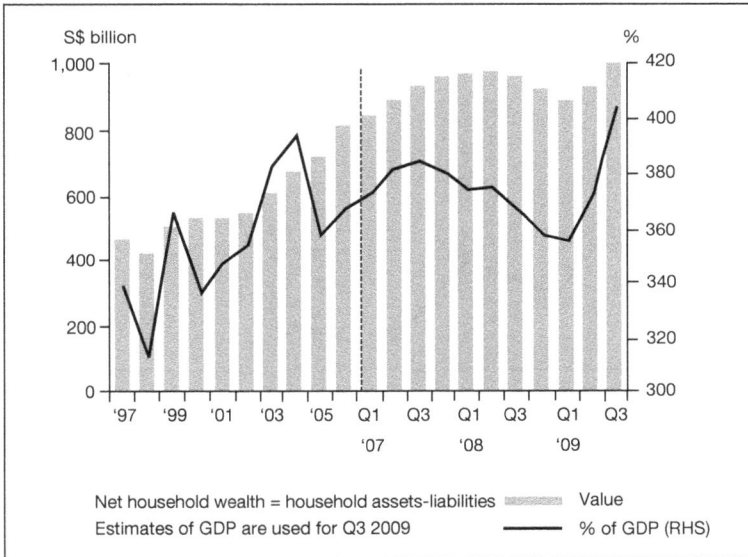

Source: MAS as cited in Siow Li Sen, "Wages rise, debts slow and Singaporeans get richer", *Business Times*, 10 November 2009.

Similar optimism was shown by export figures released by the International Enterprise (IE) Singapore. In November 2009, non-oil exports surged by 8.7 per cent, reversing an eighteen-month decline.[22]

By December 2009, there was some indication that employment prospects in 2010 would return to pre-crisis level. The Singapore arm of the global human resource consultancy Manpower Inc. released a report on employment outlook for 2010. About 700 employers from seven industries were interviewed in October 2009. About 65 per cent would retain their headcount in Q1 of 2010. Another 27 per cent

FIGURE 3.2
GDP Growth Rate, 2008–09

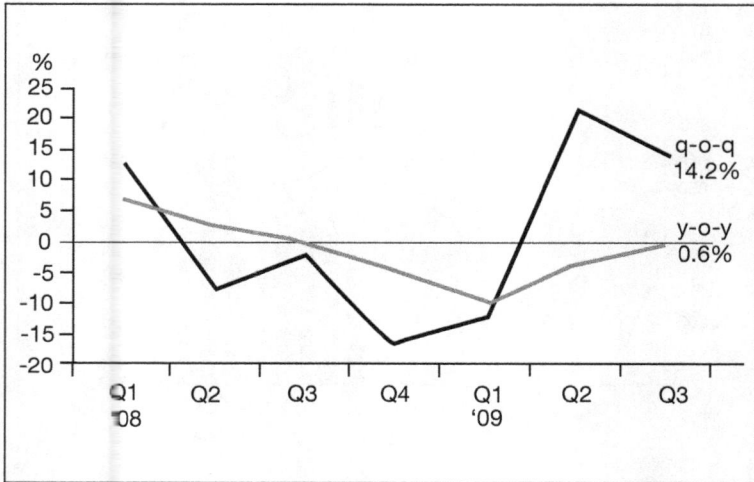

Source: Anna Teo, "No easy ride, but MTI bets on 3–5 per cent growth for 2010", *Business Times*, 20 November 2009.

planned to increase headcount while only 5 per cent planned to reduce staff. Job prospects seemed to be brightest in the finance, insurance and real estate sectors. Total employment rose by 15,400 jobs in the third quarter of 2009, ending losses in the first and second quarters (Teh 2009).

According to a survey commissioned by payment service provider PayPal, about 75 per cent of small and medium businesses in Singapore are optimistic about business growth in 2010. In this survey, about 300 businesses with staff strength of 5 to 50 were surveyed (Zhang 2009).

Future Measures

As revealed in the MAS Financial Stability Review released in November 2009, during the first half of 2009, as a result of the low interest environment, the cost of financing was substantially reduced, thus causing a surge in demand for properties. If unchecked, this could lead to a spiral of demand and prices as more property buyers and speculators entered the market. In order to prevent speculative bubble from forming, the government introduced the following measures in September 2009.[23]

(i) It banned interest-only housing loans and interest absorption scheme that allowed developers to absorb interest payments for apartments that were still under construction.

(ii) The Ministry of National Development restarted its confirmed list of Government Land Sales programme. To meet the strong demand for private homes, during the first six months of 2010, it would place eight residential sites on the confirmed list.

The aim of these measures was to curb erratic price hikes arising from excessive speculation or market manipulation. On 23 November 2009, as disclosed by National Development Minister Mah Bow Tan, these measures have taken some effect on the property market. According to the Urban Redevelopment Authority (URA), developers sold 822 units in October, down 29 per cent from 1,143 units in September, and September's volume was itself 37 per cent less than the 1,805 units sold in August (Yap 2009).

The MAS will review its corporate governance regulations for banks and insurance companies. The objective is to set more stringent standards on these financial institutions. The review will tighten the definition of independence of directors and require the nominating committee to consider the length of service of these directors. It will focus on the effectiveness of risk management at the board level. The board has to align its compensation policies with the nature of risk taking in line with the principles published by the International Financial Stability Board.[24]

During the financial crisis, international credit rating agencies were criticized for not downgrading the ratings for troubled companies. The National University of Singapore (NUS) plans to launch its own credit rating system to rate some 500 Asian companies by 2011. The non-profit rating system will suggest new methods that will face off against rating systems currently used. The project will be funded by the NUS Risk Management Institute (RMI), which in turn is partly funded by the Financial Sector Development Fund from the Monetary Authority of Singapore (MAS). The system will challenge the "one-dimensional" rating system adopted by present credit rating agencies. Critics have commented that present rating agencies have conflicting interests since debt issuers pay them for rating. This has led to the call for independent research and more transparency in the methods used by these agencies. The ratings market has been dominated by global agencies Moody's, Standard and Poor's and Fitch.[25]

The financial crisis has taught us that globalization has its costs. While international trade, investment and finance have benefited the world greatly to improve economic prosperity, they come with negative effects. First, the economic gains are not distributed evenly among nations. While some have benefited from cheaper imports, others remain below the poverty line. Second, private capital flow could inflict serious economic damages when there is a sudden capital flow reversal. During the crisis, many countries felt the impact as multinational banks redeemed their funds to cover huge non-performing loans associated with the U.S. subprime bubble. Third, environmental quality is compromised when global activities put stress on resources and the ecosystem.[26]

Part of the cause of the financial crisis was the inadequate training provided by banks. This was disclosed by a survey done by PricewaterhouseCoopers (PwC) from December 2008 to March 2009. It polled 240 private banks and wealth managers in forty countries, with 16 per cent from the Asia Pacific. The study disclosed that client trust and confidence had declined. There was an urgent need for wealth managers to improve the skills of their relationship managers (Cua 2009).

The financial crisis has revealed that during the past two decades, there was a regulatory gap in the interconnected global financial markets. While banks were international and capital flows crossed national borders, supervision and regulation was largely domestic. As highlighted by Singapore's Minister for Finance Tharman Shanmugaratnam, the crisis is not about the failure of the global market economy, but about failure of regulation. The invisible hand of the market requires the visible hand of the regulator if it is to work well. Governments and central banks must play a supporting role in a free market system by setting rules to mitigate the build-up of excesses (Shanmugaratnam 2009).

It is timely to consider Harvard Professor Elizabeth Warren's suggestion of a Financial Product Commission in the United States or a similar institution in other countries. Information about financial products should be disclosed in a manner that investors can understand. In the wealth management industry, professionals should rebalance their incentives from transaction revenue to assets under management. In order to regain trust from clients, they should switch their role from salesmanship to guardianship (Fong and Low 2009).

Any proposed financial reform need to address not only the underlying causes of the crisis, but also protect the real economy from the excesses of the financial sector. Professionals in the financial markets must be able to identify and manage systemic risks better. Perverse incentives in the industry need to be monitored. The shadow banking sector must be regulated along the same lines as the core banking sector.[27]

As observed by Dean Hawawini of INSEAD, one lesson that the global finance community can learn from recent events is that no country is isolated from a major crisis, particularly one that originates from the United States. As countries become more connected to one another through international trade, so do the banks. This global connection comes with inter-related risks and costs. While hoping to gain from the benefits, nations must also be prepared for the worst (Hawawini 2009).

As suggested by Dean Cooley at the Stern School of Business, New York University, business students must understand that the pursuit of profits may lead to a systemic breakdown that destroys the credibility of institutions and the wealth of their customers. They must understand what happened, which incentive systems broke down, and why the system of checks and balances failed. Business students must learn analytical tools that will help them understand this crisis and prevent, or at least, manage the next one. The structure of financial markets, the regulatory system, the credit rating agencies, financial derivatives, mortgage finance, incentives and compensation — all these issues should become the focus of business school research for years to come (Cooley 2009).

In the search for a lesson from the financial crisis, it is timely for bankers, investors and business leaders to do some self-examination. Business executive education should equip participants how to make better decisions under risky conditions. They must understand the range of possible outcomes of their decisions and the potential consequences of such outcomes (Arvey 2009).

In the context of managing personal finance, the crisis revealed that many individual investors were victims of herd behaviour. They believed that when everyone was making money, they too bought the same fund. Some could have done it under the persistent persuasion of financial advisers at the bank. Regardless of the situation, there is no substitute for independent thinking and critical enquiry (David Lee 2009).

APPENDIX

Abstract of Budget 2009 Key Budget Initiatives

Key Initiatives 1 — Jobs for Singaporeans

(A) Jobs Credit

Employers receive a 12 per cent cash grant on the first $2,500 of each month's wages for each employee on their CPF payroll. Job Credits is for one year.

(B) SPUR for Workers and Professionals

SPUR provides higher course fee support for companies and individuals and absentee payroll for companies that send their workers for training. Course fee subsidies for PMET-level courses will be increased from 80 per cent to 90 per cent.

(C) Workfare Income Supplement (WIS) Special Payment

Low-income workers will get a temporary WIS Special Payment to supplement their pay and to stay employed.

(D) Government Hiring

18,000 public sector jobs will be made available over the next two years.

— 7,500 jobs in teaching positions
— 4,500 jobs in healthcare positions
— 1,400 jobs for the Home Team
— 2,000 jobs for MINDEF
— 2,600 jobs for the rest of public service

Key Initiatives 2 — Stimulating Bank Lending

(A) Special Risk-Sharing Initiative (SRI)

The objective is to ensure that viable companies continue to have credit access to sustain their operations and keep jobs.
— New Bridging Loan Programme
— Trade Finance Scheme
— Loan Insurance Scheme — Plus
— Trade Credit Insurance Programme (TCIP)

(B) Enhancements to Existing Credit Measures

Existing loan schemes have been enhanced:
— Local Enterprise Finance Scheme
— Micro Loan Programme
— Internationalization Finance Scheme

(C) Other Credit-related Measures

Extension of Tax Deduction on Loan Loss Provisions for Banks.

Key Initiatives 3 — Enhancing Business Cash-flow and Competitiveness

(A) Easing Business Cash-flow

— Property tax rebate for industrial and commercial properties
— Rental rebates by JTC, HDB and SLA
— Enhancements to loss carry-back scheme
— Tax exemption on remittance of foreign-sourced income
— Transport rebates and concessions
— Further extension of the government fee freeze
— Measures for property developers
— Deferment of increase in assessment rate for hotels

(B) Reducing Taxes to Encourage Investments

— Corporate income tax rate cut
— Accelerated capital allowance
— Writing down of renovation and refurbishment expenses
— New tax framework for corporate amalgamations

(C) Sector Specific Taxes and Duties

For Financial Sector Activities:
— Enhancements to and streamlining of Fund Management Initiatives

— Recovery of GST for qualifying local funds
— Expansion of scope of tax exemption under Fund Management and Trust Incentives
— Enhancements to Financial Sector Initiative — Headquarter Service Scheme
— Extension and enhancement of Commodity Derivatives Traders (CDT) Scheme

For Maintenance, Repair and Overhaul (MRO) Activities:
— Zero-rating for the aerospace industry

For Auction, Exhibition and Specialized Storage Activities:
— Suspension of GST and duty on goods temporarily removed from zero-GST or Licenses warehouses

For Wine Trading Activities:
— Exemption of duty to facilitate wine trading activities

For Maritime Activities:
— Withholding tax exemption for maritime industry

(D) Making Innovation Pervasive

— Accelerated Writing-Down Allowance (WDA) for acquisition of intellectual property rights for media and digital entertainment content
— Test-bedding fund
— Government taking the lead in innovation

Key Initiatives 4 — Supporting Families

(A) Direct Assistance to Households

— Goods and Services Tax (GST) credits and senior citizens'
   bonus
— Service and conservancy charges (S&CC) rebates
— Rental rebate
— Personal income tax rebate
— Installment option for personal income tax payment
— Property tax rebate
— Removal of tax on net annual value of property
— Increase in additional CPF housing grant

(B) Targeted Help for the Most Vulnerable Groups

— Public Transport Fund (PTF) top-up
— Financial assistance scheme for education
— Public assistance rate
— Singapore Allowance

(C) Support for Charitable Giving and the Community

— Citizens' Consultative Committees ComCare Fund and
   Self-Help Groups
— Increased tax deduction and additional grant for
   government-funded voluntary welfare organizations
   (VWOs)

— Extending business measures to VWOs
— Extending start-up exemption to companies limited by guarantee

Key Initiatives 5 — Building a Home for the Future

(A) Expanding and Accelerating Public Sector Infrastructure Spending

The government will increase public sector construction spending to between $18 billion and $20 billion in 2009.

(B) Developing Suburban Nodes and Rejuvenating Neighbourhoods

— Invest in new regional commercial nodes such as Jurong Lake District, Kallang Riverside and Paya Lebar Central
— Rejuvenating existing public housing neighbourhoods

(C) Pushing Ahead on Sustainable Development

The government will spend $1 billion over the next five years on sustainable development initiatives.

(D) Spending More on Education and Healthcare

— Enhancing school education
— Expanding healthcare capacity

NOTES

1. Examples are Bamber and Spencer (2008); Bonner and Wiggin (2009); Bougearel (2009); Brummer (2009); Faber (2009); Foster and Magdoff (2009); Goodhart (2009); Kelley (2009); Krugman (2009); Muolo (2009); O'Brien (2009); Png (2008); Posner (2009); Ritholtz (2009); Roberts (2008); Rotman (2008); Shiller (2008); Soros (2008); Talbott (2009); Turner (2009). For full details of these sources, see list of references.
2. For detailed discussion on the impact, see Leong and Mahmood, eds. (2009).
3. For details, see Monetary Authority of Singapore (2009).
4. Monetary Authority of Singapore (2009).
5. Ibid.
6. Ibid.
7. Ibid.
8. Ibid.
9. Ibid.
10. In February 2010, this ban was lifted for some of these banks. See MAS press release, 11 February 2010.
11. See <http//www.mas.gov.sg/print/consumer/structured_products/fidrec_3_step_process.html>.
12. These guidelines are available at MAS website <www.mas.gov.sg>.
13. *Business Times*, 17 July 2009.
14. See <http://www.mas.gov.sg/print/news_room/press_releases/2010/MAS_Issues_Consultation>.
15. Conrad Tan (25 November 2009).
16. See Appendix for details.
17. Fiona Chan (17 December 2009).
18. For details on these programmes, see WDA website <www.wda.gov.sg>.

19. See National Wages Council Recommendations 2009/ 2010.
20. *Business Times*, 2 December 2009.
21. See *MAS Financial Stability Review*, November 2009.
22. Fiona Chan (18 December 2009).
23. Conrad Tan (10 November 2009).
24. Jaime Lee (20 November 2009).
25. Jaime Lee (17 July 2009).
26. Lim Chin and Bernard Yeung, "Currents, Crisis and Internal Tensions", 2009.
27. Lim Chin and Bernard Yeung, "Laying Foundations for More Stable Order", 2009.

REFERENCES

Arvey, Richard. "Leaders Need to Re-think Attitudes". In *The Financial Crisis: Impact and Implications for Singapore Business*, edited by Leong Siew Meng and Ishtiaq P. Mahmood. Singapore: NUS Business School, National University of Singapore, 2009.

Bamber, Bill and Andrew Spencer. *Bear Trap: The Fall of Bear Stearns and the Panic of 2008*. New York: Brick Tower Press, 2008.

Bonner, William and Addison Wiggin. *Financial Reckoning Day Fallout*. New Jersey: John Wiley, 2009.

Bougearel, John. *Riding the Storm Out: What So You Do As Investors Do Now?* Financial Futures Analysis Inc., 2009.

Brummer, Alex. *The Crunch: How Greed and Incompetence Sparked the Credit Crisis*. London: Random House, 2009.

Chan, Fiona. "Scramble for Government-backed Loans". *Straits Times*, 17 December 2009, p. C12.

———. "November Exports Surge Ends 18-month Decline". *Straits Times*, 18 December 2009.

Chan, Robin. "Steady Progress in Resolving Cases". *Straits Times*, December 2009.

Chay, Felda. "Fresh Grads, PMETs Benefit from SPRING". *Business Times*, 25 September 2009.

Cooley, Thomas F. "Crisis and Consequences: The Ultimate Teachable Moment". *BizEd*, January–February 2009.

Cua, Genevieve. "Crisis on Several Fronts for RMs". *Business Times*, 5 August 2009.

Faber, David. *And then the Roof Caved In: How Wall Street's Greed and Stupidity Brought Capitalism to Its Knees*. Hoboken: Wiley, 2009.

Fong, Wai Mun and Low Chee Kiat. "Restoring Trust in Bankers". In *The Financial Crisis: Impact and Implications for Singapore Business*, edited by Leong Siew Meng and Ishtiaq P. Mahmood. Singapore: NUS Business School, National University of Singapore, 2009.

Foster, John Bellamy and Fred Magdoff. *The Great Financial Crisis: Causes and Consequences. New York: Monthly Review Press, 2009.*

Goodhart, Charles A.E. *The Regulatory Response to the Financial Crisis*. Cheltenham: Edward Elgar, 2009.

Hawawini, Gabriel. "Crisis and Consequences: Preparing for the Worst". *BizEd*, January–February 2009.

Kelly, Kate. *Street Fighters: The Last 72 Hours of Bear Stearns*. New York: Portfolio Penguin Group, 2009.

Krugman, Paul. *The Return of Depression Economics and the Crisis of 2008*. New York: Norton & Co., 2009.

Lee, David. "Fund Managers Still Your Best Bet". In *The Financial Crisis: Impact and Implications for Singapore Business*, edited by Leong Siew Meng and Ishtiaq P. Mahmood. Singapore: NUS Business School, National University of Singapore, 2009.

Lee, Jaime. "NUS RMI Plans Credit Rating System". *Business Times*, 17 July 2009.

_____. "Corporate Governance Code to be Reviewed". *Business Times*, 20 November 2009.

Lee, U-Wen. "MAS Rap will Tarnish FIs' Name". *Business Times*, 21 July 2009.

Leong, David. "When the Housing Bubble Bursts: How Subprime Woes Spiraled into an Economic Slowdown". *Pulses*, August 2008, pp. 48–50.

Leong Siew Meng and Ishtiaq P. Mahmood, eds. *The Financial Crisis: Impact and Implication for Singapore Business*. Singapore: NUS Business School, National University of Singapore, 2009.

Lim Chin and Bernard Yeung. "Currents, Crisis and Internal Tensions". In *Globalization and Financial Crisis*, edited by Lim Chin. Singapore: NUS Business School, National University of Singapore, 2009.

_____. "Laying Foundations for More Stable Order". In *Globalization and Financial Crisis*, edited by Lim Chin. Singapore: NUS Business School, National University of Singapore, 2009.

Monetary Authority of Singapore. *Investigation Report on the Sale and Marketing of Structured Notes Linked to Lehman Brothers*, 7 July 2009.

Muolo, Paul. *$700 Billion Bailout: The Emergency Economic Stabilization Act*. New Jersey: John Wiley, 2009.

O'Brien, J. *Engineering A Financial Bloodbath: How Subprime Securitization Detroyed the Legitimacy of Financial Capitalism*. London: Imperial College Press, 2009.

Png, Ivan. "Options and What They Mean". *Straits Times*, 26 October 2008.

_____, ed. *Financial Crisis 2008*. Singapore: NUS Business School, National University of Singapore, 2008.

Posner, Richard A. *A Failure of Capitalism: The Crisis of 2008 and the Descent into Depression*. Massachusetts: Harvard University Press, 2009.

Ritholtz, Barry. *Bailout Nation: How Greed and Easy Money Corrupted Wall Street and Shook the World Economy.* Hoboken: Wiley, 2009.

Roberts, Lawrence. *The Great Housing Bubble: Why Did House Prices Fall?* Las Vegas: Monterey Cypress Publishing, 2008.

Rotman School of Management. *The Finance Crisis and Rescue.* Toronto: Rotman School of Management, 2008.

Shanmugaratnam, Tharman. "New Global Regulation: Learning from Facts, Not Beliefs". In *Globalisation and Financial Crisis*, edited by Lim Chin. Singapore: NUS Business School, National University of Singapore, 2009.

Shiller, Robert. *The Subprime Solution: How Today's Global Financial Crisis Happened and What to Do About It.* Princeton: Princeton University Press, 2008.

Siow, L. Sen. "Want to Invest? Take a Knowledge Test First". *Business Times*, 29 January 2010.

Sivanithy, R. "Minibonds or Megabombs?" *Pulses*, November 2008.

Soros, George. *The Crash of 2008 and What It Means: The New Paradigm for Financial Markets.* New York: Public Affairs, 2008.

Talbott, John R. *Contagion: The Financial Epidemic that is Sweeping the Global Economy — and to Protect Yourself.* Hoboken: Wiley, 2009.

Tan, Conrad. "More Action may be needed if Recent Property Measures Inadequate: MAS". *Business Times*, 10 November 2009.

————. "55 per cent take-up for UOB offer to Prudential Fund Investors". *Business Times*, 25 November 2009.

Tan, Lorna. "GE Offers to Return $250 Million to Investors". *Straits Times*, 1 August 2009.

————. "Minibond Notes Holders to Get Payouts". *Straits Times*, 4 February 2010.

Teh, Shi Ning. "Hirings in 2010 seen Hitting Pre-crisis Levels". *Business Times*, 8 December 2009.

Tilson, Whitney and Glenn Tongue. *More Mortgage Meltdown: 6 Ways to Profit in These Bad Times*. New Jersey: Wiley, 2009.

Turner, Graham. *No Way to Run an Economy, Why the System Failed and How to Put It Right*. London, Pluto Press, 2009.

Wong, Dar. "The Insurance Blowout". *Pulses*, May 2009.

Yang, Huiwen. "SIA Pilots Agree to take Pay Cut". *Straits Times*, 20 June 2009.

Yap, Emilyn. "Moves to Cool Property Market Worked: Mah". *Business Times*, 24 November 2009.

Zhang, Jiao. "Singapore SMBs Optimistic about Growth Prospects". *Business Times*, 8 December 2009.

4
The Malaysian Economy and the Impact of the Global Financial Crisis

K. K. Foong

The Malaysian economy is gradually coming out of a deep recession as clearer signs of a recovery started emerging from 2009. Stabilizing global and domestic demand conditions resuscitated manufacturing output, while large public expenditure contributed to expansion in both construction and services activities. Better consumer and business sentiments have also led to revival in private sector demand. This, along with projected recovery in exports, will lift economic growth to +3.7 per cent in 2010 and further to +5.0 per cent in 2011, from an estimated contraction of 3.3 per cent in 2009.

Economic Outlook

Malaysia experienced a much better GDP growth rate of −1.2 per cent y-o-y in 3Q09 (−3.9 per cent in 2Q09) (see Figure 4.1). This improvement was attributed to the

FIGURE 4.1
GDP Growth Trend, 2006–09

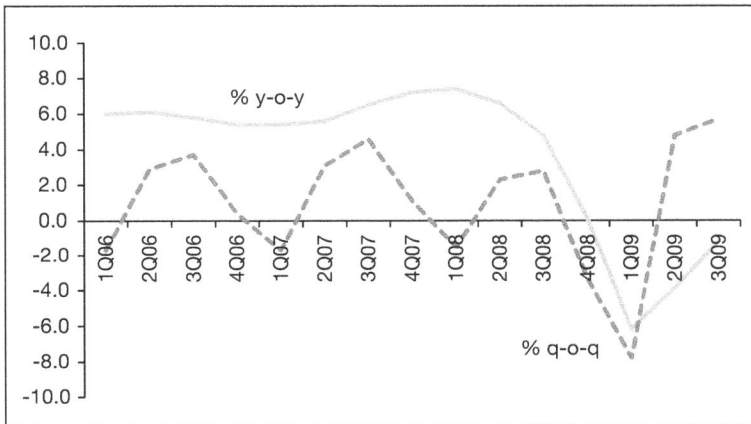

Sources: Department of Statistics; MIER calculations.

positive effects of stabilization policy measures as well as better domestic and external conditions. GDP expanded sequentially in 3Q09 by +5.7 per cent (2Q09: +4.8 per cent), reflecting an apparent upward trending path.

Dissecting GDP according to its expenditure component reveals that private consumption rose by +1.5 per cent y-o-y in 3Q09 (+0.5 per cent in 2Q09) due to improving general sentiment and labour market conditions (see Tables 4.1 and 4.2). Total investment moderated to –7.9 per cent y-o-y in 3Q09 (–9.6 per cent in 2Q09) due to the impact of higher public spending. Stabilizing conditions led to recovery in both exports and imports to –13.4 per cent y-o-y (–17.3 per cent in 2Q09) and –12.9 per cent y-o-y (–19.7 per cent in 2Q09) in 3Q09, respectively.

TABLE 4.1
GDP by Expenditure (% y-o-y), 2007–09

	2007	2008	1Q08	2Q08	3Q08	4Q08	1Q09	2Q09	3Q09
GDP	6.2	4.6	7.4	6.6	4.8	0.1	-6.2	-3.9	-1.2
Private Consumption	10.4	8.5	11.3	9.4	8.2	5.3	-0.7	0.5	1.5
Public Consumption	6.5	10.9	14.1	10.3	6.4	12.7	2.1	1.0	10.9
Gross Fixed Capital Formation	9.6	0.8	4.6	5.6	3.1	-10.2	-10.8	-9.6	-7.9
Domestic Demand	9.8	6.9	10.5	8.3	6.6	2.8	-2.9	-2.2	0.4
Exports of Goods & Services	4.5	1.3	5.9	9.5	4.5	-13.3	-15.2	-17.3	-13.4
Imports of Goods & Services	6.0	1.9	3.2	8.1	7.7	-10.2	-23.5	-19.7	-12.9

Source: Department of Statistics.

TABLE 4.2
Share of GDP by Expenditure, 2007–09

% share	2007	2008	1Q08	2Q08	3Q08	4Q08	1Q09	2Q09	3Q09
Private Consumption	50.5	52.4	52.7	50.3	52.3	54.1	55.8	52.7	53.8
Public Consumption	12.9	13.7	11.1	12.1	12.7	18.9	12.1	12.7	14.2
Gross Fixed Capital Formation	23.2	22.3	22.4	23.7	23.2	19.8	21.3	22.3	21.7
Domestic Demand	85.8	86.9	84.5	84.7	86.5	92.0	77.0	84.1	88.6
Exports of Goods & Services	122.3	118.4	117.0	123.5	124.3	108.4	105.8	106.4	109.1
Imports of Goods & Services	108.0	105.3	101.5	108.2	110.8	100.4	82.8	90.5	97.7

Source: Department of Statistics.

GDP growth analysis, in terms of key economic sectors (see Tables 4.3 and 4.4), shows that the manufacturing sector has rebounded to a smaller contraction of 8.6 per cent y-o-y in 3Q09 (−14.5 per cent in 2Q09) owing to slower rates of deceleration in export (−9.9 per cent y-o-y in 3Q09 vs. −16.4 per cent in 2Q09) and domestic-oriented industries (−5.8 per cent y-o-y in 3Q09 vs. −9.4 per cent y-o-y in 2Q09). The effects of fiscal stimulus measures propelled the construction sector to expand by +7.9 per cent y-o-y in 3Q09 (+4.5 per cent in 2Q09). Strong growth in finance, insurance, wholesale, retail trade, real estate, and tourism enabled the services sector to post +3.4 per cent y-o-y in 3Q09 (−1.6 per cent in 2Q09). Better sentiments and receding uncertainties also contributed to this expansion. The mining sector fell by 3.5 per cent y-o-y in 3Q09 (−3.6 per cent in 2Q09), while the agriculture sector contracted by 0.5 per cent y-o-y in 3Q09 (+0.3 per cent in 2Q09) due to lower production of palm oil and rubber.

Industrial Production

The IPI (see Table 4.5) reverted back to negative growth on a y-o-y and m-o-m basis in November 2009 to 1.3 per cent (October 2009: +0.9 per cent) and 6.0 per cent (October 2009: +5.9 per cent), respectively. This was due to broad-base slowdown across all sectors.

In terms of its components, manufacturing output (see Figure 4.2) moderated to +0.9 per cent y-o-y in November 2009 (−1.6 per cent in October 2009). Output of export-oriented industries rose by +1.4 per cent y-o-y (October 2009: −2.3 per cent), while domestic-oriented industries fell by 3.8 per cent y-o-y (October 2009: +5.4 per cent).

TABLE 4.3
GDP by Sector (% y-o-y), 2007–09

	2007	2008	1Q08	2Q08	3Q08	4Q08	1Q09	2Q09	3Q09
GDP	6.2	4.6	7.4	6.6	4.8	0.1	-6.2	-3.9	-1.2
Agriculture	1.4	4.0	6.5	6.3	3.3	0.5	-4.3	0.3	-0.5
Mining	2.0	-0.8	3.6	-0.5	-0.3	-5.7	-5.2	-3.6	-3.5
Manufacturing	3.1	1.3	7.0	5.6	1.8	-8.8	-17.9	-14.5	-8.6
Construction	4.7	2.1	5.3	3.9	1.2	-1.6	1.1	4.5	7.9
Services	9.6	7.2	8.4	7.9	7.1	5.7	-0.2	1.6	3.4

Source: Department of Statistics.

TABLE 4.4
Share of GDP by Sector, 2007–09

% share	2007	2008	1Q08	2Q08	3Q08	4Q08	1Q09	2Q09	3Q09
Agriculture	7.6	7.5	7.2	7.4	7.9	7.5	7.4	7.7	8.0
Mining	8.5	8.1	8.6	7.9	7.7	8.1	8.7	7.9	7.5
Manufacturing	30.1	29.1	30.1	30.0	29.5	26.8	26.3	26.7	27.4
Construction	3.0	3.0	2.9	3.1	2.9	2.9	3.1	3.4	3.2
Services	50.8	52.4	51.2	51.6	51.9	54.7	54.4	54.3	54.0

Source: Department of Statistics.

TABLE 4.5
Industrial Production Index in 2009 (% y-o-y)

% y-o-y	1Q	2Q	3Q	Jan	Feb	Mar	Apr	May	Jun	Jul	Aug	Sep	Oct	Nov
Overall IPI	-14.6	-10.9	-7.0	-17.9	-12.5	-12.7	-11.7	-11.3	-9.5	-8.1	-7.0	-6.0	0.9	-1.3
Manufacturing	-18.8	-14.9	-9.0	-23.4	-15.4	-17.1	-16.1	-15.6	-13.0	-11.3	-7.7	-8.2	1.6	0.9
Export-oriented	-20.3	-16.4	-9.9	-24.7	-17.0	-19.2	-17.9	-16.6	-14.6	-12.5	-7.2	-9.9	-2.3	1.4
Domestic-oriented	-12.2	-9.4	-5.8	-18.7	-8.9	-9.0	-9.2	-12.0	-7.0	-7.0	-4.6	-6.5	5.4	-3.8
Mining	-6.1	-3.2	-4.2	-5.8	-7.3	-3.2	-2.9	-3.0	-3.4	-2.9	-7.7	-3.0	-2.7	-7.4
Electricity	-9.1	-0.9	2.9	-12.5	-5.5	-8.9	-2.9	-2.1	2.5	3.1	3.9	4.8	11.0	5.9

Source: Department of Statistics.

FIGURE 4.2
Manufacturing Output Index (% y-o-y), 2006–09

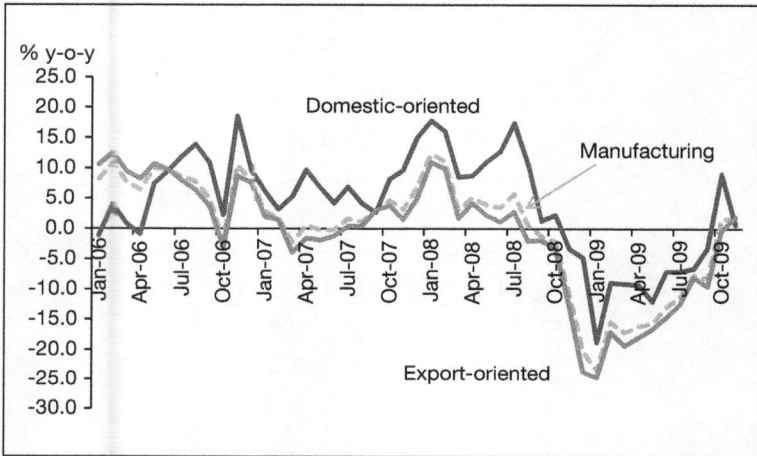

Sources: Bank Negara Malaysia; Department of Statistics.

Mining output declined by 7.4 per cent y-o-y in November 2009 (–2.7 per cent in October 2009), due to large contractions in production of crude oil (–11.1 per cent), which more than offset the increase in natural gas production (+1.7 per cent). Electricity output also grew at a slower rate of +5.9 per cent y-o-y in November 2009 (+11.0 per cent in October 2009) due to lower demand from industrial and commercial users.

MIER expects that the economy will exit out of recession in the 4Q09. This is supported by effects of the larger public infrastructural expenditure, manufacturing turnaround, improved services trade, and higher domestic spending.

External Trade Position

In November 2009, exports growth (see Table 4.6) lost its momentum by posting –3.3 per cent y-o-y and –7.7 per cent m-o-m (October 2009: +1.5 per cent y-o-y and +15.0 per cent m-o-m) due to lower shipments of electrical and electronic (E & E) products and a sharp fall in the value of liquefied natural gas.

E & E products moderated to +5.8 per cent y-o-y and –7.2 per cent m-o-m in November 2009 (+18.7 per cent y-o-y and +17.2 per cent m-o-m in October 2009) due to seasonal factors. First, semiconductors grew at a slower pace both y-o-y and m-o-m basis, namely by +20.3 per cent in November 2009 (+27.8 per cent in October 2009) and –7.0 per cent in November 2009 (+12.4 per cent in October 2009), respectively. Second, personal computers and office equipment showed a similar trend by slowing y-o-y (–4.3 per cent in November 2009 vs. +14.5 per cent in October 2009) and m-o-m (–4.2 per cent in November 2009 vs. +21.1 per cent in October 2009). Third, telecommunication equipment also recorded a similar pattern on both y-o-y and m-o-m basis. It declined 10.1 per cent y-o-y in November 2009 (+3.7 per cent in October 2009) and 12.9 per cent m-o-m in November 2009 (+24.2 per cent in October 2009).

Meanwhile, non-E & E products worsened by –9.3 per cent y-o-y in November 2009 (–8.5 per cent in October 2009) due to a large 52.0 per cent fall (October 2009: –40.7 per cent) in the export value of liquefied natural gas. Other categories improved in November 2009, notably palm oil earnings which rose +20.5 per cent (October 2009: –5.2 per cent), chemicals and chemical products higher by +16.0 per

TABLE 4.6
Trends in External Trade (% y-o-y), 2009

	Jan	Feb	Mar	Apr	May	Jun	Jul	Aug	Sep	Oct	Nov
Total Exports	-27.8	-16.0	-15.7	-26.3	-29.7	-22.7	-22.9	-19.9	-24.2	1.5	-3.3
Electrical & Electronic products	-34.3	-15.8	-4.4	-23.2	-28.3	-16.3	-15.7	-13.1	-19.2	18.7	5.8
Crude petroleum	-49.6	-57.6	-44.6	-56.9	-57.1	-53.8	-65.6	-24.2	-53.3	-29.4	-16.1
Chemicals & chemical products	-31.1	-27.4	-32.5	-26.5	-31.4	-24.5	-26.8	-19.5	-17.6	-4.9	16.0
Liquefied natural gas	58.6	43.6	23.3	-22.0	-38.8	-43.3	-31.6	-47.6	-35.6	-40.7	-52.0
Palm oil	-22.0	-24.4	-31.1	-34.7	-34.4	-17.4	-33.4	-35.3	-25.5	-5.2	20.5
Refined petroleum products	-57.2	-21.9	-43.5	-54.8	-46.4	-47.9	-31.8	-39.3	-36.5	21.9	9.0
Machinery/appliances	-31.3	-8.0	-21.5	-22.9	-31.0	-9.0	-11.6	-13.2	-8.9	6.5	-8.0
Optical/scientific instrument	-14.2	-15.7	-9.2	-36.2	-36.1	-19.7	-19.4	13.8	-11.8	8.5	-10.3
Metal manufactures	-35.3	-30.9	-42.6	-20.3	-32.2	-28.4	-30.0	-33.9	-36.1	-3.3	-13.4
Total Imports	-30.4	-27.3	-28.7	-22.4	-27.8	-20.9	-16.2	-18.7	-20.3	-2.4	2.3
Intermediate goods	-36.1	-33.8	-34.9	-26.8	-31.1	-23.7	-20.4	-23.6	-23.8	-9.6	-4.4
Capital goods	-2.3	-8.3	-12.6	-10.0	-27.2	-14.6	-7.3	-9.1	-22.7	5.0	23.3
Consumption goods	-14.1	-4.4	6.9	-7.0	-12.4	-5.5	-9.5	-2.0	-0.5	9.4	3.1
Trade Bal (RM bil)	8.1	12.1	12.5	7.4	10.0	9.1	7.8	9.6	9.3	11.5	8.9

Source: Department of Statistics.

cent (October 2009: +4.9 per cent), and crude petroleum by −16.1 per cent (October 2009: −29.4 per cent).

Imports performance (see Figure 4.3) strengthened further in November 2009 to +2.3 per cent y-o-y (October 2009: −2.4 per cent), supported by strong expansion in capital goods by +23.3 per cent y-o-y (October 2009: +5.0 per cent). This may suggest improved business sentiment, which led to higher private investment. Intermediate goods also improved to −4.4 per cent y-o-y in November 2009 (−9.6 per cent in October 2009), indicating that firms are replenishing their inventories, given gradual global economic recovery. Consumption goods moderated to +3.1 per cent y-o-y in November 2009 (+9.4 per cent in October 2009), reflecting cautious spending. On a sequential basis, imports and its components declined in November 2009, which raises concern over imports recovery ahead.

FIGURE 4.3
Import Trends (% y-o-y), 2006–09

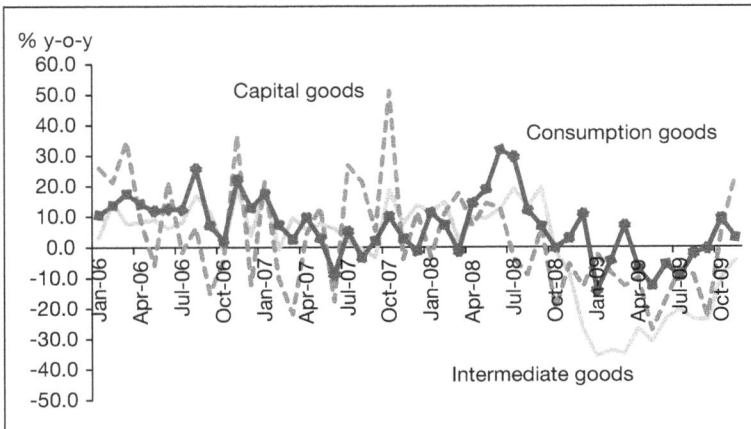

Source: Department of Statistics.

As exports declined faster than imports on a m-o-m basis, trade balance (see Figure 4.4) weakened to a smaller surplus of RM8.9 billion in November 2009 (RM11.5 billion in October 2009). Since the start of 2009, trade balance amounted to RM106.3 billion as the rates of contraction of exports and imports were 19.2 per cent y-o-y and 19.4 per cent y-o-y, respectively.

FIGURE 4.4
Export and Import Trends, 2006–09

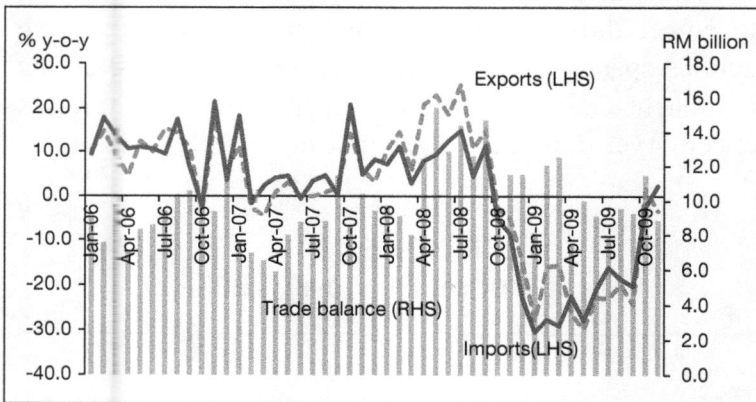

Source: Department of Statistics.

Hence, MIER expects exports growth to rebound to +9.3 per cent y-o-y in 2010 after bottoming out at –17.5 per cent y-o-y in 2009. Demand recovery from global E & E as well as improving commodity prices is expected to lift exports growth further in 2010.

Investment Trends

In 3Q09, total approved manufacturing investment (see Table 4.7) declined sharply by 71.1 per cent y-o-y or 58.2 per cent q-o-q to RM3.7 billion (2Q09: RM8.7 billion), indicating repercussions of the current global economic and financial crisis. This deterioration was attributed to the approval of a lumpy foreign chemical-based project of RM5.0 billion in 2Q09. Excluding lumpy projects, approved investment remained flat in 2Q09 and 3Q09.

Domestic investment approvals improved by 25.2 per cent q-o-q to RM1.7 billion in 3Q09 (RM1.4 billion in 2Q09), but fell on a y-o-y basis by 52.6 per cent. Of the total, RM1.2 billion was for new investment, while RM0.5 billion was for expansion or diversification of existing operations. Foreign investment approvals declined sharply on both y-o-y and q-o-q basis by 78.6 per cent and 73.8 per cent, respectively to RM1.9 billion in 3Q09.

In terms of sectoral contribution (see Table 4.8), E & E products received the largest investment value of RM723.8 million in 3Q09 (equivalent to 19.8 per cent of total approvals). The bulk of this was primarily due to a domestically-funded lithium-ion battery pack manufacturing plant of RM192.0 million in Penang. The second largest recipient was chemicals and chemical products with a sum of RM707.5 million in 3Q09 (equivalent to 19.4 per cent of total approvals). The largest approval came from locals who invested RM238.0 million in an organic compost fertilizer plant in Sarawak.

Japan was the largest foreign investor in 3Q09 (see Figure 4.5), with a total investment of RM342.7 million

TABLE 4.7
Manufacturing Investment Approvals, 2008–09

		2008	1Q08	2Q08	3Q08	4Q08	1Q09	2Q09	3Q09
Total	RM bn	62.8	22.7	16.8	12.7	10.6	7.5	8.7	3.7
	% y-o-y	4.8	247.6	-33.1	60.3	-47.8	-66.7	-47.9	-71.1
Domestic	RM bn	16.7	6.7	3.1	3.6	3.3	4.3	1.4	1.7
	% y-o-y	-37.0	165.4	-75.9	43.7	-62.4	-36.5	-54.9	-52.6
Foreign	RM bn	46.1	16.0	13.7	9.0	7.4	3.3	7.4	1.9
	% y-o-y	37.9	299.5	10.8	68.2	-36.9	-79.4	-46.4	-78.6
Number	Units	919	197	225	234	263	209	178	152
Investment/Project	RM m	68.3	115.1	74.6	54.1	40.5	36.1	49.1	24.1

Source: Malaysian Industrial Development Authority.

TABLE 4.8
Total Manufacturing Investment Approvals by Sector (RM million)

	3Q08	4Q08	1Q09	2Q09	3Q09
Total	12,661	10,648	7,547	8,741	3,656
Food manufacturing					
Domestic	702	459	293	198	183
Foreign	198	275	35	84	102
Chemical and chemical products					
Domestic	731	99	447	338	395
Foreign	348	32	876	5,648	312
Petroleum refineries products					
Domestic	414	951	694	0	8
Foreign	102	502	455	0	0
Plastic products					
Domestic	55	80	78	53	11
Foreign	24	57	294	144	60
Basic metal products					
Domestic	450	93	1,621	57	52
Foreign	0	951	51	143	0
Fabricated metal products					
Domestic	62	257	178	75	128
Foreign	288	24	424	195	87
E & E products					
Domestic	144	164	311	62	239
Foreign	7,076	4,604	816	647	485

Source: Malaysian Industrial Development Authority.

(or 17.8 per cent of total foreign approvals). Of the total, an amount of RM175.5 million was made to expand into multipurpose vehicles in the Selangor transport equipment industry. Other investors included Singapore (RM241.3 million or 12.5 per cent share), Germany (RM220.9 million or 11.5 per cent share), and the United Kingdom (RM176.8 million or 9.2 per cent share).

Ongoing economic turbulence and weak domestic business sentiments will restrict manufacturing investment prospects for the rest of the year. Lower capital expenditure will drag down foreign direct investment (FDI) due to the existence of spare capacity in various sectors, demand retrenchment, and poorer financing conditions. To confront this issue, the government liberalized twenty-seven services sub-sectors in April 2009, and also deregulated rules practised by the FIC in order to promote FDI inflows to

FIGURE 4.5
Foreign Investments by Country in 3Q09

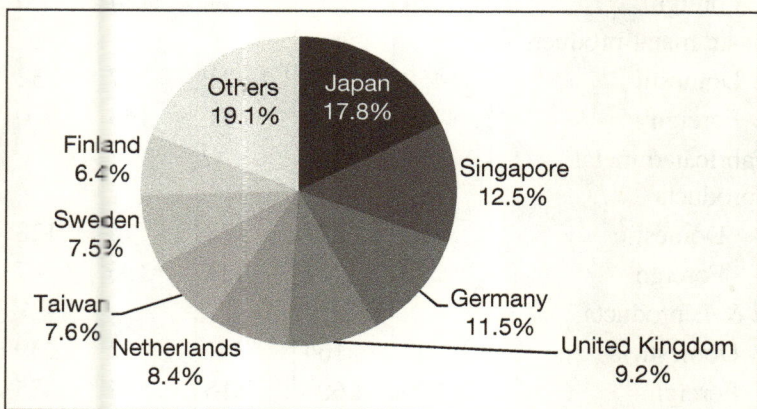

Source: Malaysian Industrial Development Authority.

Malaysia. On the local arena, domestic investors' sentiments strengthened further as indicated by the in-house Business Conditions Index (BCI) to 113.7 points in 3Q09 (105.3 points in 2Q09).

Direct investment (see Table 4.9) posted a net outflow of RM9.7 billion in 3Q09 (–RM8.1 billion in 2Q09). Investment abroad rose to RM13.3 billion in 3Q09 (RM9.0 billion in 2Q09), reflecting investments in mining (RM6.0 billion), financial and insurance (RM3.8 billion), and information and communication (RM1.8 billion). Net inflow of FDI was higher at RM3.6 billion in 3Q09 (RM0.9 billion in 2Q09) due to higher reinvested earnings (RM1.7 billion) and other capital (RM1.1 billion). The investment was directed to manufacturing (RM1.9 billion), financial and insurance (RM1.6 billion), and information and communication (RM0.5 billion).

Inflation Trends

Overall Consumer Price Index (CPI) (see Table 4.10) declined at a slower rate of 0.1 per cent y-o-y in November 2009 (–1.5 per cent in October 2009) due to effects from higher transportation cost. Sequentially, CPI increased by +0.3 per cent in November 2009 (+0.1 per cent in October 2009). Consumer inflation remained in positive at 0.5 per cent on a year-to-month basis. Meanwhile, core CPI also declined at a slower rate of 0.6 per cent y-o-y in November 2009 (–2.6 per cent in October 2009).

Prices of food and non-alcoholic beverages (see Figure 4.6) rose by 0.9 per cent y-o-y in November 2009 (0.8 per cent in October 2009). Sequentially, it rose 0.4 per cent

TABLE 4.9
Balance of Payments (Net, RM billion), 2008–09

	2008	1Q08	2Q08	3Q08	4Q08	1Q09	2Q09	3Q09
Goods & Services	171.8	33.8	49.2	48.6	39.2	39.5	34.2	33.5
Goods	170.1	33.8	48.2	49.7	38.8	37.0	33.1	33.4
Services	1.7	−0.1	1.0	1.2	0.4	2.5	1.0	0.1
Income	−24.9	−6.1	−6.6	−5.4	−5.6	−3.9	−1.5	−1.6
Current Transfers	−17.1	−4.7	−4.3	−4.5	−4.0	−4.2	−3.9	−6.7
Balance on Current Account	129.9	23.0	38.3	38.6	29.6	31.4	28.8	25.3
Financial Account	−123.6	26.5	−11.1	−62.0	−71.8	−29.8	−24.2	−11.1
Direct Investment	−20.7	−5.2	0.2	−19.6	−1.5	3.2	−8.1	−9.7
Abroad	−47.3	−8.9	−15.7	−20.0	−5.6	0.4	−9.0	−13.3
In Malaysia	26.6	3.8	15.9	0.3	4.1	2.8	0.9	3.6
Portfolio Investment	−92.3	26.1	−22.0	−55.3	−33.2	−12.2	−9.9	18.6
Other Investments	−10.6	5.5	10.7	12.9	−37.2	−20.8	−6.2	−19.9
Error & Omissions	−25.2	−1.3	−1.0	−8.0	−19.6	1.7	−2.4	
Overall Balance	−18.3	48.9	26.2	−31.5	−61.9	3.3	2.1	11.5
Foreign Reserves (US$ bil)	91.3	116.3	125.8	109.7	91.6	125.1	100.2	96.0
Months of Imports	7.3	9.5	9.9	8.9	7.6	8.3	9.0	9.2

Source: Bank Negara Malaysia.

TABLE 4.10
Consumer and Producer Price Inflation in 2009 (% y-o-y)

	Jan	Feb	Mar	Apr	May	Jun	Jul	Aug	Sep	Oct	Nov
Consumer Price Index (CPI)	3.9	3.7	3.5	3.0	2.4	-1.4	-2.4	-2.4	-2.0	-1.5	-0.1
*Core CPI inflation**	*1.1*	*1.2*	*1.1*	*1.0*	*1.1*	*-3.5*	*-4.5*	*-4.2*	*-3.4*	*-2.6*	*-0.6*
Food & non-alcoholic beverages	9.8	9.2	8.8	7.5	5.2	3.4	2.0	1.4	1.0	0.8	0.9
Housing, water, electricity	1.7	1.5	1.4	1.4	1.6	2.0	1.3	1.1	1.0	1.0	1.1
Transport	-2.1	-2.1	-2.1	-2.3	-2.5	-18.0	-19.9	-19.3	-16.2	-13.2	-6.8
Communication	-0.5	-0.5	-0.6	-0.5	-0.4	-0.5	-0.4	-0.4	-0.5	-0.5	-0.4
Producer Price Index (PPI)	-4.5	-6.3	-8.9	-9.9	-10.8	-12.2	-12.8	-10.0	-9.6	-4.3	
Adjusted PPI**	-0.2	-0.5	-1.2	-1.4	-2.0	-2.7	-3.3	-3.1	-2.4	-2.0	

Notes: *excluding food and non-alcoholic beverages
**excluding crude materials, fuels and vegetable oils
Sources: Bank Negara Malaysia and Department of Statistics.

in November 2009 (0.0 per cent in October 2009). The transport category improved to −6.8 per cent y-o-y in November 2009 (−13.2 per cent in October 2009), due to higher transportation fares from August 2009 onwards and relatively expensive RON97. Prices in the communication segment decelerated by 0.4 per cent in November 2009 (−0.5 per cent in October 2009), reflecting the impact of price competition among telecommunication companies and supply of new mobile phones.

Producer Price Index (PPI) (see Figure 4.7) fell at a slower pace of 4.3 per cent y-o-y in October 2009 (−9.6 per cent in September 2009) due to higher local production prices (−5.8 per cent in October 2009 vs. −13.1 per cent in September 2009) as well as import prices (−1.2 per cent in October 2009 vs. −2.0 per cent in September 2009).

FIGURE 4.6
Consumer Inflation Trend (% y-o-y), 2006–09

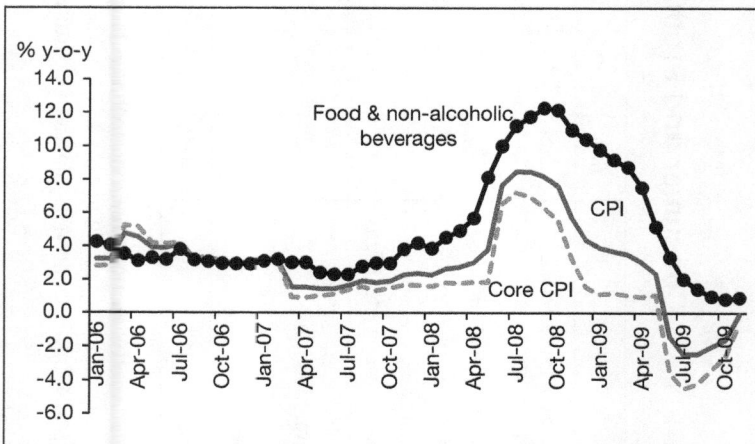

Source: Department of Statistics.

FIGURE 4.7
Producer Inflation Trend (% y-o-y), 2006–09

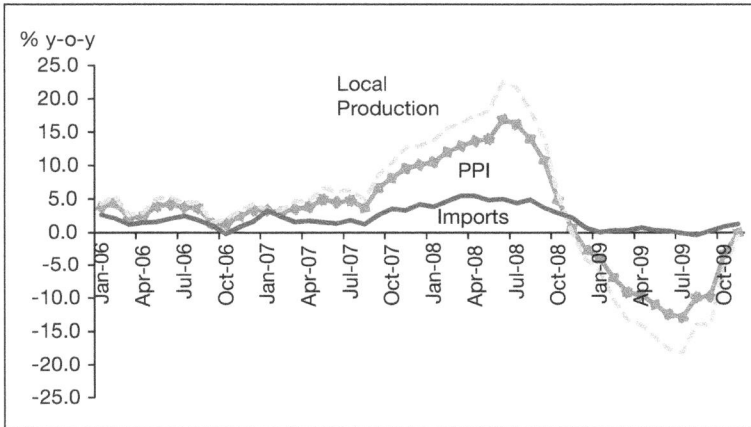

Source: Department of Statistics.

Banking and Monetary Trends

The banking system's outstanding loan growth (see Table 4.11) moderated to +7.0 per cent y-o-y in November 2009 (+7.5 per cent in October 2009). This was due to broad-base slowdown in both business (+0.6 per cent y-o-y in November 2009 vs. +1.0 per cent in October 2009) and household (+9.5 per cent y-o-y in November 2009 vs. +9.7 per cent in October 2009) loans. All forward loan indicators (see Figure 4.8) continued to expand in November 2009 due to stronger domestic demand. First, overall loan applications moderated to +36.8 per cent y-o-y in November 2009 (+39.1 per cent in October 2009). This was attributed to slower demand by the small and medium business sector of 50.4 per cent y-o-y in November 2009 (+51.1 per cent in October 2009) and the

TABLE 4.11
Selected Banking and Monetary Indicators (% y-o-y), 2008–09

	2008	2009										
	Dec	Jan	Feb	Mar	Apr	May	Jun	Jul	Aug	Sep	Oct	Nov
		Banking System										
Total Loans	12.8	11.7	10.9	10.9	10.6	8.9	8.3	8.4	7.2	7.2	7.5	7.0
Business	13.2	11.8	10.0	9.5	9.2	5.7	3.7	3.2	0.6	0.5	1.0	0.6
Household	9.1	9.1	8.9	8.8	8.5	8.4	9.1	9.0	9.1	9.1	9.7	9.5
Total Deposits	11.9	9.2	8.3	8.0	6.2	5.6	7.2	6.2	8.1	8.1	9.0	10.6
Loan-Deposit Ratio	73.5	73.3	73.6	73.7	77.9	78.3	78.2	78.5	78.4	78.9	79.0	78.0
Three-mth Net NPL Ratio	2.2	2.2	2.2	2.2	2.2	2.2	2.2	2.1	2.1	2.1	2.1	1.9
RWCR	12.6	12.9	13.1	13.6	14.2	14.2	14.1	14.4	14.6	14.6	14.6	14.6
		Monetary Trends										
Narrow money (M1)	8.3	4.7	3.9	3.5	7.4	9.3	5.5	6.0	7.8	6.4	10.5	13.6
Broad money (M3)	11.9	9.0	7.8	7.3	6.1	4.9	5.8	5.3	7.5	6.9	9.2	10.0
OPR	3.25	2.50	2.00	2.00	2.00	2.00	2.00	2.00	2.00	2.00	2.00	2.00
BLR	6.48	6.38	5.89	5.53	5.53	5.53	5.53	5.53	5.51	5.51	5.51	5.51
ALR	5.86	5.77	5.49	5.16	5.13	5.02	5.04	4.96	4.90	4.91	4.91	4.85

Source: Bank Negara Malaysia.

household sector by +39.9 per cent y-o-y in November 2009 (+61.8 per cent in October 2009). Second, loan approvals rose by +37.8 per cent y-o-y in November 2009 (+26.3 per cent in October 2009) due to revival in the business sector by +45.3 per cent y-o-y in November 2009 (+12.0 per cent in October 2009) and the household sector to +31.5 per cent y-o-y in November 2009 (+38.6 per cent in October 2009). Third, loan disbursements expanded further by 21.7 per cent y-o-y in November 2009 (10.1 per cent in October 2009). The business sector grew strongly by 17.3 per cent y-o-y in November 2009 (–2.7 per cent in October 2009), while the household sector moderated to +32.6 per cent y-o-y in November 2009 (+44.6 per cent in October 2009).

The three-month net NPL ratio improved to 1.9 per cent in November 2009 (2.1 per cent in October 2009) due to better balance sheet management by banking institutions. Accordingly, the quality of banking system assets remained strong.

Meanwhile, the Central Bank of Malaysia (BNM) continued its accommodative monetary stance by maintaining its OPR unchanged at 2.00 per cent for the sixth consecutive meetings in November 2009. According to the regulator, the current monetary policy hinges on whether economic activity and private investment are sufficiently strong or otherwise. However, current nascent domestic economic conditions as well as ongoing external volatility lead MIER to expect that the OPR will prevail until the end of 2010, given the absence of any inflationary expectation.

The rate of growth in both narrow money (M1) and broad money (M3) accelerated to +13.6 per cent y-o-y (+10.5 per cent in October 2009) and +10.0 per cent y-o-y (+9.2 per cent in October 2009) in November 2009, respectively. This

FIGURE 4.8
Forward Loan Indicators (% y-o-y), 2006–09

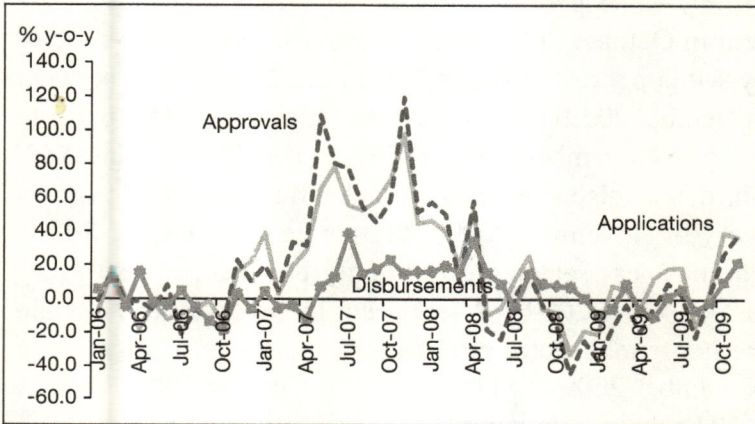

Source: Bank Negara Malaysia.

was due to higher credit to public and private sectors, as well as greater net foreign inflows.

In November 2009, the average fixed deposit rates of commercial banks remained stable; 2.00 per cent for one-month tenure and 2.50 per cent for twelve-month tenure. The base lending rate (BLR) was unchanged at 5.51 per cent, while the average lending rate (ALR) fell marginally to 4.85 per cent.

Growth in total deposits of the banking system increased by +10.6 per cent y-o-y in November 2009 (+9.0 per cent in October 2009). This was attributed to strong growth in savings and fixed deposits of +6.5 per cent y-o-y in November 2009 (+5.1 per cent in October 2009). Liquidity in the banking sector remained ample as indicated by the loan-deposit ratio of 78.0 per cent in November 2009 (79.0 per cent in October 2009).

Exchange Rates

During December 2009, the ringgit depreciated against the USD by 1.5 per cent following the Dubai debt crisis, while on a year-to-month basis it gained 0.8 per cent (see Table 4.12). Continued weakness in the greenback and the search for higher yields has led to the strength of the ringgit. Compared to other major currencies, the ringgit appreciated against the EUR (3.3 per cent), GBP (2.1 per cent), JPY (4.2 per cent), and SGD (0.3 per cent) in December 2009. Meanwhile, the ringgit depreciated against the THB (1.0 per cent), PHP (2.4 per cent), IDR (1.7 per cent), KRW (0.5 per cent), and RMB (1.4 per cent) over the same period.

External Reserves

BNM international reserves rose by US$5.3 billion to US$96.7 billion at the end of December 2009 (see Figure 4.9). This was attributed to ongoing current account surplus as well as net inflow of capital. In addition, foreign exchange revaluation gain of RM10.7 billion from the appreciation of some major foreign currencies against the ringgit in the first three quarters of 2009 also lifted external reserves. Better economic prospects and higher yields were the leading factors, which encouraged capital inflows into the region. The current reserves position is sufficient to finance 9.8 months of retained imports and is 4.1 times the short-term external debt.

As at the end of December 2009, the excess liquidity mopped up by BNM rose to RM219.2 billion. The large accumulation of excess liquidity over previous years gives BNM the capacity to release them into the financial sector if liquidity tightens.

TABLE 4.12
Trends in Ringgit Exchange Rate, 2008–09

RM/CCY	End of Period				Per Cent Change	
	Dec 08	Oct 09	Nov 09	Dec 09	End-Dec 08 – Dec 09	End-Oct 09 – Dec 09
USD	3.4640	3.4075	3.3875	3.4370	0.8	-0.9
EUR	4.8759	5.0617	5.1026	4.9345	-1.2	2.6
GBP	4.9989	5.6490	5.6165	5.4994	-10.0	2.7
100 JPY	3.8327	3.7328	3.9087	3.7463	2.3	-0.4
SGD	2.4070	2.4398	2.4497	2.4421	-1.4	-0.1
100 THB	9.9398	10.198	10.202	10.301	-3.5	-1.0
100 PHP	7.2774	7.1760	7.2151	7.3882	-1.5	-2.9
100 IDR	0.0316	0.0357	0.0358	0.0364	-15.2	-1.9
100 KRW	0.2750	0.2882	0.2920	0.2936	-6.8	-1.8
RMB	0.5076	0.4991	0.4961	0.5031	0.9	-0.8

Source: Bank Negara Malaysia.

FIGURE 4.9
External Reserves Position, 2006–09

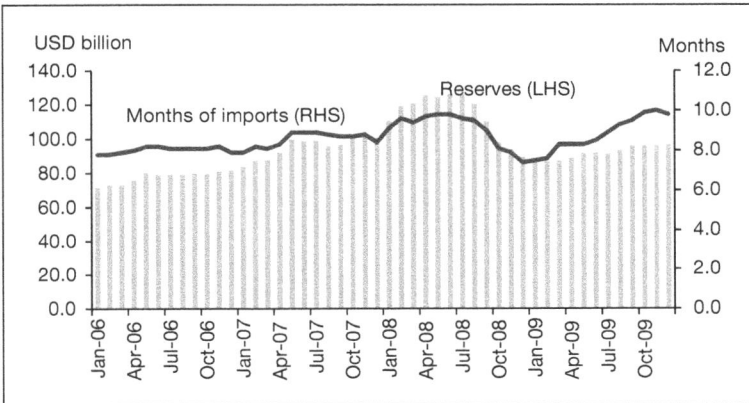

Source: Bank Negara Malaysia.

Tourist Arrivals

In December 2009, tourist arrivals grew by 4.0 per cent y-o-y due to ringgit competitiveness, better marketing, and other promotional activities (see Figure 4.10). Furthermore, this figure is astonishing, given a confluence of negative factors, which include the ongoing global crisis and the danger posed by the H1N1 virus. On a year-to-month basis, tourist arrivals rose by 7.2 per cent y-o-y.

The top ten markets for tourist arrivals were Singapore, Indonesia, Thailand, Brunei, Greater China, India, Australia, the Philippines, the United Kingdom, and Japan. Significant growth was recorded from Cambodia (38.5 per cent), Iran (38.3 per cent), Greater China (32.7 per cent), India (30.8 per cent), and Australia (29.0 per cent). However, large declines

FIGURE 4.10
Tourist Arrivals in December 2009 by Country

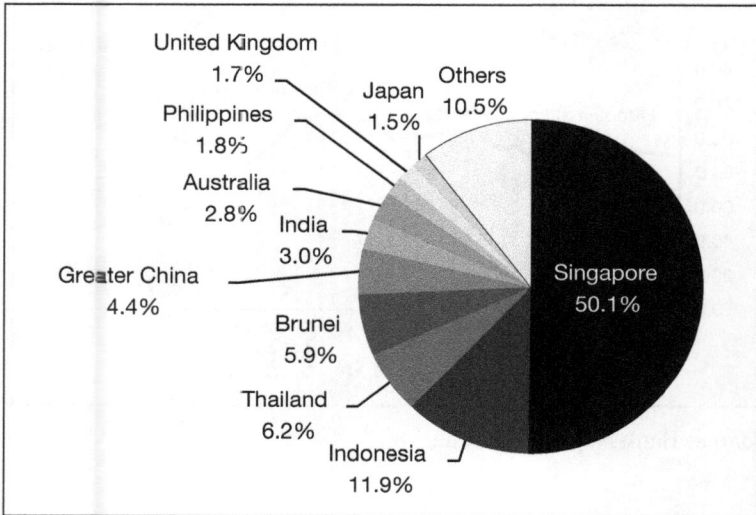

Source: Tourism Malaysia.

were registered from United Arab Emirates (31.8 per cent), Turkey (30.9 per cent), Saudi Arabia (29.6 per cent), Brunei (23.3 per cent), and Japan (12.5 per cent).

Labour Market

The labour market continued to deteriorate as ongoing economic downturn takes a toll on companies. According to data from the Ministry of Human Resources, during the period October 2008 to 2Q09, the number of workers laid off totalled 38,363, when 29,415 workers were retrenched permanently, and another 8,948 opted for voluntary separation scheme (VSS). Out of the total 38,363 retrenched workers, about 19.5 per cent or 7,477 were foreigners. Apart from that, a total of 4,753 workers were temporarily laid off and another 40,422 workers had to take pay-cuts. As the economy enters a recessionary phase, the unemployment rate is estimated to creep up to 4.8 per cent in 2009, from 3.3 per cent in 2008. More than 70 per cent of those laid off were from the manufacturing sector, while 23.0 per cent were from the services sector.

Under the second stimulus package, a total RM700 million has been allocated to create 163,000 training and job placement opportunities in public and private sectors. The government is offering RM50 million worth of short-term modular training programmes for workers wanting to upgrade their skills and earn extra income. MIER's Employment Index has increased marginally to 114.3 points in 4Q09 (112.8 points in 3Q09), as households expect the government stimulus measures to act as a buffer for the depressed labour market.

Malaysia's Economic Prospects: 2010–11

Global Outlook

The U.S. Federal Reserve and the IMF have recognized that the U.S. economy would slide into recession in 2009, while a protracted downturn has not been totally ruled out. A US$1.2 trillion plan is in the pipeline to fund the purchase of "toxic assets" in the banking sector through public-private partnership. On a positive note, jobless benefits fell more than expected in June 2009, dipping below 600,000 for the first time since early January 2009. Layoffs are slowing, but jobs are scarce, leaving nearly 7 million Americans collecting unemployment checks and retailers looking for customers. In its October 2009 review (see Table 4.13), the IMF has revised its projection for the U.S. economy in 2009 to −2.7 per cent (2008: +1.1 per cent), and to be followed by a recovery in 2010 (+1.5 per cent).

The European economy continues to decline as external demand collapses, the housing market weakens, and credit flows tighten. Recent data on new orders exhibited some improvement, but the recovery in Europe remains fragile. Europe is expected to decelerate to negative growth (−4.2 per cent) in 2009 from positive growth (0.8 per cent) in 2008. Affected by the plunge in exports, investment and consumption, the Japanese economy has slid into recession and would remain dim owing to the anaemic U.S. market.

TABLE 4.13
GDP Growth Forecasts of Major Economies
(% y-o-y), 2002–10

Country	2002	2003	2004	2005	2006	2007	2008	2009	2010
World	3.0	3.9	5.3	4.8	5.1	5.0	3.1	−1.1	3.1
United States	1.9	2.7	3.9	3.1	3.0	2.6	1.4	−2.7	1.5
Japan	−0.3	1.8	2.7	1.9	2.4	2.1	-0.7	−5.4	1.7
Europe	0.9	1.1	2.2	1.5	2.8	2.6	0.8	−4.2	0.3
Developing Asia	6.6	6.7	7.8	6.9	7.2	10.6	7.6	6.2	7.3
China	9.1	10.0	10.1	10.4	11.6	13.0	9.0	8.5	9.0
World Trade Volume	3.3	5.4	10.6	7.5	9.4	7.2	2.9	−11.9	2.5

Source: WEO (IMF).

However, business confidence in 2Q09 has improved, suggesting that the economy is bottoming out. Japan's real GDP is forecast to register a –5.4 per cent in 2009 (2008: –0.7 per cent), the sharpest contraction among the three major economies.

Despite a bleak global outlook, the IMF is predicting China to grow by 8.5 per cent in 2009 (2008: +9.0 per cent), picking up to 9.0 per cent growth in 2010. Domestic demand is expected to hold up, buoyed by the pump priming of more than US$500 billion. Dismal external demand is likely to lead to a decline in exports and reduced revenues from tourism. FDI inflows would be curtailed by the grim prospects in the global economy. China's growth should have positive spillover effects on the rest of Asia.

Near-Term Prospects

As the external sector tumbles, Malaysia's GDP contracted by a steep 6.2 per cent in 1Q09, following a stagnant 0.1 per cent growth in 4Q08. As external demand nose dived, Malaysia's exports dipped sharply in 1Q09, while investment was severely affected as well. Given the deteriorating global economic prospects, a second stimulus package amounting to RM60 billion (about 9 per cent of GDP) was unveiled in March 2009. Although the second package appears hugely larger, the actual direct spending is only RM15 billion (or 25 per cent of total) to be spent over a two-year period. The recurring concerns have been the speed and efficiency of implementation and the potential leakages. A notable point is the greater attention given to retrenched workers and unemployed graduates. With the second stimulus package, the fisca deficit is estimated to rise to 7.4 per cent of GDP in 2009, up markedly from 4.8 per cent in 2008. With this, GDP strengthened to −3.9 per cent y-o-y in 2Q09 following rebound in the external sector.

In a move to make Malaysia more attractive to investors, liberalization measures have been announced. Effective 22 April 2009, twenty-seven services sub-sectors were fully liberalized to foreign investors, on the premise that Malaysia lacks expertise and local investments in many of these sub-sectors. Among the sectors opened up are computer and related services, health and social services, tourism services, transport, recreational, business services, and shipping On 30 June 2009, the long standing 30 per cent Bumiputra equity requirement for newly listed companies was removed, making investment conditions less restrictive. This will bring Malaysia's equity market closer to regional benchmarks, but the impact remains to be seen since there are many factors influencing investment decisions.

To promote discretionary expenditure, the personal income tax rate will be reduced from 27.0 per cent in 2009 to 26.0 per cent in 2010 (see Table 4.14). Individual relief and tax deduction will also be increased from 2010. However, the impact on consumption may be limited since only 1 million out of 10.5 million workers pay income taxes. Moreover, the income tax cut only affects those earning more than RM100,000 per year. The absence of a civil servant bonus is another negative factor.

In terms of investment, the reintroduction of a 5.0 per cent property gains tax will lower property sales (see Table 4.15). Furthermore, slightly lower development expenditure in 2010 may reduce public investment, as some major

TABLE 4.14
Key Budget 2010 Measures and Impacts, by Level of Income

Income Level	Measures	Impacts
All	Allow EPF contributors to use current and future savings in Account 2, to get higher financing to purchase higher value or additional houses, but limited to purchase of a house at any one time. Effective from January 2010.	More property sales, but few details announced.
	Employees' EPF contribution rises to 11.0 per cent on a voluntary basis effective immediately, although from January 2011 it will be fixed at 11.0 per cent.	Individuals may choose to delay higher contribution rate so as to maintain higher disposable income temporarily.
	Formation of 1 Malaysia Retirement Scheme to allow self-employed individuals and those without fixed income to contribute voluntarily to EPF. For every RM100 contributed, the government will give 5.0 per cent, capped at RM60 yearly.	Increases personal savings for retirement purposes, and lowers current disposable income.
Civil Servants	Computer loans of up to RM5,000 from the government once every three years.	
	Special financial contribution of RM500 to all civil servants from Grades 41–54 and those on mandatory retirement, to be paid in December 2009.	
Low Income	Federal welfare assistance on the first day of each month, starting September 2009 for Peninsular and January 2010 for East Malaysia.	Welfare consequences are generally felt over a long-time period.
	Provide RM48 million for urban poverty eradication programmes, welfare aid, and housing rental.	
	To give 74,000 low-cost houses to be rented in 2010 by the National Housing Department. Allocate RM200 million for upgrading of existing low-cost houses.	

TABLE 4.14 — cont'd

Low Income	To extend Skim Pembangunan Kesejahteraan Rakyat with an amount of RM180 million for skills training and micro-credit facilities.	
Middle Income	Higher personal relief of RM9,000 from current RM8,000 with effect from 2010.	Relatively small rise in yearly disposable income.
	Personal tax relief of RM6,000 for EPF contribution and life insurance premiums to be increased to RM7,000 from January 2010.	
	Tax relief on broadband subscription fee up to RM500 a year from 2010–12.	
	A more targeted fuel subsidy from 2010 using MyKad and existing infrastructure.	Luxury vehicle owners will bear higher fuel cost.
	A yearly credit card service tax of RM50 on each principal cardholder and RM25 for each supplementary card from January 2010.	Some negative effect on consumption trend.
Upper Income	Reduction of personal income tax rate from 27.0 per cent (2009) to 26.0 per cent (2010).	Only applicable for individuals earning in excess of RM100,000 per year and thus limited impact on overall consumption.
	Other measures include those given to middle wage earners.	
Special Case	Local residents and foreigners who work and stay in Iskandar Malaysia will be taxed at a rate of 15.0 per cent. The incentive is available for those who apply and start work before the end of 2015, and will be given indefinitely.	Limited impact since measure restricted to Iskandar region. Poor working and living conditions will weigh out this special tax effect.

Source: Economic Report 2009/10.

TABLE 4.15

Key Budget 2010 Measures and Impacts, by Economic Sector

Sector	Measures	Impacts
Property	A tax of 5.0 per cent to be imposed on gains from disposal of property from January 2010.	Negative impact on sales of property; also not attractive in promoting investment.
	Start of an initiative to allow EPF contributors to use current and future savings in Account 2 to get financing for purchase of higher value or extra houses.	No concrete measures yet.
	To further develop Putrajaya and Cyberjaya into livelier, vibrant townships. Public transport will be upgraded too.	Possibly higher investment in these and surrounding areas.
	The government has identified several land and buildings, which can be jointly developed or sold to government linked companies. Examples include Brickfields, Jalan Stonor, Bukit Ledang, Sungai Buloh, Jalan Ampang, and Jalan Cochrane.	Government linked entities will likely benefit.
	Special tax rate of 15.0 per cent for those who work and stay in Iskandar Malaysia	Possibly more property investments in the region and surrounding areas as well.
Finance	Liberalize commission sharing between brokers and remisiers in two stages to foster retail participation. Initially, allow flexible brokerage sharing at a minimum rate of 40.0 per cent for remisiers, and later fully liberalize from January 2011 onwards.	Lower brokerages income and profitability of the industry.
	Allow full foreign equity participation in corporate finance and financial planning entities.	Improve competitiveness of the industry. Need to be properly regulated to prevent financial contagion.
	All publicly listed companies to offer e-dividend to shareholders to improve efficiency of the payment system.	
	Stamp duty exemption of 20.0 per cent on Islamic financing instruments. Tax exemption on banking and Takaful profits derived from overseas operations. Tax exemption on profits received from non-ringgit Sukuk originating from Malaysia.	Long-term development of Islamic finance in Malaysia.

TABLE 4.15 — *cont'd*

Finance	Annual service tax of RM50 and RM25 on principal and supplementary credit cards from 2010.	Individuals may deter from credit cards usage with negative effect on providers' earnings.
Telecom	Tax relief for individual taxpayers on broadband subscription fee up to RM500 per year from 2010–12.	A boost to internet penetration rate across the country; more income streams to service providers.
	Computer loans of up to RM5,000 for all civil servants, once in three years.	Muted impact since only available to civil servants.
	Implementation of High Speed Broadband (HSBB) in 2010. Funding from government (RM2.4 billion) and TM (RM8.9 billion).	
Infrastructure	A total of RM9.0 billion to upgrade roads, bridges, water supply, sewerages, rails, ports, and airports across the country.	Improve welfare of the citizens over the long run; not much immediate impact however.
	Further RM3.5 billion for basic amenities, training programmes, and other socio-economic activities.	
	Tax deduction for small and medium enterprises on expenses incurred in the registration of patents and trademarks.	To foster greater degree of innovation; again, measure will benefit on a long-term basis.
Automobile	Imposition of RM10,000 for each approved permit (AP) to open AP holders, for the distribution of AP in 2010.	Automobile dealers will try to pass the AP cost to end users and increase prices for imported cars. National and CKD car-makers will benefit most.

Source: Economic Report 2009/10.

infrastructure projects could be funded off-budget, with slow rollout.

Importantly, GDP growth posted a smaller decline of 1.2 per cent y-o-y in the 3Q09 (−3.9 per cent y-o-y in 2Q09) due to rebound in both construction and services sectors. The effects of stimuli packages led to the strong growth of 7.9 per cent y-o-y in the construction sector (+4.5 per cent y-o-y in 2Q09). Better sentiment in the marketplace along with stabilizing economic conditions generated 3.4 per cent y-o-y growth in the services sector (+1.6 per cent y-o-y in 2Q09). In 3Q09, the rate of contraction of exports and imports moderated to 13.4 per cent y-o-y (2Q09: −17.3 per cent) and 12.9 per cent y-o-y (2Q09: −19.7 per cent), respectively.

The Central Bank of Malaysia has left the Overnight Policy Rate (OPR) unchanged at 2.00 per cent for the sixth consecutive meeting in November 2009. While the economic contraction is expected to decrease from 3Q09, the monetary policy stance is expected to be fairly accommodative for the remainder of the year. This is also facilitated by the absence of inflationary expectations in the near term. Hence, MIER expects the OPR to be relatively unchanged at least until the end of 2010.

Against this background, both the in-house Consumer Sentiments Index (CSI) and Business Conditions Index (BCI) continued to show improvement. In the 4Q09, CSI rose 4.2 points q-o-q to settle at 109.6 points (3Q09: 105.4), while the BCI was higher by 5.1 points q-o-q to 118.8 points (3Q09: 113.7). Nevertheless, the hardship posed by the global financial crisis, domestic labour market rigidity, rising inflation, and early policy exit strategy may affect sentiments ahead.

There are glimmer signs that the global downturn has stabilized somewhat, but the recovery is expected to be sluggish and uneven. The healing from the current crisis will be difficult compared to previous ones because of the synchronised nature of the downturn. It will take time and huge resources to revive the deeply entangled U.S. financial sector while policy options are running out. The weak external sector will impede a faster recovery, and the lower commodity prices are not helping either. Banks are becoming more cautious as bad loans could rise soon, limiting the flow of funds to firms. The services sector will be the pillar of strength amidst a glum manufacturing sector. The technical recession is likely to end in the 4Q09. However, Malaysia may not regain more strength until the global economy is back on track, which is going to be at a disappointingly slow pace.

In view of improving macro-indicators, and somewhat better CSI and BCI as well as the sectoral indices, MIER is maintaining its GDP growth forecast of −3.3 per cent y-o-y in 2009 and +3.7 per cent y-o-y in 2010, while projecting 2011 GDP growth rate of +5.0 per cent y-o-y (see Table 4.16). Downside risks are still prevalent and might perturb the road to recovery, but there are stronger positive influences that led to MIER's projections (see Figure 4.11).

Demand-side Prognosis

Given the slump in the external sector, domestic demand has taken over to become the main engine of growth. Public spending has been stepped up with two stimulus packages announced so far, in November 2008 (RM7 billion) and

TABLE 4.16
Malaysia: GDP Growth by Expenditure (% y-o-y), 2003–10

	MOF								BNM	MIER	
	2003	2004	2005	2006	2007	2008	2009	2010	2009	2009	2010
Private Consumption	8.1	9.8	9.1	6.8	10.4	8.5	1.6	2.9	3.5	1.2	4.5
Public Consumption	8.6	7.6	6.5	5.0	6.5	10.9	2.2	–3.4	7.8	8.5	5.3
Gross Fixed Capital Formation	2.8	3.6	5.0	7.5	9.6	0.8	1.0	–0.0	–0.3	–9.8	4.6
Exports of Goods & Services	5.1	16.1	8.3	6.6	4.5	1.3	–15.6	3.5	–16.4	–17.5	9.3
Imports of Goods & Services	4.5	19.6	8.9	8.1	6.0	1.9	–14.4	5.2	–14.9	–16.6	11.1
GDP	5.8	6.8	5.3	5.8	6.2	4.6	–3.0	2.5	±1.0	–3.3	3.7

Sources: Economic Report 2009/10; BNM; and MIER calculations.

FIGURE 4.11
Leading Index and IPI (% y-o-y), 2006–09

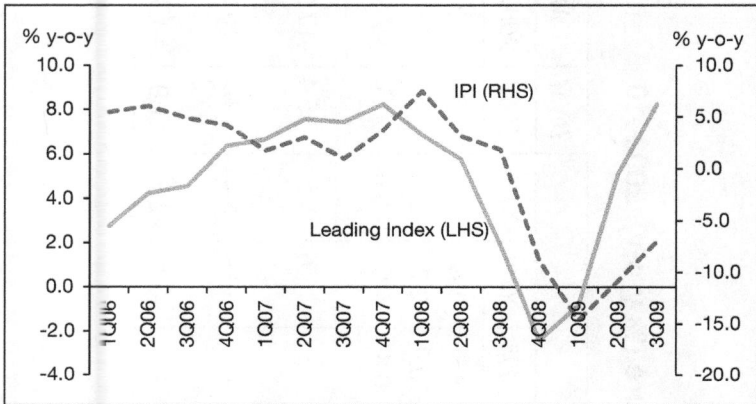

Source: Department of Statistics.

March 2009 (RM60 billion). The first package was deemed insufficient as global economic prospects continued to worsen, and hence, the need for the second package. There will be some lag before the effects of the fiscal spending are felt, making the speed and efficiency of implementation critical.

Private consumption, which has a share of about 50.0 per cent of GDP, is expected to moderate in 2009, owing to the reduction in incomes, a dismal labour market, a volatile stock market and lower commodity prices. Despite ongoing uncertainties, MIER's CSI rose to 109.6 points in 4Q09 (see Figure 4.12). Private consumption growth is estimated to moderate to 1.8 per cent in 2009 (2008: 8.5 per cent), as the global crisis takes its toll on the domestic economy. To encourage consumption, employees have been given the option of reducing EPF contributions from 11.0 per cent

FIGURE 4.12
BCI, CSI, and GDP Growth, 2006–09

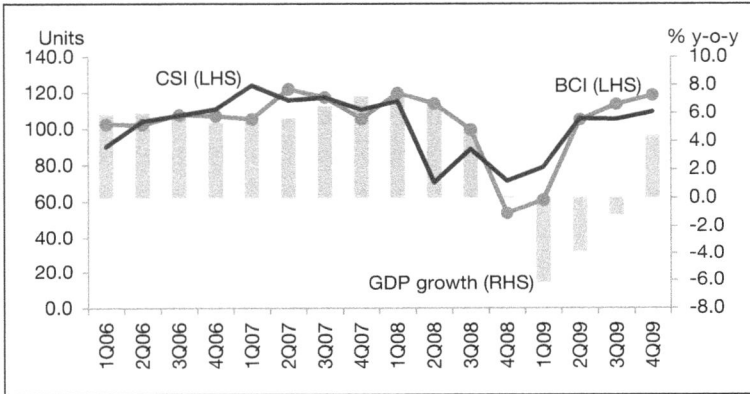

Sources: Department of Statistics and MIER calculations.

to 9.0 per cent. In the second stimulus package, greater attention has been given to retrenched workers to get them back on their feet.

Private investment is likely to contract in 2009, as businesses become financially strapped due to falling demand. Given the deep downturn in the global economy, FDI inflows have been badly affected, as indicated by plunging MIDA approvals. As business climate slumps, private investment is expected to decline by a large 25.4 per cent in 2009 (2008: 1.5 per cent). Loans applications, approvals, and disbursements have rebounded from November 2008, signalling a revival in lending activities. Possibly capturing expectations as well, MIER's BCI indicates that business confidence has improved in 4Q09, indicating the worst may have passed.

With the economy slipping to low gear, and realizing that the RM7 billion was insufficient, the government embarked on a much larger RM60 billion stimulus package (about 9.0 per cent of GDP) in March 2009. The latest package has pushed the planned deficit to 7.4 per cent of GDP in 2009 (2008: 4.8 per cent of GDP), in the hope of cushioning the economy from the global downturn. Securing tax revenue will be more challenging in 2009 with the declining oil prices and a cooling economy. The federal government's debt level at 41.4 per cent of GDP in 2008 is considered to be manageable, with most of the debts being sourced locally.

As external conditions worsen in 2009, real exports are projected to decline sharply in 2009 (–21.8 per cent). Exports have been hit hard by the down-cycle in electronics, depressing both volume and prices. Even resource-based products such as chemicals and rubber products are not spared, with demand dwindling markedly. Though still weak, new orders in the United States and Europe have improved somewhat, which could translate into export potential soon.

All sectoral indices have breached the crucial 100-points level, to record expansion in 4Q09. However, they continue to suggest a somewhat cautious mode due to ongoing uncertainties.

The CEO Confidence Index improved by 20.2 points q-o-q to 122.9 points in 4Q09 (102.7: 3Q09) due to better business condition and consumer sentiment. The Residential Property Index (RPI) rose 10.4 points q-o-q to 122.4 points in 4Q09 (112.0: 3Q09), the highest in two years (see Figure 4.13). Construction and home sales rose along with improved finances from banking institutions. Despite a confluence of

FIGURE 4.13
MIER Sectoral Indices and GDP Trend, 2006–09

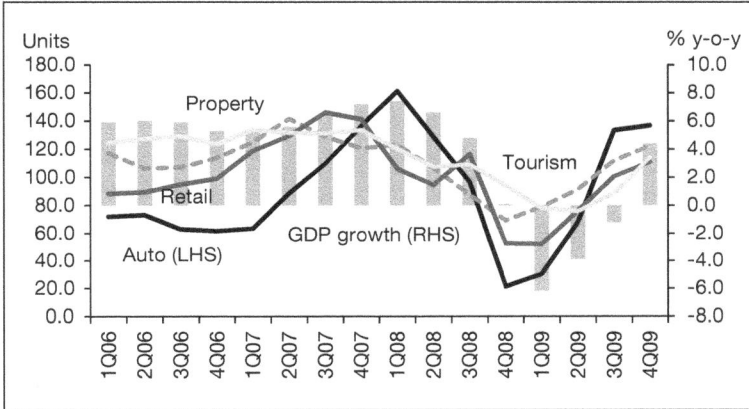

Source: MIER calculations.

negative factors, the Tourism Market Index (TMI) rebounded strongly to 114.1 points in 4Q09 (88.7: 3Q09) due to year-end season effects.

While the Retail Trade Index (RTI) surged 10.3 points q-o-q to 111.0 points in 4Q09 (100.7: 3Q09), it continued to exhibit a cautious outlook ahead. The launching of new car models at competitive prices helped to push the Automotive Industry Index (AII) higher to 136.8 points in 4Q09 (133.5: 3Q09). Nevertheless, it is not immune to ongoing economic and financial turbulence, which may affect sales in 2010.

Supply-side Prospects

On the supply side, the prospects for 2009 have become bleak with the dimming global outlook and the possibility of a protracted downturn. The main growth driver is the services sector (54.6 per cent share of GDP in 2008) amid an underperforming manufacturing sector (29.7 per cent of GDP). Exposed to the sharp contraction in global demand, the manufacturing sector has been the worst sector hit by the externally driven crisis. Domestic demand has picked up momentum to become the engine of growth and act as a buffer against the external weakness.

Battered by the global downturn, the manufacturing sector is projected to contract in 2009, due to the slump in the E & E industry and the general decline in demand, notwithstanding some support from construction-related industries and resource-based sectors. We project the growth of the manufacturing sector to decline by a steep −11.5 per cent in 2009 (2008: 1.3 per cent), dampened by a lacklustre export sector. The construction sector is likely to sustain positive but modest growth in the next few years, supported by ongoing nine MP projects, the fiscal stimulus, and development in regional corridors.

As domestic demand becomes more sedated, the services sector is likely to see growth turning sluggish in 2009 (+2.0 per cent) before improving slightly in 2010 (5.3 per cent). Services sub-sectors that depend on domestic demand, such as finance and wholesale and retail trade, may register much slower growth. Sectors that are dependent on external activity, such as trade-related services and tourism, would see a more pronounced contraction. With increasing contribution from emerging sectors such as ICT and Islamic finance, the services sector may possibly register a moderate growth, but that can only partly offset the weakness in manufacturing.

The mining sector is projected to decline slightly in 2009 (see Table 4.17), in anticipation of the lower petroleum

TABLE 4.17
Malaysia: GDP Growth by Sector, 2008–11

Sector	% y-o-y				% share of total output			
	2008	2009	2010	2011	2008	2009	2010	2011
Agriculture	3.8	–3.5	2.4	2.3	7.6	7.6	7.5	7.4
Mining	–0.8	–3.1	1.6	1.5	8.1	8.1	7.9	7.5
Manufacturing	1.3	–11.5	4.2	4.1	29.7	26.9	27.1	26.7
Construction	2.1	1.9	2.8	3.0	3.0	3.1	3.1	3.1
Services	7.3	2.0	5.3	5.5	54.6	58.5	59.4	59.8
Total Output	4.6	-3.3	3.7	5.0				

Source: MIER calculations.

production, but gas output may increase in relation to new demand. After a fairly moderate gain in 2008, the agriculture sector output is projected to dip in 2009, as output may be suppressed by the falling prices of commodities. Measures and efforts previously put in place may bear results with higher production of fisheries, livestock, fruits and vegetables, which may partly offset the fall in palm oil and rubber production.

Downside Risks in 2010–11

1) Global risks
   a) Deteriorating global imbalances
   b) A double dip in the United States
   c) Relapses in the European and Japanese economies
   d) Emerging protectionism
   e) Asset bubbles

f) Sudden changes in risk appetite
g) Abnormal capital movement
h) Influenza A (H1N1)
2) Domestic risks
  a) Widening fiscal deficit
  b) Volatile exchange rates
  c) Inflationary pressure

REFERENCES

Bank Negara Malaysia (BNM), at <http://www.bnm.gov.my>.

Department of Statistics (DOS), Malaysia, at <http://www.statistics.gov.my>.

Malaysian Industrial Development Authority, at <http://mida.gov.my>.

Malaysian Institute of Economic Research. *Automotive Industry Survey Report* 4. Kuala Lumpur: MIER, 2010.

———. *Business Conditions Survey Report* 4. Kuala Lumpur: MIER, 2010.

———. *Consumer Sentiments Report* 4. Kuala Lumpur: MIER, 2010.

———. *Residential Property Survey* 4. Kuala Lumpur: MIER, 2010.

———. *Retail Trade Survey Report* 4. Kuala Lumpur: MIER, 2010.

———. *Tourism Market Survey Report* 4. Kuala Lumpur: MIER, 2010.

Ministry of Finance, Malaysia. *Economic Report 2009/10*, 2009, at <http://www.treasury.gov.my/index.php?option=com_content&view=section&id=24&Itemid=29&lang=my>.

International Monetary Fund. *World Economic Outlook*, October 2009, at <http://www.imf.org/external/pubs/ft/weo/2009/01/index.htm>.

Tourism Malaysia, at <http://www.tourism.gov.my/corporate>.

5
Thailand's Economic Performance and Responses to the Global Financial Crisis

Suthiphand Chirathivat and Sothitorn Mallikamas

Introduction

It has become known that the U.S. sub-prime crisis which began in the summer of 2007 pulled the United States and world economy into its deepest slump since the Second World War (Eichengreen 2008, Reinhart and Rogoff 2008, Taylor 2008). Presently, it seems like the worst of the global financial crisis has been overcome, but the consequences of the economic recession will still be with almost all countries for a while. While many are opting for optimism rather than a gloomy outlook backed by growing expectation over a global economic recovery, others keep their guard about the prospects for early improvement of the global economy. At least in the United States and Europe, many more jobs will be lost next year, which will make it difficult to predict the impact of higher unemployment, while it would be no surprise to see another round of bailouts of financial institutions, with disastrous repercussions on government budgets.

Thailand, not that close to the epicentre of the crisis, but like Asia as a whole, has also been affected, less by the turmoil of the U.S. and European financial sectors, but more with subsequent global slowdown in demand that had sharply been shrinking the Thai economy in terms of tumbling exports, sharply reducing growth and employment prospects, clearly shown since the last quarter of 2008. It is clear that Thailand has not "decoupled" from the global economy, in particular, those developed markets, as the country has become even more export-oriented reliance since the recovery of the last Asian financial crisis, so the sharp slowdown of these exports causes real concerns about the nature of prosperity depending solely on the external sector. The current context of the crisis also gives rise for the discussion on the way Thailand is also part of the global imbalances in recent years and that there is an increasing need for the country to focus more on domestic and regional demand of finished goods.

The crisis also provides an excellent opportunity to assess the impact and policy responses and to discuss the options for restoring economic growth and reducing the social impact. In the context of the Thai economy, Thailand has its own difficulties to come up with a proper policy response as the country is still in serious troubles with its own domestic political crisis for some years now. In particular, in 2008, there were several changes in government, so it is difficult to put in place any kind of fiscal policy even though there was such a need before then to respond to the hardship of the crisis. By chance, the elections at the end of 2008 allowed the new government to be formed in early 2009 and right away to start implementing its first fiscal stimulus packages in the first quarter of 2008. Since then, the government had time to propose the even more ambitious second three-year fiscal stimulus packages, aiming to build a stronger and fairer economy while Thailand will make an inroad to economic recovery.

This chapter aims to discuss the impact of the global financial crisis on Thailand as the global crisis transmission is quite different from one sector to another. The assessment of each particular sector will allow one to have a clearer view of relevant issues related to the Thai economy. The urgent need to put public finances so the economy could be back on a sustainable growth will also be discussed extensively as these challenges will remain for the Thai economy and society as a whole in the years to come. Some of these packages address the immediate and short-term needs while many others have long-term economic targets. With an expansionary fiscal policy, it is crucial to look at how the Thai economy could achieve its own recovery, both in the real and financial sector, in conjunction with the global economy, before conclusion will be drawn.

Impact of Crisis

Thailand has lived with two financial crises in ten years: the Asian turmoil of 1997–98 and this present crisis of 2007–09, which represent indeed quite different experiences. The former one is home-grown as part of a prolonged and spectacular economic boom for many years since the second half of the 1980s that led to easy loans from abroad in the early 1990s up to before the crisis with the belief of limited risks at the margin. The crisis was so damaging that it took many years to recover, for Thailand, around five years after the crisis to resume 5 per cent of GDP growth in 2002, thanks in big part to the good health of the global economy (Chirathivat 2007).

The present crisis is the one that Thailand imports and it is damaging the Thai economy quite differently from the one of 1997–98. However, this time Thailand has been much less exposed to credit-debt default risks, unlike the last time. It has been hard hit for its exports clearly in the last quarter of 2009, and is still unlikely to recover soon as the pick-up process is also globally dependent and the global economic environment is reversed as compared to the last Asian financial crisis. This leaves tasks to economists, policy-makers and businessmen to think of differential impact and any possibly recovery process that might take place.

Shock Transmissions

As Thailand is not immune or "decoupled" from the global financial crisis, the issue that follows is in what way it impacts concretely on the economy as a whole. Thailand is known since the last crisis for its outward-orientation and has become increasingly dependent on the global economy. When the crisis burst outside the region, damaging firstly major financial institutions in the United States and Europe, creating credit-default shocks to the financial markets, melting down global stock markets, and finally provoking real effects on the industrialized countries with a deep recession, Thailand, like many other countries outside the crisis centres, is subject to receive the full brunt of such a crisis impact (IMF 2009).

In general, Thailand was mostly spared in the first round of crisis shock in late 2007 that hit major financial institutions that were directly exposed to credit-debt defaults. Only a few Thai financial institutions held such financial instruments. It is only a matter of time when fear and uncertainty seeped in for those directly involved crisis-occurred countries that the second shock wave was followed soon that led to panic. Cash redemption and capital flight to safety of the U.S. bond markets caused a freeze in the credit market and a meltdown in global stock markets. In this second round, Thailand financial and stock markets were not spared, as there were starting hit on the liquidity scene clearly in the second half of 2008 that directly results from companies' cash flow repositioning and the reverse flows of funds back to the United States and Europe. The Thai stock market index had much fluctuated and moved downward with the retreat of foreign funds in the market of more than 2 billion U.S. dollars in the space of a few months' time.

The last major shock wave began soon with the transmission of real economic shocks. And for this round, Thailand is starting to see the upcoming tide of real shock wave, unlike the two former ones, that hit directly on the real sector of its economy. With both the United States and the major economies in Europe already in recession, falling asset prices squeeze that imposed constraints on investment, raised unemployment and finally touches upon the external sector of their economies. A sharp reduction of imports in the United States and Europe has then started to see the effects of dampened exports and growth of outward-oriented Asian economies, including Thailand, evidently since late 2008 (Lim Chin 2008).

Impact on the Real Sector

As a result, Thailand is starting to see a sharp drop of its trade since November 2008 affecting directly its growth of 2008 to a mere rate of 2.5 per cent, and with a deep decrease in 2009, particularly in the first quarter that saw a negative growth rate of 7.1 per cent, then another two negative rates of 4.9 per cent and 2.8 per cent in the second and third quarters consecutively (see Table 5.1). With a good recovery in the last quarter, Thailand's economic growth of 2009 is projected to possess an overall negative rate of around 2.3 per cent.

Trade

To a certain extent, since 2001, Thailand's economic expansion has become even more dependent on its external sector since the size of trade is for the first time greater than the size of country's GDP. By 2008, it is growing to a new level with 1.3 times, the size of Thailand's GDP, particularly with the export dependence passing from 46.5 per cent in 1997 to 72.9 per cent in 2008. Despite a sharp slowdown of exports in the last quarter of 2008, the country is able to manage having a good level of trade value of US$356.5 billion or a growth rate of 21.3 per cent, with a slightly trade deficit of US$1 billion (see Table 5.2). Indeed, trade balance has generally been favourable for Thailand since

TABLE 5.1
Thailand's GDP and Trade, 1994–2008

Unit: Billions of Baht

Year	GDP Value	GDP Growth (%)	Export Value	Export Growth (%)	Import Value	Import Growth (%)	Total Trade Value	Total Trade Growth (%)	Export of GDP (%)
1994	2,740	9.0	1,200	14.3	1,286	14.4	2,487	14.4	43.8
1995	2,955	9.2	1,386	15.4	1,543	20.0	2,929	17.8	46.9
1996	3,075	5.9	1,309	−5.5	1,534	−0.6	2,843	−2.9	42.6
1997	3,018	−1.4	1,404	7.2	1,360	−11.3	2,765	−2.8	46.5
1998	2,711	−10.5	1,519	8.2	1,066	−21.6	2,586	−6.5	56.1
1999	2,852	4.4	1,657	9.0	1,178	10.5	2,835	9.6	58.1
2000	2,973	4.8	1,947	17.5	1,497	27.1	3,444	21.5	65.5
2001	3,064	2.2	1,865	−4.2	1,415	−5.5	3,280	−4.8	60.9
2002	3,226	5.3	2,088	12.0	1,609	13.7	3,698	12.7	64.7
2003	3,453	7.1	2,236	7.1	1,744	8.4	3,981	7.7	64.8
2004	3,668	6.3	2,451	9.6	1,977	13.4	4,429	11.3	66.8
2005	3,831	4.6	2,554	4.2	2,155	9.0	4,710	6.4	66.7
2006	4,033	5.1	2,788	9.1	2,227	3.3	5,015	6.5	69.1
2007	4,232	4.9	3,006	7.8	2,326	4.4	5,332	6.3	71.0
2008	4,333	2.5	3,159	5.1	2,523	8.5	5,683	6.6	72.9
2009p1	4,237	−2.3	2,759	−12.7	1,974	−21.8	4,733	−16.7	65.1
Q1	1,029	−7.1	666	−16.7	423	−30.5	1,089	−22.6	64.7
Q2	1,026	−4.9	623	−21.7	466	−25.6	1,089	−23.4	60.7
Q3	1,066	−2.8	710	−15.0	517	−23.8	1,228	−18.6	66.8
Q4	1,116	5.8	757	4.1	567	7.6	1,324	−1.2	67.9

Source: Office of the National Economic and Social Development Board (NESDB).

TABLE 5.2
Thailand's Trade Value and Trade Balance, 1995–2008

Unit: Billions of USD

Year	Export		Import		Total Trade		Balance Trade
	Value	*Growth (%)*	*Value*	*Growth (%)*	*Value*	*Growth (%)*	
1995	56.7		70.7		127.4		−14.0
1996	56.0	−1.3	72.2	2.2	128.2	0.6	−16.3
1997	58.4	4.4	63.3	−12.4	121.7	−5.1	−4.9
1998	54.5	−6.8	42.4	−33.0	96.9	−20.4	12.1
1999	58.5	7.4	49.9	17.7	108.4	11.9	8.6
2000	69.8	19.3	62.2	24.6	132.0	21.7	7.6
2001	65.2	−6.6	61.8	−0.7	126.9	−3.8	3.4
2002	68.2	4.6	64.2	4.0	132.4	4.3	3.9
2003	80.0	17.4	75.0	16.8	155.1	17.1	5.0
2004	96.5	20.6	94.0	25.3	190.5	22.9	2.5
2005	110.9	15.0	118.2	25.7	229.1	20.2	−7.2
2006	129.7	16.9	128.8	9.0	258.5	12.8	0.9
2007	153.9	18.6	140.0	8.7	293.8	13.7	13.9
2008	177.8	15.5	178.7	27.7	356.5	21.3	−1.0
2009	152.5	−14.2	133.8	−25.3	286.3	−19.7	18.7
Q1	33.8	−20.6	26.7	−36.9	60.5	−28.7	7.0
Q2	34.4	−26.2	30.5	−33.3	64.9	−29.7	3.9
Q3	41.1	−17.7	36.3	−28.0	77.4	−22.9	4.8
Q4	43.3	11.9	40.3	0.3	83.6	6.1	3.0

Source: Bank of Thailand.

the last Asian financial crisis which has helped to replenish its foreign reserves and put Thailand's external position in a positive territory.

However, when the crisis hit hard, Thailand also saw a sharp drop in its trade, both exports and imports. It was clear that the country's exports were continuously reducing at an average rate of around 20 per cent monthly from November 2008 up to July 2009. The same applies for the country's imports which saw even more reduction at the monthly rate of around 30 per cent for the same period. The worst of both exports and imports sharp reduction was situated in the first two quarters of 2009 (see Figure 5.1).

Thailand's G-3 markets — the United States, Japan and the EU — suffered great losses of its trade from these recession-hit economies, with Thailand's input and raw materials' exports to the Chinese market also hard hit as well as Thailand's trade of crude oil with the Middle East. It is important to remark here though that the crisis impact could be harder only if Thailand kept that same share of G-3 export dependence like a decade ago. Some important changes that took place between time have shown that the G-3 markets' share represents around half of Thailand's total exports in 2000. But the same share, however, has much reduced to represent only around one third in 2008 until before the global financial crisis. This is due essentially to the increasing importance of other markets; with ASEAN's share of Thai exports maintained its proportion, while the ones of China and other markets have much expanded during this period.

A closer look at Thailand's top ten export items, represented almost half of Thailand's recent total exports,

FIGURE 5.1
Export and Import Sharp Reduction, 2007–10

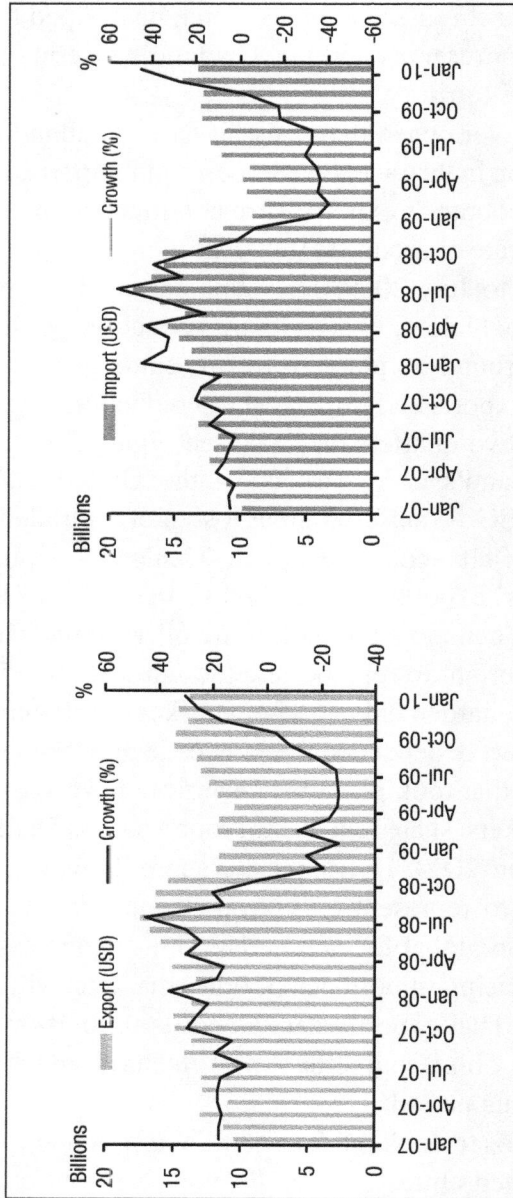

Source: Ministry of Commerce, Thailand.

also show a net reduction sharper than the overall rate, since the crisis hit the overall exports from the last quarter of 2008 (see Figure 5.2). Any single monthly rate of reduction shows that the top ten export items fall sharper than the rest of the country's exports with the exception of February. Items like automatic data processing and machine; motor cars, parts and accessories; electronic integrated circuits; rubber; refined fuels; polymers of ethylene, propylene, etc.; all of these have fallen sharply as a result of the demand contraction in those related markets. The same observation could be made for Thailand's top ten import items which saw its sharp reduction much higher than the overall country's total imports. Items like crude oil; electrical machinery and parts; chemicals; iron, steel and products; electronic integrate circuits; computers, parts and accessories; other metal ores, metal waste scrap, all have seen a sharp drop in its imports into Thailand.

As for Thailand's service trade, the country has been able to maintain over the years a positive balance of around US$5 billion per year since 2000, mainly due to the net receipt from travel. Indeed, travel alone has generally contributed more than half of Thailand's service receipts, with a total of US$18 billion or 14.6 million visitors in 2008 (see Table 5.3). The first half of 2009 saw a 16 per cent decline in arrivals, due to combined effects of the global financial crisis, fears of the H1N1 flu pandemic and the lingering fallout from the eight-day closure of Suvarnabhumi airport in late 2008.

The overall Thai tourism industry is projected a total of around 14 million arrivals in 2009, down just 4 per cent over 2008. Arrivals from Northeast Asia were worst hit with a reduction of more than 30 per cent, followed by the

FIGURE 5.2

Thailand's Top Ten Exports and Imports, 2009

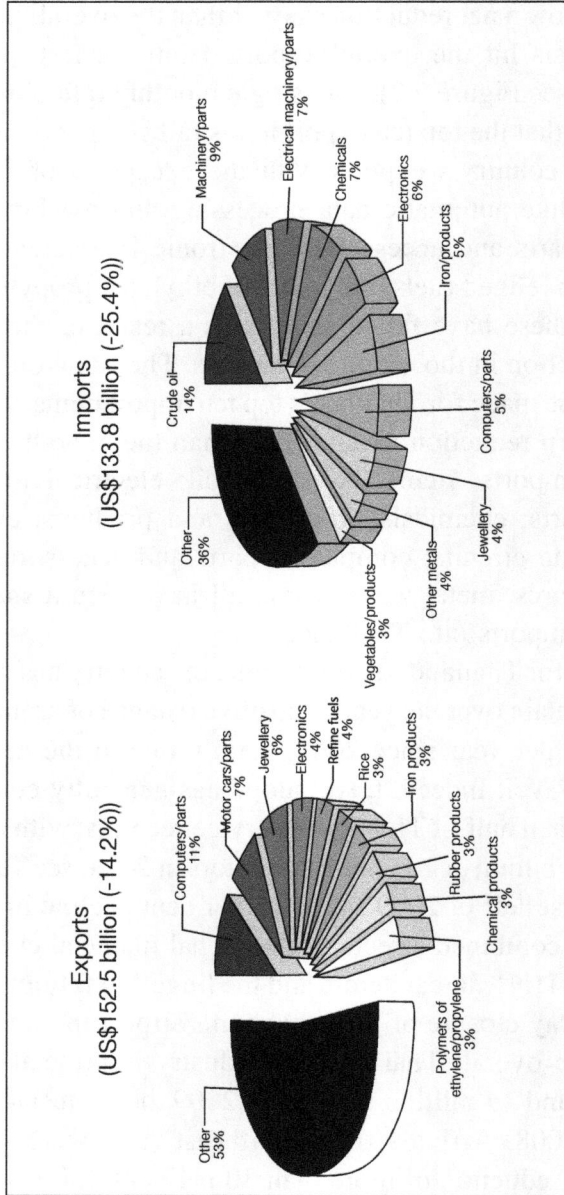

Exports
(US$152.5 billion (-14.2%))

Computers/parts
11%

Motor cars/parts
7%

Jewellery
6%

Electronics
4%

Refine fuels
4%

Rice
3%

Iron products
3%

Rubber products
3%

Chemical products
3%

Polymers of
ethylene/propylene
3%

Other
53%

Imports
(US$133.8 billion (-25.4%))

Machinery/parts
9%

Electrical machinery/parts
7%

Chemicals
7%

Electronics
6%

Iron/products
5%

Computers/parts
5%

Jewellery
4%

Other metals
4%

Vegetables/products
3%

Crude oil
14%

Other
36%

Source: Information and Communication Technology Center with cooperation of the customs department.

TABLE 5.3
International Tourists and Travel Receipts and Payments, 1997–2009

Year	Tourist (Million)[1]				Travel Receipts and Payments (Million U.S. dollars)[2]			
	Arrivals	Change (%)	Outgoing	Change (%)	Receipts	Change (%)	Payments	Change (%)
1997	7.22	0.41	–	–	7,677	–15.61	–3,425	–20.14
1998	7.76	7.53	1.39	–14.88	6,202	–19.21	–1,970	–42.48
1999	8.58	10.5	1.65	18.72	7,040	13.51	–2,476	25.69
2000	9.51	10.82	1.91	15.36	7,489	6.38	–2,775	12.08
2001	10.06	5.82	2.01	5.33	7,077	–5.50	–2,923	5.33
2002	10.8	7.33	2.25	11.89	7,902	11.66	–3,303	13.00
2003	10	–7.36	1.52	–32.48	7,855	–0.59	–2,921	–11.57
2004	11.65	16.46	1.98	30.57	10,057	28.03	–4,516	54.60
2005	11.52	–1.15	3.05	53.61	9,576	–4.78	–3,803	–15.78
2006	13.82	19.95	3.38	11.00	13,401	39.94	–4,599	20.93
2007	14.46	4.63	4.02	18.81	16,669	24.39	–5,144	11.83
2008	14.58	0.82	n.a	n.a.	18,173	9.02	–5,012	–2.56
2009								
Q1	3.65	–15.75	n.a.	n.a.	4,333.2	–28.32	–958.3	–13.73
Q2	2.96	–16.49	n.a.	n.a.	2,785.6	–30.75	–1,019.8	–27.48
Q3	3.28	–2.85	n.a.	n.a.	3,516.8	–13.10	–941.1	–24.56

Sources: Ministry of Tourism and Sports, Thailand and Bank of Thailand.

American and Oceania markets. The ASEAN and European markets were not too badly hit and the South Asia and Middle East markets maintained growth rates. The situation has been improving steady since August 2009, with the number of arrivals declined by only 5 per cent, then moved up to a positive 10 per cent increase in September 2009. These same increases seem to maintain steadily in the last quarter of 2009.

Private Consumption

As a result of prolonged impact of the global financial crisis, private consumption has also been affected, again, for the first time contraction, since the last financial crisis of 1997–98, fallen into a negative growth in 2009. With the falls of external sector's revenue, household consumption expenditure also contracted to a slower pace. Indeed, household consumption had started to slow down to a rate of 2.1 per cent in the last quarter of 2008 before contracting even further to negative rates of 2.5 and 2.2 per cent in the first and second quarters of 2009 respectively.

The third quarter had seen positive improvements with a decrease in contraction to a rate of 1.3 per cent, thus giving hope of a slight recovery in the last quarter of the year (see Table 5.4). Favourable factors for these improvements include: increase of employment in manufacturing and hotel industry gradual rise of farm income as a result of price increase for agricultural products; and boosting consumer confidence due to the approval of the government's second stimulus package (or SP2 — "Thai Khem Kaeng"). Nevertheless, these improvements have seen its limits due

TABLE 5.4
Private Consumption, 2008–09

	2008 (% y-o-y)				2009 (% y-o-y)			
	Year	*H1*	*Q3*	*Q4*	*Q1*	*Q2*	*Q3*	*Share (%)*
Private Consumption	2.5	2.6	2.7	2.1	–2.5	–2.2	–1.3	–2.0
Durable goods	9.5	10.7	9.4	7.3	–18.1	–13.7	–8.5	–13.4
Semi-durable goods	1.7	3.5	3.3	–3.1	–8.6	–8.4	–10.3	–9.3
Non-durable goods	0.9	1.8	–0.3	0.3	–1.6	–1.7	0.8	–0.7
Food	1.4	1.8	–0.1	2.4	1.8	–0.1	3.2	1.4
Non-food	0.6	1.8	–0.4	–1.1	–4.2	–2.9	–1.0	–2.3
Services	3.0	0.3	5.1	6.2	6.8	4.4	2.8	4.8

Source: Office of the National Economic and Social Development Board (NESDB).

to uncertainty in the global economic environment as well as the domestic political situation which still weighs on the pace of economic recovery and subdues the consumer confidence.

Private Investment

It is naturally known that the private investment could not be safe either when the crisis hit hard the real economy and domestic production (see Figures 5.3 and 5.4). The first two quarters of 2009 saw a strong contraction of private investment by 17.8 and 16.1 per cent before a mild recovery with a decreasing rate of 12.2 per cent in the third quarter. Such a decrease in private investment was mainly attributed by the reduction of investment in machinery and equipment as well as the contraction in investment in the construction sector.

FIGURE 5.3
Private Investment Index (PII), 2007–09

	2008	2009					
		H1	Q1	Q2	Q3	Oct	Nov
PII	176.7	149.5	149.4	149.6	159.6	161.8	164.6
%YoY	2.9	-15.9	-16.1	-15.7	-11.1	-10.1	-6.9
%QoQ, %MoM	-14.8	-12.9	0.2	6.6	1.4	1.8	

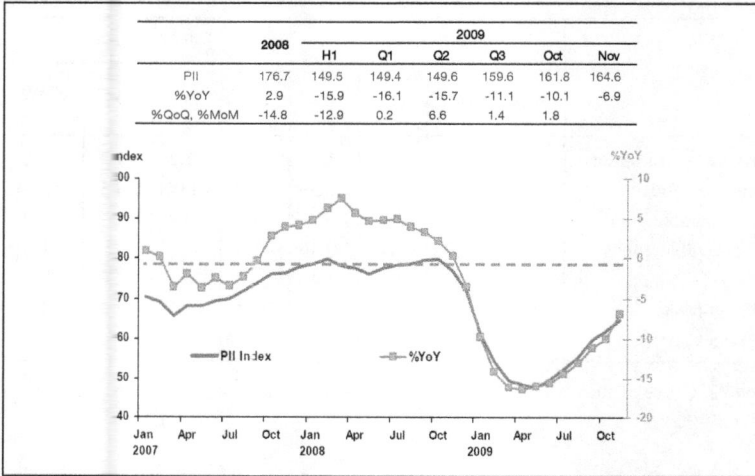

Source: Bank of Thailand.

FIGURE 5.4
Business Sentiment Index, 2006–09

	2008	2009					
		H1	Q1	Q2	Q3	Oct	Nov
BSI	41.5	40.8	37.9	43.6	46.7	50.3	49.0
Expected BSI	46.2	45.4	41.9	48.9	53.4	53.0	54.3

Feb 09 = 54.3
Nov 09 = 49.0

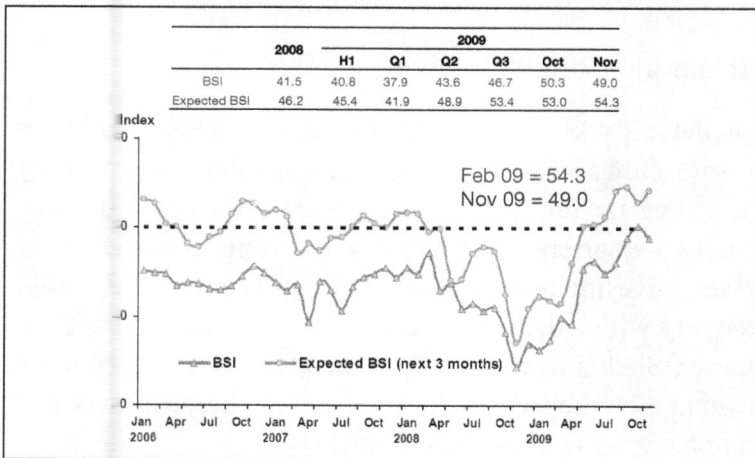

Source: Bank of Thailand.

Investment in machinery and equipment contracted at a much slower pace was in line with the imports of capital goods as well as the total capacity utilization in the production. Some negative factors that weigh much on investors' decision are: unutilized capacity of production; sluggish improvement in domestic and external demand; and delay in solving problems like the seventy-six large industrial projects related to the Maptapud industrial development.

As for the investment in the construction sector, housing and commercial building demand still remained in contraction, looking for a sign of domestic economic recovery. Overall, private investment has made positive improvements by the second half of 2009, following the increase in machinery and equipment, due to imports of machinery and equipment used for electronics, electrical appliances and automobile industries. The picking up of the construction sector however remained low. Most of the private investment was for the needs to replenishment of depreciated machinery and equipment.

Production

Among the three sectors involved, agriculture had seen the best year in 2008 for Thai farmers, with increase in farm production by 9.0 per cent, farm income by 33.0 per cent and farm price by 22.0. As a result of global food crisis, Thai farmers had benefited from the exports of several major items like rice, rubber, seafood, etc. The 2009 picture, however, was different as there was a sharp drop in crop prices and farm income, particularly in the second and third quarters, before a slight recovery by the end of the year. Simply put, the production had overall been slightly affected but rather not as a result of the global financial crisis but less significantly as compared to the price and income.

For the manufacturing production, the capacity utilization of the sector had particularly been affected by the crisis at least for the first and second quarters of 2009 as compared to the earlier year of a capacity utilization of 67.6 per cent. Somehow, it has slightly improved from the third quarter and returned to a satisfactory recovery in the last quarter with some differences among different sectors (see Figures 5.5 and 5.6). Those sectors like vehicles, electrical appliances, iron and steel, leather products, had been mostly affected by the sharp decline of the production (see Table 5.5 and Figure 5.7). This trend also seems to correspond with the producers' capacity utilization of those related industries which had seen a sharp decline to less than half of their available capacity of production.

A few words could be mentioned as well for the service sector, particularly, the tourist industry in Thailand which is considered to be among the biggest industries. Following the global financial crisis, the closure of Suvarnabhumi airport in December 2008, and the spread of H1N1 in 2009, the Thai tourist scene had gone through a series of difficulties. The room occupancy rate had been reduced from an average level of 56.2 per cent in 2008 to less than 50 per cent for most of first three quarters of 2009. Only recently that the tourist industry has seen a recovery particularly in the last quarter of 2009 so we expect that the occupancy rate will continue to improve up to at least the beginning of 2010 (see Table 5.6 and Figure 5.8).

FIGURE 5.5
Farm Income from Major Crops

	2008	2009					
		H1	Q1	Q2	Q3	Oct	Nov
Farm Income	33.0	-11.0	0.4	-21.6	-18.2	-1.0	-0.9
Production	9.0	-2.3	0.7	-6.1	-3.4	1.8	-2.1
Price	22.0	-9.1	-0.3	-16.4	-15.3	-2.8	1.3

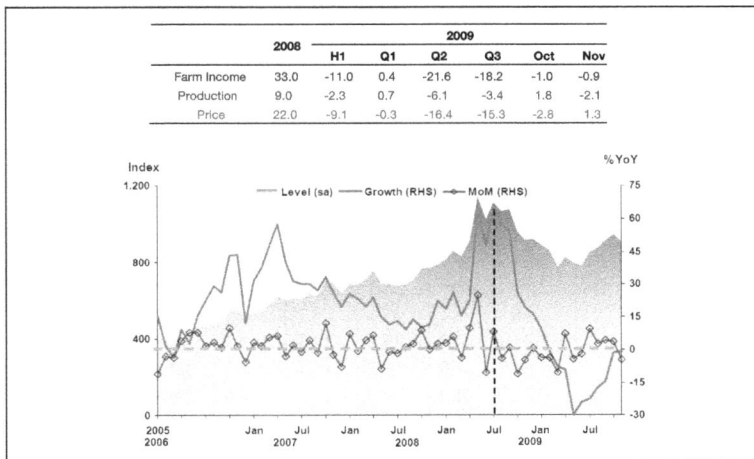

Source: Bank of Thailand.

FIGURE 5.6
Manufacturing Production Index (MPI)

	2008	2009					
		H1	Q1	Q2	Q3	Oct	Nov
MPI Level	190.2	167.2	162.5	171.9	186.0	195.7	192.3
% YoY	5.3	-13.9	-18.5	-9.2	-5.0	0.5	8.9
% QoQ	-	-	-9.3	10.1	5.3	-0.1	-0.4

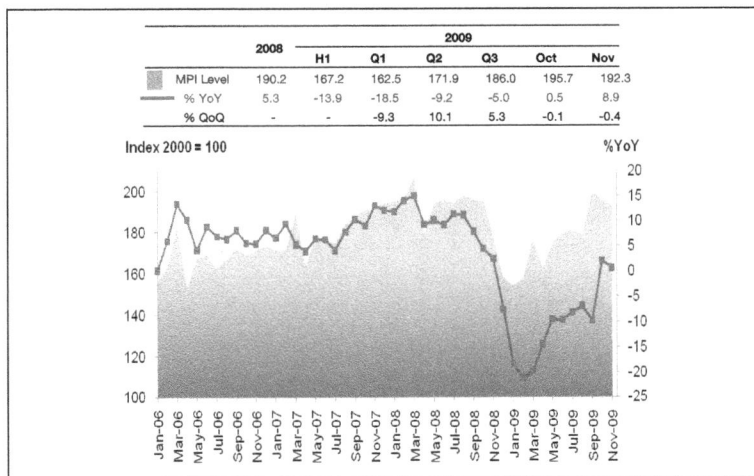

Source: Bank of Thailand.

TABLE 5.5
Manufacturing Production Index (MPI)

(% y-o-y)	Weight 2000	2008	2009					
			H1	Q1	Q2	Q3	Oct	Nov[P]
Textiles	12.23	–2.1	–4.0	–2.5	–5.4	–9.5	–5.6	–10.1
Electronics	10.31	14.9	–11.0	–22.6	1.0	2.4	0.8	12.3
Petroleum	9.48	2.7	–0.7	–2.3	0.9	10.1	2.8	15.3
Vehicles	6.85	14.8	–40.0	–42.7	–37.3	–19.3	–4.3	4.8
Food	6.82	3.1	–3.6	–6.6	1.1	–2.1	0.2	10.8
Beverages	5.11	2.9	–7.1	–1.8	–12.8	–21.2	–0.4	2.8
Electrical app.	5.05	4.9	–27.7	–37.7	–16.8	–10.4	10.9	14.1
Leather	2.79	–68.9	–25.7	–36.1	–10.2	–12.6	–4.7	–3.5
Chemical	2.36	–6.1	–4.6	–5.7	–3.5	5.7	16.7	32.4
Iron & steel	2.21	–9.8	–35.2	–38.3	–32.3	–11.3	92.6	85.9
Construction	1.84	–8.6	–9.2	–13.1	–4.9	–2.4	–2.3	12.9
Others	10.62	–4.9	–9.0	–10.5	–7.5	–6.9	–5.5	7.0
Tobacco	1.20	–0.9	–5.1	–3.7	–6.5	–22.5	–3.7	12.3
MPI (76 products	75.68	5.3	–13.9	–18.5	–9.2	–5.0	0.5	8.9
MPI (sa) % from last period	75.68	–	–	–	–9.3	10.1	5.3	–0.1	–0.4

Source: Bank of Thailand.

FIGURE 5.7
Capacity Utilization and Capacity Index

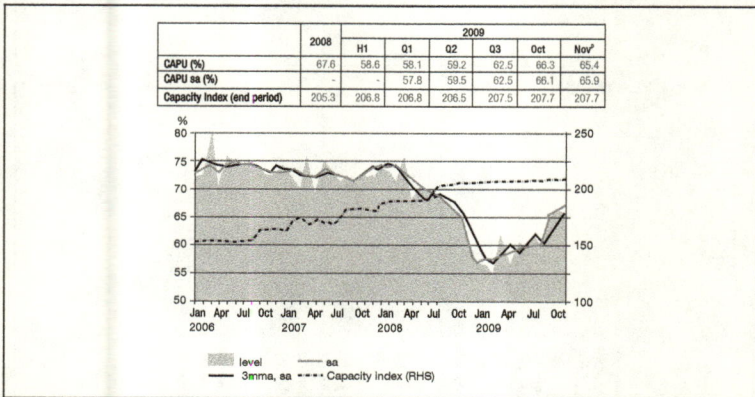

	2008	2009					
		H1	Q1	Q2	Q3	Oct	Nov[P]
CAPU (%)	67.6	58.6	58.1	59.2	62.5	66.3	65.4
CAPU sa (%)	-	-	57.8	59.5	62.5	66.1	65.9
Capacity Index (end period)	205.3	206.8	206.8	206.5	207.5	207.7	207.7

Note: CAPU constructed by using sixty-nine industry categories which represent 59.1 per cent of V.A. in manufacturing sector.
Source: Bank of Thailand.

TABLE 5.6
Capacity Utilization, 2008–09

(%)	Weight 2000	2008	2009					
			H1	Q1	Q2	Q3	Oct	Nov[P]
Electronics	10.3	67.2	52.7	45.9	59.6	68.8	72.2	69.0
Petroleum	9.5	81.7	81.2	80.7	81.6	83.2	83.7	77.6
Vehicles	6.9	75.1	44.8	43.7	45.9	59.9	72.2	75.2
Beverages	5.1	74.3	68.4	73.9	62.8	52.8	60.7	68.6
Electrical app.	5.1	61.6	47.8	42.9	52.8	57.3	63.3	60.3
Food	4.3	60.6	68.0	80.9	55.0	46.1	50.6	52.7
Leather	2.8	25.8	25.3	26.1	24.5	24.8	28.1	27.2
Chemical	2.4	88.4	85.2	83.2	87.2	93.3	90.0	81.6
Iron & steel	2.2	50.7	38.6	36.8	40.5	45.7	58.3	53.5
Construction	1.8	73.3	67.2	66.7	67.8	69.2	67.3	69.3
Paper	1.5	81.0	74.0	70.5	77.6	82.4	83.3	78.6
Rubber	1.4	60.5	51.3	56.7	45.8	51.0	55.8	60.6
Others	5.9	55.5	50.3	49.8	50.8	53.4	49.5	50.9
Tobacco	1.2	53.2	50.9	52.4	49.5	44.2	43.8	50.0
CAPU (69 products)	59.1	67.6	58.6	58.1	59.2	62.5	66.3	65.4
CAPU sa	59.1	–	–	57.8	59.5	62.5	66.1	66.9

Source: Bank of Thailand.

FIGURE 5.8
Tourism, 2008–09

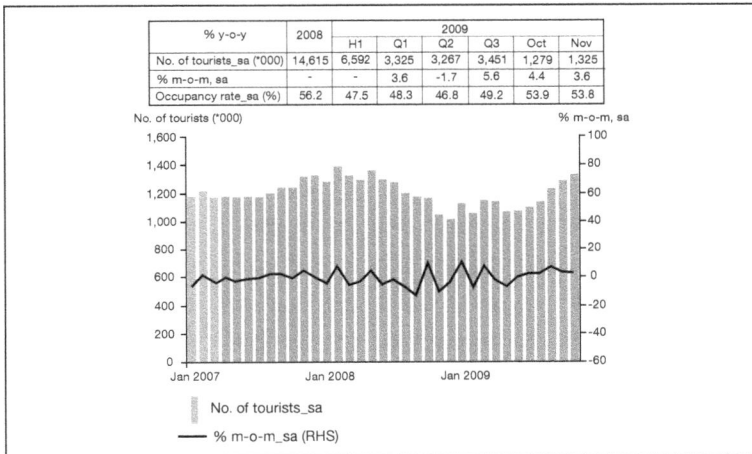

Source: Tourism Authority of Thailand.

Employment

Economic recession is critical to job creation, while demographic changes and growth in the working-age population, among other factors, influence labour force growth. In Thailand, the labour force increased at an annual rate of around 1.5 per cent from 2001 up to before the recent financial crisis, with a combined overall labour force of 37.6 million persons. Since the global financial crisis hit the domestic economy, the labour force growth was still strong until the last quarter of 2008 when such a growth turned into a negative rate of 1.9 per cent. The situation turned even worse in the first two quarters of 2009 before it took a mild recovery in the third quarter. Government job creation programmes, especially for young graduates, are indeed a positive development.

In general, labour market performance of the country cannot be simply judged solely on the number of jobs created, other criteria is also important like the quality of jobs related to the working conditions, wages and benefits. Job quality, in turn, significantly depends upon labour productivity growth. In the case of Thailand, low unemployment reflects the conditions of labour market which have somehow continuously improved before the crisis, with migrant workers at home and abroad, constituted a major bulk of non-skilled labour in the urban economy.

The jobless rates in Thailand are found to be insignificant, never over 1.5 per cent in a normal period (see Table 5.7). Even with the impact of the global financial crisis, unemployment reaches the highest level in January 2009, with a total of 900,000 unemployed persons. With the special package programme of government, known as SP1,

TABLE 5.7
Employment Trend, 2008–09

Unit: Billions of Baht

Labour Force	2008	2008				2009		
		Q1	*Q2*	*Q3*	*Q4*	*Q1*	*Q2*	*Q3*
Labour force (1,000 persons)	37,647	36.673	37,543	38,279	38,093	37,487	38,487	38,807
Unemployed (1,000 persons)	514	583	511	457	504	768	673	460
Unemployment rate	1.4	1.6	1.4	1.2	1.3	2.0	1.8	1.2

Sources: National Statistics Office and Bank of Thailand.

it seems that such a programme had met at least one of its objectives to minimize the crisis impact on unemployment standing at around 400,000 persons in August 2009. One has to take into consideration that this figure suggests Thailand statistics have yet to include the unemployed persons in the informal sector which constitutes quite a large section of the country's employed.

In general, the country's employment grew faster in manufacturing and services than in agriculture. This shift in composition of job growth played a vital role in enhancing Thailand's productivity growth as labour productivity is generally higher in manufacturing and services than in agriculture. Therefore, Thailand's economy with extensive linkages to the global and regional chains suggests that increasing pressures from the global crisis are perhaps much more on the employment and labour productivity in the labour market, particularly after the last quarter of 2008 (see Son and San Andres 2009). The fall in employment in manufacturing activities ranged from around 5 per cent in the first quarter of 2008 to almost 10 per cent in the second quarter of 2009.

Impact on the Financial Sector

In this section, impacts of the global crisis on Thailand's financial sector will be investigated. First, we will explore how the crisis has directly led to financial turmoil in Thailand's financial sector by analysing the value of toxic assets such as CDO and CDS held by financial institutions and the panic sale of assets held by international investors in stock and bond markets. Second, we will analyse the second round effect of a sharp decline in economic demand on the banking sector.

Direct Impact on the Financial Sector

In order to investigate the direct impact of the global financial crisis, we would like: (1) to analyse the impacts of international financial assets held by financial institutions in Thailand and (2) to analyse the impacts on financial markets. According to Chantarang and Chartpaisal (2009), there were two main sources of international investment on securities: Thailand's commercial banks and Thailand's funds and other financial institutions.

Commercial Banks' Assets

First, commercial banks held some foreign currencies and other risky securities including CDOs under restricted regulation on foreign exchange position limit and internal risk management. Between 2002 and 2007, commercial banks maintain squared position on foreign securities. They held some foreign assets to service mainly international transaction of their clients. However, during the second half of 2007, due to excess liquidity in financial system, commercial banks began to invest in foreign securities mostly in private debt and structural notes which include CDO for higher yield. In this period, Thailand's monetary policy kept the policy rate lower in order to stimulate sluggish economy while most developed countries raised the policy rate to curb inflation. This caused a big gap between domestic and foreign interest rates.

However, at the beginning of 2008, thanks to better internal risk control and conservatism, the banks continuously reduced their risky position in foreign private debt and CDO and increased their holding on safer foreign government debt (Chantarang and Chartpaisal 2009). At the end of October 2008, the value of commercial banks' foreign securities stood at US$2.4 billion which accounted for only around 1.03 per cent of the total asset. Among these foreign assets, the banks invested largely in safe and liquidity government bond. For risky debt securities such as CDO, Thai commercial banks had continuously sold them out. As a result, Thailand's banking system has experienced very small direct negative impact of the U.S. financial crisis.

Assets of Funds and Other Financial Institutions

The second source of international investment came from Thailand's funds and other financial institutions such as mutual funds, provident funds, social securities funds, life insurance and specialized banks. Between 2002 and the first half of 2007, the value of investment in foreign securities was very small due to high return of domestic assets, strong baht trend, and capability problems of domestic funds to invest abroad. However, since the second half of 2007, international investment by funds began to increase due to higher foreign yield particularly in Korea, Australia and New Zealand, higher demand diversification of portfolio risk and limit of supply of domestic bonds. In addition to investment through mutual fund channel, in 2008, further deregulation on investment abroad allowed individuals to directly invest abroad through local brokers.

The value of international assets of funds and other financial institution increased from only US$2.5 billion at the end of 2006 to US$13 billion at the end of 2007. The value of asset fluctuated and decreased in 2008 due to subprime crisis and maturity of foreign bond holding. Among these investments, about 76 per cent came from mutual funds, 10 per cent from life insurance and 9 per cent from Government Pension Fund.

When we analysed foreign exposures by looking at the relative size of international investment in comparison to their total asset of funds, we found that international investment was still small. At the end of September 2008, the percentage of foreign asset to total asset was 23 per cent for mutual funds, 6 per cent for life insurance and 13.4 per cent for the Government Pension Fund (see Table 5.8).

In addition, when looking at the types of assets held by these funds and the sources of assets, we found that

TABLE 5.8
Investment in Foreign Assets of Thailand's Institutional Investors

Investors	Net Asset Value (billion baht)	Foreign Assets/NAV (%)
Government Pension Fund	318.8	13.4
Social Security Fund	552.4	4
Insurance Companies	866.5	6
Mutual Funds	1,577.2	23
Provident Funds	387.8	0.3

Source: Chantarang and Chartphaisal (2009).

risk exposure to the subprime crisis is quite limited. Since investment policy of funds is mainly for low risk foreign assets which provided high yield than very low yield domestic bonds. About 82 per cent of investment fund were invested in debt securities and 18 per cent in equities. The shares of investment in debt securities were 67 per cent for mutual funds, 70 per cent for provident funds and 100 per cent for social securities funds. In addition, currency risk was limited by currency risk hedging. F/X hedging ratios were 60 per cent for mutual funds, 70 per cent for provident funds, and 80 per cent for social securities. Fixed income securities were almost completely F/X risk hedging while equity securities were no hedge (see Table 5.9).

Regarding investment destination for debt securities, Korea and the United States accounted for 75 per cent and 19 per cent of Thai funds' total investment in foreign debt securities respectively. Thai funds were heavily invested in Korea government bonds. Some went for structured

TABLE 5.9
Foreign Assets Held by Thailand's Institutional Investors and F/X Hedge

Investors	% of Investment by Type of Assets				FX Hedging (%)
	Equity	Debt	Mix	Unit Trust	
Foreign Investment Mutual Funds	6	67	27	–	60
Provident Funds	–	70.4		25.6	70
Government Pension Fund	68	32		–	n.a.
Social Security Fund	–	100		–	80
Insurance Companies	–	90		–	n.a.

Source: Chantarang and Chartphaisal (2009).

notes issued by foreign financial institutions. For equity investment, Hong Kong as a financial centre accounted for 79 per cent of the share.

Regarding types of securities, debt investment, which was about 82 per cent of total investment and largely in terms of safe government bond, had a small impact from the financial crisis. Credit rating was at least A–, well above the investment grade. In addition, these investments were full F/X hedging. As a result, the NAV in the fourth quarter declined by only 0.24 per cent from the third quarter of 2008.

Thailand's investment in foreign equity, unlike debt investment, faced severe impacts from the global financial crisis. The NAV of equity portfolio was declined by 22 per cent in the fourth quarter or 40 per cent for the whole 2008. However, when compared to SET Index, the domestic equity index declined by 23 per cent and 45 per cent in the fourth quarter and in 2008 respectively. As a result, the financial crisis had slightly less negative impact on the value of foreign equity funds than domestic equity funds. In addition, the policy of these funds were long-term investment in which the value of the equity investment picked up as the stock market rebounded during the second half of 2009.

Money and Foreign Exchange

Right after Lehman failure announcement in September 2008 which shocked the global financial market, the money market in Thailand faced minor liquidity tightening. There was no information regarding the quality of assets of Thai banks. How much toxic foreign assets were held by Thai banks? How much of their assets would foreign investors withdraw from Thailand? Fortunately, all banks confirmed that they held a very small amount of foreign assets of only 1.2 per cent of total assets and the value of toxic assets such as CDO and CDS was just only 0.04 per cent of the banks' total asset. As the balance sheets were relatively cleaner than before, this means that worries lie on the general liquidity situation rather than the risk from bad bank assets. The worries led to a higher interbank rate by 40–60 basis point between September and November 2008 while the interbank spread over the rate of government T-bills was around 20–100 basis points between July 2008 and April 2009 (see Figure 5.9).

Regarding the liquidity issue, Thai banks did not rely on foreign money for their liquidity since they had excess

FIGURE 5.9
Interbank and Corporate Debenture Spreads over T-Bills, 2008–09

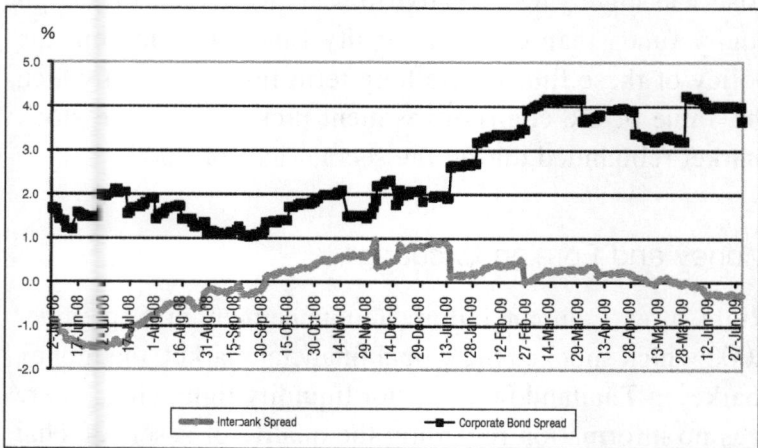

Source: CEIC Data.

liquidity in the system. The ratio of loan to deposit was less than 0.9 in 2008 and 2009 compared to 1.2 in 1997. The capital outflows largely came from the panic sale of stock investment of US$2 billion during the third quarter of 2008. Foreign investment in bond market had been very limited. When compared with huge liquidity in bank system and the large amount of international reserve of over US$105 billion, the capital outflow had trivial impact on liquidity in the money and F/X market in Thailand.

Exchange Rate

Between 2006 and mid-2008, the value of the baht kept strengthening from 40 baht/$ to 32 baht/$ due to the country's strong macroeconomic condition and yen carry trade leading to capital inflow. However, since April 2008, weak U.S. financial institutions led to a withdrawal of capital from Asia to USA, resulting in weakening of the baht to 34.3 baht/$ in September 2008. Even though the baht weakened against the U.S. dollar, the value moved in the middle range among most regional currencies. The main reason is that Thailand faced less capital outflows than some other Asian countries such as Korea. In addition, with a large international reserve of over 100 billion, the Bank of Thailand successfully managed and limited the volatility of Thailand's currency.

However, after the crisis resolution, risk appetite of international investors started to improve since May 2009, leading to capital inflow into Thailand's stock market. The baht value has been continuously strengthened to 33.3 baht/$ in December 2009 (see Figure 5.10).

FIGURE 5.10
Relative Value of Regional Exchange Rates (2008=100), 2008–09

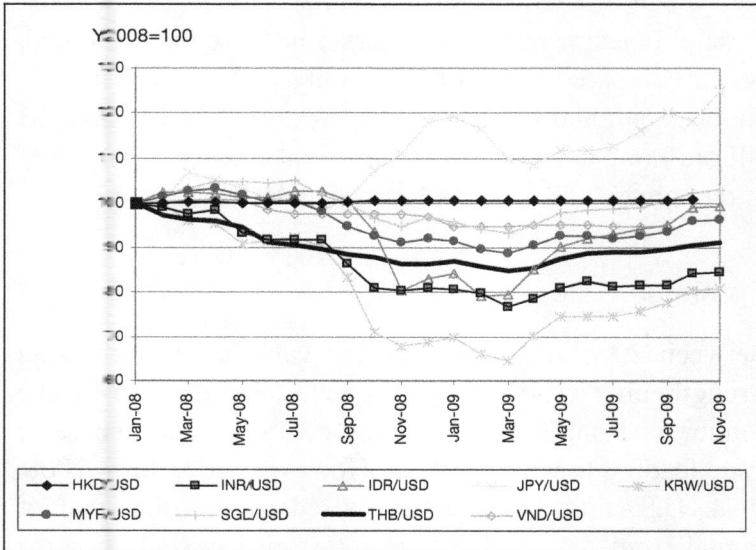

Source: CEIC Data.

Monetary Policy Rate

Between July 2007 and July 2008, the monetary policy rate, 1 day repurchase rate, was kept low at 3.25 per cent to stimulate the sluggish economy from political turmoil. However, between July and August 2008, the rate was raised to 3.75 per cent to slow down rising inflation caused by commodities bubbles. In October 2008, inflation concern caused the monetary policy committee to maintain the same policy rate and failed to react to the global crisis. However, on 3 December 2008, in order to aggressively respond to global crisis, the policy rate was sharply cut down by 1 per cent to 2.75 per cent and the rate has been kept at 1.25 per cent since April 2009 (see Figure 5.11).

Stock Market

Before 2008 financial crisis, like other Asian financial markets, Thailand's stock market had enjoyed market rally due to commodities bubble and the yen carry trade. Even though the stock prices increased significantly, Thailand stock market did not face a bubble. The market P/E ratio was around 17 in December 2007 which was much lower than that of other Asian markets. Local political problems largely contributed to the relatively lower stock prices (see Figure 5.12).

Due to its small market capitalization and low liquidity, foreign investment has a significant impact on Thailand's stock market. Between January 2005 and June 2007, foreign investors came back to the Thai market after their departure during the 1997 Asian financial crisis. During this period, foreigners had accumulated Thai stock worth 329 billion baht. However, between August 2007 and February 2009, foreigners dumped their equity investment in Thailand worth 243 billion baht. As a result, the SET Index dropped from its peak of 884 points in May 2008 to the lowest point of 413 in March 2009 or 53 per cent decrease. This indicated that although the crisis originated in the United States, the global financial crisis can sharply hit Thailand's stock market due to the capital flight to safe haven and liquidity problems. However, since March 2009, the SET Index has continuously increased to the level of 720 in December 2009 or 18 per cent decline from its peak in May 2008.

FIGURE 5.11
Monetary Policy Target Rates, 2001–09

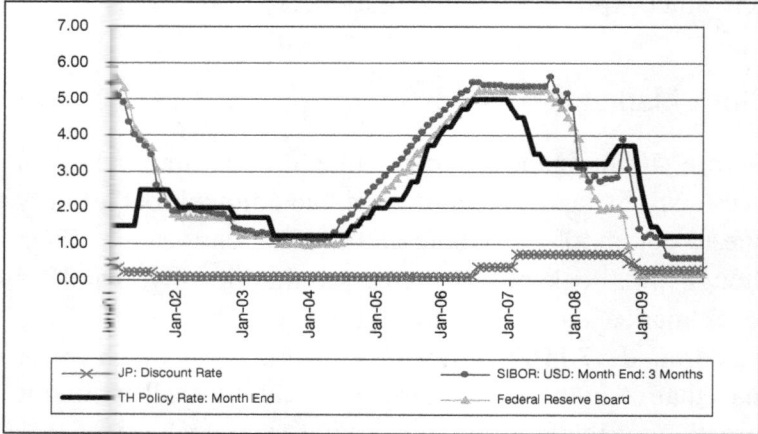

Source: CEIC Data.

FIGURE 5.12
Relative Stock Prices and Net Foreign Purchases
(2005=100), 2005–09

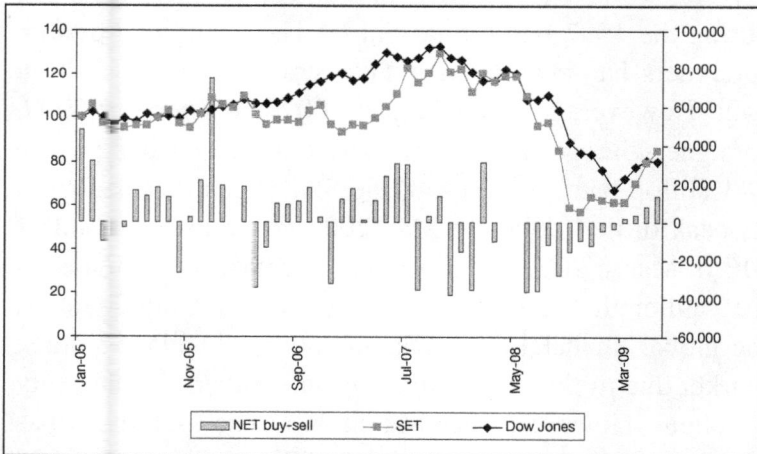

Source: CEIC Data and SET.

Secondary Impact on Thailand's Banking System

This section will explain the secondary impact of the global financial crisis on the health of Thailand's banking system. Unlike the small direct impacts of the crisis on our banks, the secondary impacts from significant slowdown in economic activities caused by a sharp drop in export sectors, are relatively more significant. With the 1997 experiences, Thailand's banks worried about the decline in quality of loan resulting from the decline in aggregate demand particularly the export of manufacturing products and tourism. Overall loan started to decline in the fourth quarter of 2008 and the y-o-y growth of the third quarter of 2009 stood at –3.1 per cent while the loan growth for corporate sector was only at –6.5 per cent y-o-y in the third quarter of 2009. As a result, the corporate sector, particularly in construction and manufacturing sectors, faced credit tightening. In addition, loans to SMEs declined by 8.7 per cent y-o-y in the second quarter of 2009. Credit squeezes started to ease in the third quarter 2009. Surprisingly, the consumer lending, including credit cards, mortgages, automobiles and other private loans, continued to grow despite the crisis.

On the quality of bank assets, the NPL and delinquency rate increased only in first quarter of 2009. After its peak of 45 per cent NPL rate in 1998, the ratio of NPL and delinquency to total loan went down continuously and gradually to 5.3 per cent at the end of 2008. However, the secondary impact of the crisis caused the quality of loan to decline slightly. The ratio of NPL and delinquency to total loan increased slightly to 5.5 per cent and 4.0 per cent respectively during the first quarter of 2009 (see Table 5.10).

TABLE 5.10
Thailand's Banking System Indicators, 2007–09

Year	Liquidity (Loan/Deposit + B/E) (per cent)	Loan Growth (per cent y-o-y)			Quality of Loan (per cent)		Profitability (billion baht)		Capital Adequacy Tiar I+II (per cent)
		Total	Corporate	Consumer	NPL	Delinquency	Operating profit	Net profit	
2007	86.5	4.7	1.5	16.2	7.3	2.7	157	24	14.9
2008	88.3	11.4	10.5	14	5.3	3.9	196	99	14.1
Q1	84.7	7.3	5.5	13.7	6.8	2.9	56	30	14.7
Q2	89.8	11	9.5	16	6.4	3.1	50	27	15.2
Q3	90.9	13.2	12.3	16.1	6	3.5	54	24	15.7
Q4	88.3	11.4	10.5	14	5.3	3.9	44	18	14.1
2009									
Q1	83.5	5.4	3.2	14.1	5.5	4	46	22	15
Q2	85.3	0.6	–2.4	13.2	5.4	3.6	44	24	15.9
Q3	85.4	–3.1	–6.5	7.3	5.3	3.5	49	26	16.5

Source: Bank of Thailand.

Beside a slight decline in asset quality, overall financial health of Thailand's banking sector has been very strong. Liquidity in banking system remained abundant. The ratio of loan to deposit ratio and loan to deposit plus B/E ratio has been in the range of 92–95 per cent and 84–88 per cent between the third quarter of 2008 and 2009. Despite a sharp drop in overall output of the country, all banks in Thailand were able to show profit. Banks showed remarkable operating profit of 196 billion baht in 2008, compared to 157 billion baht in 2007. However, the profitability declined slightly during the first quarter of 2009. Bank's capital has been very strong. The Capital Adequacy Ratio has ranged between 14.1 per cent and 16.5 per cent since early 2008 while the requirement by BIS is at 8.5 per cent.

Policy Responses

It is necessary for Thai Government to adopt the so-called Keynesian economic stimulus policy to boost the domestic demand since the global economic crisis hit Thailand's economy very hard mainly through the export channel. The quarter GDP declined 4.2 per cent in Q4 of 2008 and 7.1 per cent in Q1 of 2009 (see Table 5.11).

Monetary Policy

Initially, during the September panic in the U.S. financial market, the Bank of Thailand successfully calmed down Thailand's banking system by providing sufficient liquidity in the banking system and stabilized the exchange rate.

TABLE 5.11
Thailand's Economic Indicators, 1996–99

Year	GDP Growth (%)	Headline Inflation (%)	Unemploy- ment (%)	Gov Cash Deficit/ GDP (%)	Public Debt/ GDP (%)	Current Account/ GDP (%)	International Reserves ($ billion)	International Debt ($ billion)	Interest Rate % (prime rate)	Exchange Rate (baht: $)
1996	5.8	5.9	1.1	2.3	15.9	−7.8	38.7	108.7	13	25.34
1997	−1.4	5.6	0.9	−1.9	19.8	−2	27	109.2	15.25	31.37
1998	−10.5	8	3.4	−2.4	27.0	12.7	29.5	105	11.5	41.37
1999	4.4	0.3	3.0	−2.2	42.3	10.2	29.5	95	8.25	37.84
2007	4.9	2.3	1.4	−1.1	34.6	5.7	87.4	61.7	6.85	34.56
2008	2.5	5.5	1.4	−0.3	36.9	0.6	111	65	6.75	33.36
Q1	0.5	5.3	1.3	−3.3	38.7	5.7	109.8	66.9	6.87	31.45
Q2	−5.3	8.9	1.2	−4.7	35.8	0.3	105.7	66.7	7.25	33.2
Q3	−0.1	6	1.2	5.3	35.9	−1.4	102.4	64.8	7.25	34.3
Q4	0.8	0.4	1.3	1.7	36.9	−2.4	111	65	6.75	35
2009	−3	0.25	1.2	−4.8	45.6	8.5	135.2	65.9	5.85	33.41
Q1	−2.6	−0.3	2.1	−1.6	38.1	15.5	116.2	62	6	35.78
Q2	−3	−2.8	1.7	−2.7	42.0	4.4	120.8	62.8	5.87	34.13
Q3	2.1	−2.2	1.2	−3.8	43.6	5.6	131.8	65.9	5.87	33.8
2010	4.3	4		−1	45.6		135.3			

Note: 2009 numbers are forecast figures by BOT.
Source: Bank of Thailand.

In response to global demand slump, however, the monetary policy rate cut was quite cautious at the early stage. This is because the monetary policy committee had been more worried about the inflation problems caused by commodity price bubble and kept waiting for impact analysis of export decline. Between July 2007 and July 2008, the monetary policy rate, 1 day repurchase rate, was kept rather low at 3.25 per cent to stimulate the sluggish economy from political turmoil. However, between July and December 2008, the rate was raised to 3.75 per cent to slow down rising inflation caused by commodity's bubbles. However, after realizing that the secondary impacts via export slowdown cause Thailand's output and employment sharply reduced, the monetary committee, in 3 December 2009, aggressively cut down the 1 day repurchase rate by 1 per cent to 2.75 per cent and the rate has been kept at 1.25 per cent since April 2009 (see Figure 5.12).

Fiscal Policy

The Thai Government's initial response to the external crisis was very late due to internal political turmoil and government transitions. Thailand had four governments within 2008. The U.S. financial crisis occurred during the rough transition between Samak and Somchai governments in September. During the three-month-old Somchai government, the economic team tried to set up stimulus packages consisting of large infrastructure projects which had been delayed for several years. But Somchai government lasted only three months due to new coalitions of political parties led by Democratic Party instead of Pheu Thai Party.

In January 2009, after a three-month delay for final policy formulation, Abhisit's government immediately announced its different stimulus package right after taking control of the administration. This first stimulus package is designed to increase the domestic demand as soon as possible. In addition, the government later announced the second stimulus package for 2010–12 aiming to stimulate aggregate demand as well as increase economic productivity.

Stimulus Package 1

The 2009 stimulus package, which was announced in January and started to implement in March, consisted of three components: spending, tax reduction measures and financial measures.

Spending

Abhisit's government announced its 115 billion spending of the supplementary stimulation in the middle of January 2009. The key idea is that in order to have effective stimulation, we need to put money in people's hand as quickly as possible. It took too long for investment projects to be implemented. Therefore, Abhisit's government decided to concentrate more on consumption rather than investment. The government targeted seven groups of people, namely farmers, low income earners, parents, SMEs, community-based enterprises, senior citizens and the self-employed (see Table 5.12).

There are seventeen projects which were announced. First group of these projects is to reduce expenses and increase

TABLE 5.12
Stimulus Package 1

Plan and Projects	Budget (billion baht)	Start Date	People Coverage (million)
1. Income Increasing & Expense Reduction Measures	**62.4**	April 08	
— B2000 living allowance for low income earners	18.9	Feb-July 08	9.45
— Free utilities: water, electricity, bus, train	11.4	April 08	people in cities
— inexpensive products for low income earners	1	May 08	
— Free 15 year education	19	April-Sept 08	8.5
— B500 living allowance for senior citizens	9	April-Sept 08	3
— B600 living allowance of village health volunteers	3		65,000 villages
2. Infrastructure Construction Measures	**7.2**		
— small water development projects for farmers	2	Q2 08	
— asphalt road in village (490 kms)	1.5	Q2 08	
— river and canal development	0.8	Q2 08	
— housing for policemen	1.8	Q2 08	
— public health centre development	1.1	Q2 08	
3. Productivity Improvement for Unemployed Measures	**6.9**		
— trainings for unemployed workers	6.9	Q2 08	0.24
4. Tourism Promotion Measures	**1**		
— tourism promotion	1	Q2 08	
5. Supportive Measures for Food Sector & SMEs	**0.5**		
— supports for food industries and SMEs	0.5	Q2 08	
6. Image Promotion and Village Funds	**15.53**		
— country's image promotions	0.3	Q2 08	
— sufficiency economy village funds	15.2	Apr 08	
7. Reserves	**4**		
8. Finance Budget Deficit	**19.1**		
Total	**116.7**		

Source: Ministry of Finance, Thailand.

income Free education project of 19 billion baht is to support free tuition fees, books, uniforms, and materials for 8.5 million students. The current government has expanded free education from twelve years to fifteen years by adding three years of pre-school education. In addition, it aims to make compulsory education actually free, not only free by laws. The measures started in May 2009.

For low income earners (below 15,000 baht per month) under the social securities as well as the civil servant system, 2,000-baht living allowance support is provided for low income earners. This helicopter drop project, which will use 18 billion baht, has been most subject to criticism of vote buying and short-term effect. However, the government argued that this would be the fastest way to increase spending via consumption rather than investment.

For senior citizens over sixty and without pension programme, 500-baht monthly living allowance programme costs 9 billion baht. It is estimated that 5 million senior citizen will receive the benefit. This programme, started by Thaksin's government, allows each village to decide who is most eligible to receive the support. The current government is going to expand the programme for every senior citizen.

In addition, 13 billion baht is set aside for reducing the cost of living for another six months such as free electricity and water supply for small units and free bus and train. Several cost-cutting programmes were initiated by the Samak government in mid-2008 when the prices of commodities sharply increased. However, the three-baht excise tax reduction for gasoline measure was cancelled since the gas prices went down. In addition, the Ministry of Commerce under the Blue Flag Program has offered low cost products for sale.

Second, there are several projects aiming to improve public infrastructure in rural villages. Two billion baht, 1.5 billion baht and 1 billion baht are also provided to small water resource development projects, asphalt road projects of 490 kms and village health centre development projects respectively.

Third group of projects aimed to increase the productivity of unemployed workers. Training programmes for unemployed workers costing 6.9 million baht is to retain employment and to promote jobs in communities. The budget is set to cover the training cost for 240,000 unemployed workers over 100 training programmes as well as 5,000-baht living allowance per month. More money is to be arranged in 2010 so that trainings will be provided for 500,000 workers. In addition, the government has tried to make sure that the training will better fit with the actual job opportunities. For example, the Education Ministry and the Public Health Ministry will open new positions such as teaching and health care promotion in villages and offer free training for the unemployed, particularly new graduates, to fill in these positions.

Fourth, the Sufficiency Economy Village Fund project of 15 billion baht is to support community development by community-based enterprises. The government will give 1 million baht for each village for their small projects. The village fund, which is fiscal decentralization programme aims to promote grass root participation in all fiscal decision-making process. Unlike village fund under Thaksin's regime, the Sufficiency Economy Village funds focus mainly on small investment projects not consumption.

Fifth, 0.57 billion baht will be used in the country's image building and export promotion projects. Since the recent image of Thailand has been quite poor due to political instability, particular the temporary closure of Suvarnabhumi Airport in November 2008, the government set the budget to promote the country's tourism and export.

Even though these stimulus projects were set directly to support farmers who are the poorest group of the population, the government had prepared 150 billion for its regular budget to support prices of agriculture products which face sharp decline such as rice, corn, rubber, tapioca, fruits and palm.

Tax Reduction

On 20 January 2009, the government has announced its second stimulus package of 50 billion baht tax reduction plan. This policy is targeted at three groups including: (1) property business, (2) SMEs and community enterprises, and (3) tourism business.

To increase new home purchase in 2009, the government has increased income tax deduction on new home purchase from 100,000 baht to 300,000 baht. In addition, tax rate on property transfer and registration fee will be reduced. It is estimated that these two measures will stimulate 50,000 new home purchases, while causing a drop in government revenue by 36.5 billion baht. These measures will benefit home buyers, property developers, construction material producers, banks, and construction labours.

In addition, the government aims to reduce income burden for SMEs, community enterprises, small hotels and debt restructuring firms by increasing the minimum corporate taxable income from 60,000 baht to 1 million baht per year.

Moreover, income tax deductibles for corporate training and seminar held in Thailand will increase from 100 per cent to 200 per cent of the spending on training in order to promote local tourism. Under low numbers of foreign tourist visits, hotels and resorts will be utilized for these training and seminars.

Quasi-fiscal Policy

The government also adopted quasi-fiscal policy through its government financial institutions. For farmers, the government not only planned to spend about 150 billion baht from regular budget to support prices of agriculture products which face sharp decline such as rice, corn, rubber, tapioca, fruits and palm, but also increased financial support to its agricultural bank so that it can provide additional loan of 110 billion baht. For SMEs and exporters, credit guarantee was provided to encourage more bank lending. In addition, the government speeded up its disbursement of regular investment spending which has been typically slow.

In order to revitalize the economy and develop infrastructure, the government has announced its plan to borrow 200 billion baht from local banks and 70 billion baht ($7.7 billion) from World Bank, ADB and JICA. The domestic borrowing of 200 billion is used to increase liquidity of state enterprises such as THAI. The foreign borrowing of 70 billion will be used: (1) to raise the equity of government banks such as the Agricultural and Cooperative Bank, EXIM banks, SMEs banks, and (2) for urgent infrastructure development projects. As a result, with higher capital, these banks will provide more loan and credit guarantee for farmers, exporters, importers and SMEs, who may face a sharp decline in loan from private banks.

Thirty billion baht of credit guarantee provided by Small Business Credit Guarantee Corp (SBCG) will be another measure to increase commercial banks' lending. Since the credit risk has been increasing, commercial banks are likely to reduce their lending. Target recipients include hotels, restaurants and exporters. Each segment will receive a guarantee of up to 20 million baht, with a fee of 1.75 per cent. It is expected to increase bank lending by three times the amount they otherwise would and to cost the government 2 billion baht due to the possibility of non-performing loans.

Stimulus Package 2

Following the implementation of Stimulus Package 1 to help minimize the crisis impact, this package was, however, seen as not desirable in its scope for stimulating economic growth as it was only designed as an immediate short-term fix to encourage more consumption and to lessen the hardship of the people, particularly those unemployed people. In mid-2009, the Abhisit Vejjajiva government made another strong response to the prolonged global economic crisis with Stimulus Package 2 or SP2, formally referred as the "Thailand: Investing from Strength to Strength", more commonly known in Thai as the "Thai Khem Kaeng" economic stimulus scheme.

The bulk of this actual stimulus will come from the off-budget, 1.43 trillion baht, three-year SP2 stimulus package (2010–12) (SP2 consists of 1.11 trillion baht government projects and 321 billion baht state-owned enterprise investment projects), in funding to tens of thousands of investment infrastructure programmes nationwide, with major objectives to revive economic growth and raise the country's productivity and competitiveness in the medium and long term. In a sense, Thailand's public investment in infrastructure has lagged for quite sometime since the last financial crisis of 1997. This might help to explain why the SP2 had its aims high during the three years of its implementation.

Nearly 60 per cent of the SP2 package consist of "hard" infrastructure — transport and logistics (mainly roads and rail) and irrigation projects — categories where disbursement typically is back-loaded. Current government estimates assume a fairly aggressive implementation and disbursement schedule, somewhat higher than what historical disbursement rates would suggest. Applying both actual and historical disbursement patterns to each category of package spending suggests a more back-loaded disbursement schedule. Due to statutory limits on the size of the budget deficit resulting in budget cut, it is possible that a good part of the SP2 package is also replacing foregone on-budget investment spending (see Figure 5.13).

However, there is still the critical issue which is always the implementation of all these projects. At the end of September 2009, the project disbursement under SP2 amounted to only around 20 billion baht, with 14.5 billion for recapitalizing Specialized Financial Institutions (SFIs) under the "Community Level Investment Sector"

FIGURE 5.13
Government Investment Plan (on-budget and SP2), 2005–10

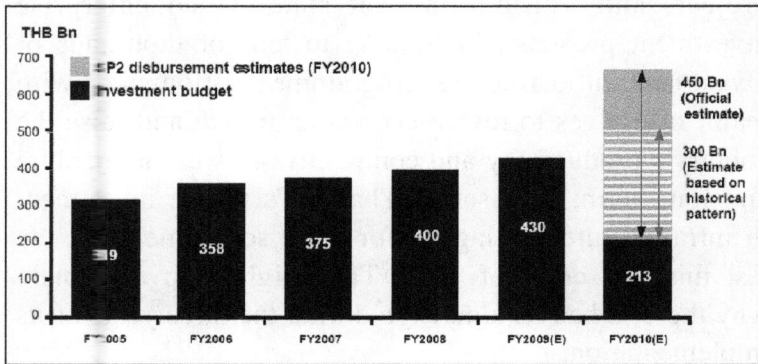

Note: Historical pattern estimate is based on projects which are most likely to begin in FY2010 (known as Tier-1 projects), with historical disbursement pattern applied to major construction projects. Assume that 90 per cent of Tier-1 projects are implemented and that projects begin in FY2010 Q2 to allow for (minimum) one-quarter lag for procurement.
Sources: Ministry of Finance; Bureau of the Budget; Local Newspaper; and SCB EIC analysis.

programme. As a result, 330 billion baht funding under the SP2 programme originally due to be disbursed in the fiscal year of 2009 would instead be drawn in 2010. Meanwhile, the fiscal 2010 budget contains investment projects worth 200 billion baht, with a projected disbursement rate of 80 per cent. Overall, nearly 500 billion baht in fiscal stimulus spending will help to expand the economy in 2010.

According to the Thai Government, the investment plans are sufficient to help stimulate economic growth up to 4 per cent in 2010 and at least up to more than 5 per cent in 2011–12 if the disbursement is kept on track, even if the private investment has yet to recover. In the pre-crisis years of the 1990s, total investment made up around 40 per cent of GDP; with 10 per cent public investment and another 30 per cent private investment. However, during 2004–08, public investment made up only around 5.3–5.9 per cent of GDP and private investment was only 16.6–17.5 per cent of GDP. Considering quite a variety of investment projects (see Table 5.13) — including transport and logistics, irrigations management and irrigations for agriculture, energy and alternative energy, education, health, support for community development including sufficiency economy initiatives, communications, creative economy, science and technology, tourism infrastructure, social welfare, natural resources and environment — this Keynesian approach to spending is also

TABLE 5.13
Key Areas of Public Investment under SP2

Sector	Amount (billion baht)	Percentage of the Total
1. Transportation and logistics	572	39.9
2. Irrigation management and irrigation for agriculture	239	16.7
3. Energy and alternative energy	206	14.4
4. Education	136	9.6
5. Public healthcare	100	6.9
6. Others	178	12.5
Total	**1,431**	**100.0**

Source: Ministry of Finance, Thailand.

widely viewed as creating more public debt. Again, from the government projections, public debt to GDP could reach its peak by 2013 of around 60 per cent, after that, it could decrease (see Figure 5.14). By the end of September 2009, public debt stood at 4,001,942 million baht, equivalent to 45.6 per cent of GDP, increased from outstanding debts at the end of June 2009, which was at 43.6 per cent of GDP. See NESDB (2009).

To cover all of the spending, the government needs additional funding so it also sets a target for public borrowing of around 800 billion baht; with a plan for Parliament's approval of special borrowing legislation of 400 billion baht by January 2010 and another 400 billion baht seeking for approval at a later date (see Table 5.14). From government's

FIGURE 5.14
Size of Public Debt to GDP (%), 1996–2018

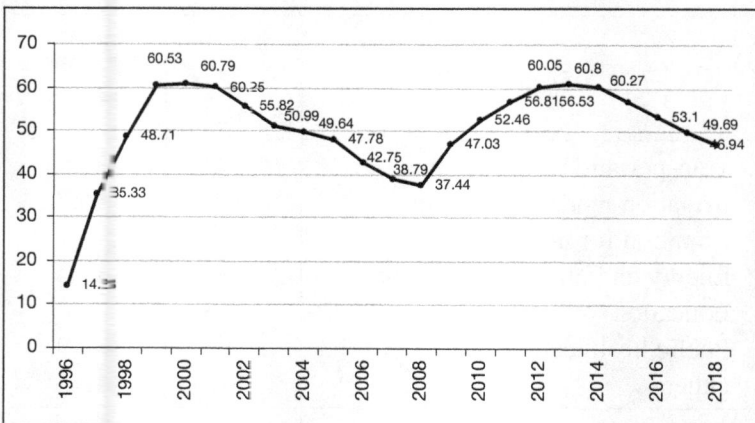

Source: Forecast by Fiscal Policy Office, Ministry of Finance, Thailand.

TABLE 5.14
Estimates of Borrowing Needs for SP2

	Amount (billion baht)	In Percentage of SP2 Total
Budget	170.2	11.9
State-owned enterprises contribution	179.6	12.5
Domestic borrowing under the usual law	115.7	8.1
Foreign borrowings under the usual law	234.1	16.4
Public private partnership	27.7	1.9
Total special borrowing needs under SP2	**703.9**	**49.2**

Source: Ministry of Finance, Thailand.

perspective, borrowing costs for the government on average stand at around 4.5 per cent per year. If economic growth could produce between 4 and 5 per cent per year, then all of public borrowing could be squared. And if such an economic growth could produce beyond that level, Thailand would be in a good position to service its public debt burden quite comfortably in a reasonably rather than a longer time period.

Path to Recovery

For the whole year of 2009, the Thai economy is expected to contract around 3 per cent, after a sign of recovery in the third quarter with a contraction of 2.8 per cent, a much improvement from the sharp contractions of 7.1 and 4.9 per cent in the first and second quarters respectively. Household consumption, private investment and exports continued to improve as a result of government economic stimulus programmes and global economic recovery following the economic stimulus measures applying in most countries of the world. Confidence of foreign travellers to Thailand has also regained after the domestic political conflict has been eased. A slight recovery, hopefully, will gain its momentum, as the Thai economy has also seen the expansion in export-oriented industries, with an increase in capacity utilization and a lower unemployment rate.

With the last quarter growth turning out to be positive as compared to the same period last year, this represents the first positive expansion since the country has slept into the crisis impact. The issue is still by far whether such growth in Thailand will be sustained in the next few years considering the crisis impact around the world is still real with most of the G-3 still mired in recession. In the Thai case, it is hopeful that such growth will continue to be supported by positive contributing factors; these are the global recovery directly benefited the exports and tourism, the improvement of household consumption following an increase in income and employment, and the implementation of Thai Khem Kaeng 2012 programme at the time when the private investment has yet to recover.

Export Challenges

Surely in the Thai case, a more durable recovery from this global crisis will come from the export sector as the Thai economy has been much exposed to the global economy, particularly even more since the last Asian financial crisis. Any recovery from 2010 onwards will depend how much different sectors of the Thai industry will adjust to the so-called "new normal" in G-3 countries (Chirathivat 2009). In between, the global crisis has caused debate about their export dependence and the instability that is related to it. For sure, if Thailand could find a recovery from those crisis-affected markets in the coming years, then one could not continue to blame the validity of the export growth model.

The crisis also presents other challenges differently from that of the Asian crisis a decade earlier. Any recovery, apart from the domestic level, can be achieved more substantially in the medium-term period through regional demand, rather than depending solely on the crisis-hit Western countries. This potential could come from those emerging markets around the world and particularly in developing Asia like China, India and a few other countries of ASEAN which have sizable domestic consumption to cater to the downturn of Thailand's exports. Future potential growth of the region and increasing intra-regional trade and investment suggest that the demand for final goods and services in the region could increase much more than the present level.

A recent study (Cheewatrakulwongse 2009) has shown how much the export reduction could affect the macroeconomic variables of the Thai economy as well as various sectors of production according to the Thailand's input-output table. The result had clearly demonstrated that the crisis had directly impacted on national income, import and private investment more than production, employment and capital, with the manufacturing and service sector more affected than the agricultural sector (see Table 5.15). The same study had classified the impact of those related industries according to the forward and backward linkages. The findings are that there are twenty-six industries like hotels and restaurants, construction, machinery, vehicles, metals plastics, that are highly sensitive to the crisis impact, perhaps due to its linkages to the trade decrease and the highly elastic demand. These industries still need assistance in funding their cash flows and to a certain extent, employment measures to cater to their difficulties. The same study also finds another thirty-five industries that are highly linked to the rest of the industries. These are for example, steel, motor vehicles and vehicles, construction, plastics, animal feeds, cassava with their changes affected much the whole of Thailand's industrial linkages. Thailand

TABLE 5.15
Crisis Impact on Thailand's Macroeconomic Variables

Variable	Net Result (%)	Direct Impact (%)	Indirect Impact (%)	
			Trade	Third Country
GDP	−7.7	−4.33	−3.44	
Export	−8.34	−3.66	−4.24	−0.66
Import	−11.21	−4.46	−6.38	−0.37
Production	−6.42	−1.16	−5.26	
Private Consumption	−7.7	−4.33	−5.44	
Non-Skilled Labour	−5.83	−0.83	−4.99	
Skilled Labour	−6.27	−0.55	−5.72	
Capital	−6.73	−0.95	−5.80	

Source: Karnkarun Cheewatrakulwongse and al. (2010).

needs to improve the competitiveness of these industries thus included the issues like research and development, productivity improvement and production and market adaptability. Finally, there are also seven industries that are subject to the crisis impact and are closely linked as well to other industries; these are textiles, construction, public services, air transport, other food, land transport, canned seafood, plastics, which are all in need of government proper measures to build proper short-term assistance and long-term competitiveness (see Table 5.16).

In short, there is nothing wrong with the way Thailand has become an export-oriented economy. Rather, it depends on how Thailand would like to improve in the longer term especially its labour productivity together with product and market competitiveness. Also, the crisis has reflected the situation that with an export-oriented economy, this has pulled Thailand into the puzzle of global imbalances. Accordingly, the immediate short-term discussion has been directed towards global issues like how Thailand should participate with the Asian region or follow-up closely the discussion with G-20.

Stimulus Packages' Effectiveness

As shown earlier, Thailand's stimulus packages consisted mainly of SP1, implemented starting from the first quarter of 2009 and SP2 partly from the budget year of 2009, but formally known for the three years' implementation from 2010–12. Major differences between the two have become evident. The former was designed, for short term, to stimulate domestic demand as well as to alleviate domestic producers

TABLE 5.16
Crisis Impact on Export and Import by Major Sector

Export	Net Result (%)	Direct Impact (%)	Indirect Impact (%)	
			Trade	Third Country
Agriculture	−4.60	−0.89	−3.38	−0.33
Natural Resource	−9.04	−2.14	−6.55	−0.35
Food Industry	−6.20	−3.14	−2.23	−0.83
Industry	−8.54	−3.70	−4.48	−0.36
Services	−9.14	−4.23	−4.33	−0.58
Total	−8.34	−3.66	−4.24	−0.44

Import	Net Result (%)	Direct Impact (%)	Indirect Impact (%)	
			Trade	Third Country
Agriculture	−8.71	−2.67	−5.51	−0.44
Natural Resource	−13.50	−4.05	−9.45	−0.00
Food Industry	−8.79	−3.24	−4.66	−0.89
Industry	−11.21	−4.52	−6.43	−0.26
Services	−9.66	−5.01	−3.39	−1.26
Total	−11.21	−4.46	−6.38	−0.37

Source: Komkarun Cheewatrakulwongse and al. (2010).

due to the collapse of the external demand and partly to prevent job losses from a sharp adjustment in production decrease in different industries.

The latter has much broader objectives, both in its scopes and depths especially for various projects to be implemented. Starting from the concept of a three-year stimulus plan, one could question the motives behind, whether they are economic, social and political, and why this total figure had been decided once and for all, with a total budget of 1.43 trillion baht to be spent during these three years. Of course, there are also the issues about in what ways all these projects of infrastructural investment once implemented could help Thailand's economic and social future, like infrastructural improvement, increase in productivity and creativity, competitiveness enhancement, poverty alleviation and more equitable and sustainable development.

For instance, analyses from the Bank of Thailand, by using the social accounting matrix, have shown that the SP1, with its spending power of 135 billion baht, could increase Thailand's GDP by 0.9 per cent. In addition, when applying the macroeconomic model, the SP1 could also help to increase Thailand's GDP between 0.77 and 1.12 per cent. The same study expected the impact from government spending to be much faster than the impact from tax reduction under the environment of the recession that Thailand had gone through. Spending stimulus would have its significant impact from the last quarter of 2009 while the tax reduction would be in its effectiveness during the second quarter of 2009 after the tax payment deadline (Premsil and Vanichthanunkul 2009).

As for job creation, the SP1 would help to increase employment of around a total value of 160 billion baht or around 0.4 per cent of Thailand's total labour force of 38 million. Government spending package would lead to a total value of 100 billion baht of job creation while government tax reduction would lead to a total value of 60 billion baht of job creation. Also shown from the study is more job creations in those related service sectors like properties, construction and tourism, rather than the production sectors like manufacturing and agriculture.

At the end of 2009, however, it was estimated that only less than 50 billion baht of SP1 had been spent, probably due to the complexity in public disbursement and the slowness of responsible government agencies, thus included the problems of investment returns, governance and corruption. In order to yield more results from the economic stimulus, the government had finally decided to speed up the spending process with the inclusion of several non-spending budget lines of SP1 to the next budget year of 2010, in conjunction with the application of the SP2, publicly known as the Thai Khem Kaeng scheme, or literally translated as "Thailand from strength to strength". The government has finally set this three-year fiscal plan in which the total spending could be 7.44 trillion baht while the total revenue was projected to be 5.24 trillion. A huge fiscal deficit of 2.2 trillion baht would require the government to fulfill the gap, thus the borrowing from the public, both domestic and abroad, to be designed accordingly as well.

Thus, from the same source of analyses from the Bank of Thailand by applying the social accounting matrix, the SP2 would help Thailand's GDP increase by 1.3 per cent per year, with a job creation's total value of 870 billion baht between 2010 and 2014. As a result, Thailand's economic growth in 2010 is expected to be around 3.5 to 4.0 per cent, largely on the part of a recovery in manufacturing and exports. Manufacturing and related service sectors account for nearly 65 per cent of GDP and are expected to contribute well over a growth of 2 per cent in 2010 on the back of the global recovery. Service sectors tied to tourism like hotels, restaurants and transportation are likely to lag somehow the recovery (see Figure 5.15).

FIGURE 5.15
Headline GDP Growth Largely Driven by Recovery in Manufacturing and Related Services

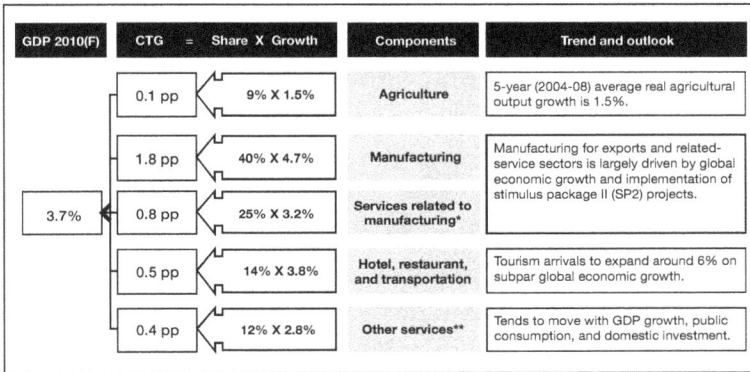

GDP 2010(F)	CTG	= Share X Growth	Components	Trend and outlook
	0.1 pp	9% X 1.5%	Agriculture	5-year (2004-08) average real agricultural output growth is 1.5%.
	1.8 pp	40% X 4.7%	Manufacturing	Manufacturing for exports and related-service sectors is largely driven by global economic growth and implementation of stimulus package II (SP2) projects.
3.7%	0.8 pp	25% X 3.2%	Services related to manufacturing*	
	0.5 pp	14% X 3.8%	Hotel, restaurant, and transportation	Tourism arrivals to expand around 6% on subpar global economic growth.
	0.4 pp	12% X 2.8%	Other services**	Tends to move with GDP growth, public consumption, and domestic investment.

Notes: Numbers may not add up due to rounding.
   * Services related to manufacturing includes mining, utilities, construction, real estate, trade.
   ** Other services include financial, public administration, education, health and social work, private household with employed persons.
   Pp = percentage point
Sources: National Economic and Social Development Board (NESDB) and SCB EIC analysis.

Public Debt Sustainability

While the public expenditures in conjunction with the stimulus packages could spur the Thai economy to be back on track, the total spending, however, could push the country into a new trajectory of mounting public debt. It is estimated that, if fully utilized, the stimulus packages of 2009 could result in an increasing budget deficit up to 6.5 per cent of GDP for the 2009 fiscal year, thus making a public debt of GDP up to 48.3 per cent by the end of 2009 fiscal year. With the pursuits of SP2 between 2010 and 2012, it will certainly aggravate the share of public debt to GDP to rise even further. For this reason, the Bank of Thailand expects the public debt to GDP to reach its peak at around 59 per cent in 2013, then falling downward afterward. With a more sustainable economic recovery, the stimulus packages will phase out by then, thus the public debt is supposed to decline after 2013.

It is worthy to note here that following the Asian financial crisis of 1997, Thailand's public debt was also ballooned to around 58 per cent in 2000 as a result of government spending and stimulus policy, while the government revenue continued to decline. However, Thailand's economic recovery became clear in 2002 onwards which had helped the government to reduce spending and to collect tax revenue, thus balancing the overall government budget and reducing the ratio of public debt to GDP. Therefore, it might be following this past experience that the government seems to be confident about the country's ability to manage the mounting public debt in this round of fighting against the economic downturn although the scenario of an economic recovery looks different from the last time.

As a matter of fact, the Ministry of Finance had recently shown that the actual budget deficit of 2009 was only around 344 billion baht or around 3.4 per cent of Thailand's GDP, mainly due to the delay in budget spending. In addition, with global economic recovery starting to show its sign by late 2009 continuing into 2010, and private sector in the domestic economy also showing a recovery sign in late 2009, all these seems to provide a better look at the way in which stimulus packages should be adjusted like the total packages spending of 350 billion baht to be used in 2010. At the end of the day, Thailand's public debt to GDP should not pass beyond the level of 60 per cent which is the threshold set by international standard.

Exit Policy and Implications from Global Rebalancing

Since the end of 2009, the Thai economy has clearly started to recover from the global financial crisis. There is, however, an issue of how durable this recovery would be, as this is directly related to the exit policy of government rescued packages. For the moment, fiscal policy has seen sign of relaxation and it is possible that some urgent, short-term packages could be scaled down. Between time, the Thai Government looks to coordinate its fiscal policy in accordance with what would happen with the global recovery.

In conjunction with the recovery of the Thai economy and possibly exit policy, the monetary policy might also move back to its neutral stance, let alone the economy would have to handle a rise in interest rate. More recently, the Bank of Thailand clearly indicated that the upward trend of interest rate would probably start soon once it reaches the bottom for sometime. In this regard, it is expected that the Bank of Thailand will allow the rise of interest rate sometime during mid-2010. This is in line with the Fed policy measures. This rise could be in the order of 0.5 per cent by the end of 2010.

For these reasons, both Thailand's financial and real sector has to be well prepared in the face of a possible exit policy and new adjustments in the country's macroeconomic policy coordination once the global recovery become more certain. Other related major concern of the Thai economy to this global recovery is the new baht value according to the impact of global rebalancing as a result of U.S. current account possibly being started to make its long-term correction. If that correction might be the case, then medium-term correction of global imbalance will cause a seemingly substantial U.S. dollar depreciation against other currencies, particularly the ones in Asia, including the Thai baht. The issue is how the Bank of Thailand will manage a possibly strong baht during the rebalancing period. How could Thailand's real sector, particularly the export sector, manage its competitiveness, relative to a decline in the value of the U.S. dollar? There is also a major concern about the volatile capital flows as a result of major financial movements that might take place. All these new arising issues will put the country into its own responses to these global and regional challenges.

Conclusion

The current global financial crisis, which has not yet ended, has caused the global economy to drop into a negative growth in 2009, the first time since the end of the World War II. By and large, Asian exports and growth had evidently been much affected because of their over dependence on the external sector to the developed countries, namely, the United States and Europe. Thailand, like many other Asian countries, had seen the collapse of its trade in 2009 by 16.7 per cent, as much as a sharp reduction of its GDP growth rate to −2.3 per cent. The country had also seen the recession for three consecutive quarters of 2009 before the recent strong recovery in the last quarter. The extent of the global crisis also reaches the travel industry, private consumption, private investment, production and employment which requires strong adjustments in all sectors involved.

However, the impact of the global financial crisis on the Thai financial sector was quite limited. The last Asian financial crisis of 1997–98 has helped the Thai banks in some ways to be much more conservative in its lending approach. Indeed, they were more reluctant to expose themselves to risky foreign assets hence high risks for their business. As a result, they had not been exposed to any toxic assets or rising NPLs due to Thailand's economic decline. When the panic set in at the global level, the Bank of Thailand including the financial institutions at the local level had continued to manage successfully the liquidity in the banking system as well as the baht value. Even though foreign investors made a clear sell-off of the Thai equity, the amount of capital outflows was relatively small when compared to the stock of Thailand's international reserves. At one point, the equity market was hard hit as the SET Index was subject to decline at the global level, in particular, the influence of U.S. stock index decline.

Despite the domestic political turmoil throughout 2008, the Democrat government once in power, at the beginning of 2009, had immediately started to roll out its first stimulus package during the first quarter of 2009. This stimulus package aims to stimulate consumers' spending of different, well-target groups of population. These measures are 2,000-baht income allowances, 500-baht monthly allowances for senior citizens, free utilities for the poor, education and training for the young and unemployed, and small infrastructure development in rural areas. The government often refers to these measures as welfare benefits to the needy Thais and not the populist policies as often applied in the former Thaksin government.

The following government stimulus package two, formally known as "Thai Khem Kaeng" was a natural response to the medium and long-term programmes that aim to improve the country's productivity, competitiveness and infrastructure. Whether and how the government would meet these objectives is another issue. Indeed, Thailand has missed a significant public investment since the last Asian financial crisis. Therefore, the stimulus package two has, in its design, a three-year programme of its implementation, with nearly 60 per cent, consisting of hard infrastructure, transport and logistics, and irrigation projects. The issue of public spending and debt is still a natural concern as Thailand moves along this path.

While the overall economic recovery of Thailand is well on track since the last quarter of 2009, this path to recovery is still hinging on several issues. Firstly, this recovery has again depended upon the export sector. The export dependence and its instability is still a concern. Also, the global crisis had shown the falling exports from China reduced the country's demand for raw materials and intermediate goods. In the medium term, Thailand has to work closer with those emerging economies, particularly, China, India and ASEAN through its production and market linkages, both for goods and services. Secondly, the government stimulus packages are still the order of the day as the global crisis might be prolonged. The scopes and depths for various projects must be scrutinized while moving onto their implementation. For Thailand, the government also aims to use these funds to stimulate economic growth, expected to be at least 3.5 per cent in 2010. Thirdly, in relation to the public spending, would be the issue of public debt. Whether this public debt is sustainable when Thailand expects the share of public debt to GDP to reach its peak at around 60 per cent in 2013 is still debatable. Last but not least, Thailand is to consider its exit policy in terms of government rescued packages once the economic recovery is on its path. The Bank of Thailand also needs to adjust the monetary policy with the interest rate back to its neutral stance and the baht currency in line with the new global rebalancing, particularly, a possibly medium-term correction of global imbalance causing the U.S. dollar to depreciate and particularly, Asian currencies, including the Thai baht, to appreciate.

ANNEX 1
Sectors with Strong Crisis Impact and Linkages to Other Sectors

	Sector with Strong Crisis Impact		Sector with High Backward Linkages and Raw Material Uses		Sector with Crisis Impact and Linkages to Other Sectors
084	Restaurants and drinking places	057	Iron and steel	041	Wearing apparel
097	Education	100	Unclassified	082	Non-residential building construction
094	Real estate	031	Tapioca milling	089	Air transport
041	Wearing apparel	025	Canning and preservation of meat	100	Unclassified
098	Hospital	024	Slaughtering	034	Other food products
096	Public administration	071	Motor vehicles	087	Road passenger transport
082	Non-residential building construction	015	Swine	028	Canning and preservation of fish and other seafoods
085	Hotels and places of loading	035	Animal feed	054	Plastic ware
099	Other service not classified elsewhere	081	Non-residential building construction		
074	Tanneries and leather finishing and leather products	078	Pipeline and gas distribution		
		029	Coconut and palm oil		
089	Air transport	028	Canning and preservation of fish and other seafoods		
100	Unclassified	054	Plastic ware		
034	Other food products	041	Wearing apparel		
064	Special industrial machinery	087	Road passenger transport		
075	Saw mills	016	Poultry and poultry products		
049	Other chemical products	058	Secondary steel products		
067	Radio, television and communication equipment and apparatus	072	Repair of motor vehicles		

ANNEX 1 – *cont'd*

Sector with Strong Crisis Impact	Sector with High Backward Linkages and Raw Material Uses	Sector with Crisis Impact and Linkages to Other Sectors
083 Trade	080 Residential building construction	
065 Office and household machinery and appliances	040 Knitting	
076 Other manufactured goods	089 Air transport	
087 Road passenger transport	030 Rice milling	
028 Canning and preservation of fish and other seafoods	026 Dairy products	
070 Motor vehicles	095 Business services	
060 Structure metal products	047 Paints	
054 Plastic ware	039 Spinning, Weaving and Bleaching	
066 Electrical industrial machinery and appliances	034 Other food products	
	062 Agricultural machinery and equipment	
	042 Other textile products	
	027 Canning and preservation of fruit and vegetables	
	052 Types and tubes	
	082 Non-residential building construction	
	037 Soft drinks and carbonated water	
	056 Other non-metallic products	
	053 Other rubber products	

Source: Kornkarun Cheewatrakulwongse and al. (2010).

ANNEX 2
Sectors with Strong Crisis Impact and Linkages to Other Sectors

Sector with Strong Crisis Impact		Sector with Strong Impact on Total Income		Sector with Crisis Impact on Individual Income	
084	Restaurants and drinking places	001	Paddy	041	Wearing apparel
097	Education	032	Grinding of maize	066	Electrical industrial machinery and appliances
096	Public administration	015	Swine	075	Saw mills
041	Wearing apparel	003	Cassava	085	Hotels and places of loading
098	Hospital	018	Other forest products	089	Air transport
096	Public administration	030	Rice milling	096	Public administration
082	Non-residential building construction	026	Dairy products	097	Education
085	Hotels and places of loading	035	Animal feed	098	Hospital
099	Other service not classified elsewhere	092	Banking services	099	Other service not classified elsewhere
074	Tanneries and leather finishing and leather products	075	Saw mills		
089	Air transport	033	Sugar		
100	Unclassified	053	Other rubber products		
034	Other food products	096	Public administration		
064	Special industrial machinery	086	Railways		
075	Saw mills	097	Education		
049	Other chemical products	098	Hospital		
067	Radio, television and communication equipment and apparatus	002	Maize		
		077	Electricity		
		089	Air transport		

ANNEX 2 – *cont'd*

Sector with Strong Crisis Impact		Sector with Strong Impact on Total Income		Sector with Crisis Impact on Individual Income
083	Trade	099	Other service not classified elsewhere	
065	Office and household machinery and appliances	007	Sugar cane	
076	Other manufactured goods	079	Water work and supply	
087	Road passenger transport	093	Insurance services	
028	Canning and preservation of fish and other seafoods	085	Hotels and places of loading	
		066	Electrical industrial machinery and appliances	
070	Motor vehicles	062	Agricultural machinery and equipment	
060	Structural metal products			
054	Plastic ware	031	Tapioca milling	
066	Electrical industrial machinery and appliances	091	Post and telecommunication	
		080	Residential building construction	
		040	Knitting	
		058	Secondary steel products	
		057	Iron and steel	
		073	Other motor vehicles	
		041	Wearing apparel	

Source: Kornkarun Cheewatrakullwongse and al. (2010).

REFERENCES

Bank of Thailand. BOT News nos. 6 and 42 (2008).

_____. BOT Monthly Economic and Financial Report, November 2009.

_____. BOT News no. 51 (2009).

Chantarang U. and Chartpaisal. *International Investment in Foreign Securities and Impacts on Financial Crisis*. WE-MEG Discussion Paper No. 11, Bank of Thailand, 2009.

Cheewatrakulwongse, K. and al. "Study of the Global Financial Crisis Impact on Thailand's Real Sector through Trade Transmissions". Mimeographed. Research work in progress, 19 August 2009.

Chirathivat, S. "Ten Years after the Asian Crisis: Toward Economic Sustainability in Southeast Asia". *Dialogue and Cooperation*. Singapore: Friedrich Ebert Stiftung, 2007.

_____. "Global Financial Crisis and Broader Regional Cooperation in Asia". Mimeographed. Paper presented at the High-Level Conference on "Financial Crisis, Global Economic Governance and Development: Responses of Asia and Global South". Organized as part of the RIS 25th Anniversary, New Delhi, 6–7 February 2009.

Eichengreen, Barry. "The Global Credit Crisis as History". Mimeographed. December 2008.

International Monetary Fund. *World Economic Outlook*. Washington, D.C., 2009.

Kindleberger, C. *Manias, Panics and Crashes*. New York: Basic Books, 1978.

Lim Chin. "Asia's Change to Ease the Crisis". *Bangkok Post*, 6 December 2008.

Ministry of Finance. "Macroeconomic Analysis Briefing" [in Thai]. Mimeographed. Fiscal Policy Office, Macroeconomic Policy Division. 1 July 2009.

National Economic and Social Development Board (NESDB). "Thai Economic Performance in Q3 and Outlook for 2010". Mimeographed. Macroeconomic Strategy and Planning Office, 23 November 2009.

Premsil J. and Vanichthanunkul J. "The Appropriate Stimulus Fiscal Policy". WE-MPG Discussion Paper 15, Bank of Thailand, 2009.

Reinhart, C. and K. Rogoff. "Is the 2007 U.S. Financial Crisis So Different?". *American Economic Review* 98, no. 2 (2008): 339–44.

Siam Commercial Bank. "2010 Thailand Macroeconomic and Sectoral Outlook". SCB Insight by Economic Intelligent Center, August–September 2009.

Son, H.H. and E.A. San Andres. "How Has Asia Fare in the Global Crisis? A Tale of Three Countries: Republic of Korea, Philippines and Thailand". ADB Economics Working Paper Series No. 174. Asian Development Bank, October 2009.

Taylor, John B. "The Financial Crisis and the Policy Responses: An Empirical Analysis of What Went Wrong". Mimeographed. November 2008.

6
Tackling the Global Financial Crisis in Vietnam

Vo Tri Thanh
and Nguyen Anh Duong

Introduction

The past couple of years marked a memorable experience for
Vietnam. After a long period of continuous high growth and
macroeconomic stability, Vietnam offered foreign investors
one of the most attractive investment destinations. However,
after a short period of overly optimistic expectations in the
first half of 2007, Vietnam had to start worrying about the
overall economic situation. The accumulated inflationary
pressures from continuous credit and public investment
expansions, in combination with the external shocks such
as rising energy and rice prices, and inappropriateness
of the policy responses to a surge in capital inflows in
2007, sent the country to macroeconomic turbulence
and the perplexity in formulating a proper stabilization
policy. A policy package for dealing with macroeconomic
instability has been implemented since March 2008. As the
macroeconomic situation improved somehow by the end of

2008, the country has suffered from very negative impacts of the global financial crisis and recession.

This chapter discusses the main economic developments in Vietnam in 2009. In doing so, the chapter also makes comparison with the changes in macroeconomic conditions in Vietnam in line with the external shocks after the country became a member of the World Trade Organization (WTO) in 2007. Besides, the chapter describes Vietnam's policy responses during the crisis and summarizes some economic projections for the economy in 2010.

The rest of the chapter is structured as follows. The first section analyses the economic development in 2008–09, focusing on merchandise trade, investment, economic growth, inflation, balance of payments, and the financial system. The next section then reviews the policy response in 2009, before providing a summary of several key economic projections for Vietnam in 2010. The concluding remarks, finally, list several challenges and issues that the country should consider in the years from 2010 onwards.

Vietnam's Economic Development in 2008–09

For many years since *Doi Moi* (*Renovation*), particularly since 2000, Vietnam focused its policies on promoting high economic growth and on sustaining macroeconomic stability. However, till 2007 the promotion of high economic growth depended heavily on expanding investment and credit. Total investment grew on average by 15.3 per cent per year in the years 2000–07, while the 2007 rate of growth in investment alone was 27.0 per cent. Similarly, outstanding credit increased by almost 53.9 per cent in 2007.

Vietnam's accession to the WTO in 2007 made foreign investors more confident on the country's development prospect. This led to the dramatic surge in capital inflows even prior to the recession. Foreign direct investment (FDI) increased dramatically, from over US$6.8 billion (US$3.3 billion) in 2005 to above US$12 billion (US$4.1 billion) in 2006 and US$21.3 billion (US$8.0 billion) in 2007. The figures reflected registered capital of FDI projects, while those in brackets were values of implemented capital. Portfolio investment also rose from US$865 million in 2006 to US$1,313 million and US$6,243 million in 2007 and 2008 respectively. These surges in foreign capital inflows resulted largely from increasing investment in the securities and real estate markets (see Figure 6.1)

In addition, Vietnam also suffered from the external shocks and the inappropriateness of policies in response to the surge in capital inflows. The rising energy and rice prices presented sources of unfavourable impacts on Vietnam's domestic prices level. Meanwhile, facing the sudden surge in capital inflows while keeping the crawling-peg exchange rate regime to promote export growth, Vietnam had to increase its supply of domestic currency in exchange for foreign currencies. However, the country did not carry out sterilization measures to a reasonable extent, leading to the dramatic increase in money supply. Together with the inflationary pressures building up after a long period of investment- and credit-led growth, this put Vietnam in serious macroeconomic turbulence, with inflation sky-rocketing to a high level in the first eight months of 2008. This gave rise to the implementation of a policy package

FIGURE 6.1
Analytical Framework of Post-WTO Impacts on Vietnam's Economy

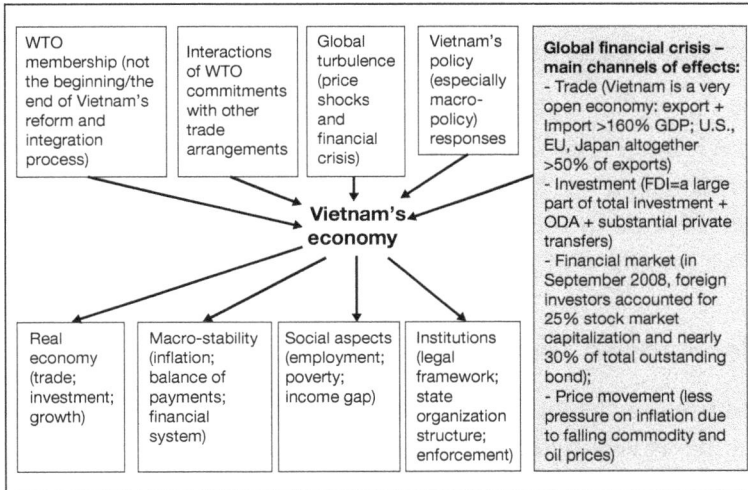

WTO membership (not the beginning/the end of Vietnam's reform and integration process)	Interactions of WTO commitments with other trade arrangements	Global turbulence (price shocks and financial crisis)	Vietnam's policy (especially macro-policy) responses	**Global financial crisis – main channels of effects:**
				- Trade (Vietnam is a very open economy: export + Import >160% GDP; U.S., EU, Japan altogether >50% of exports)
		Vietnam's economy		- Investment (FDI=a large part of total investment + ODA + substantial private transfers)
				- Financial market (in September 2008, foreign investors accounted for 25% stock market capitalization and nearly 30% of total outstanding bond);
Real economy (trade; investment; growth)	Macro-stability (inflation; balance of payments; financial system)	Social aspects (employment; poverty; income gap)	Institutions (legal framework; state organization structure; enforcement)	- Price movement (less pressure on inflation due to falling commodity and oil prices)

Source: Authors' modification from Vo and Nguyen (2009).

for dealing with macroeconomic instability since March 2008.

However, since the fourth quarter of 2008, Vietnam has again suffered from significant negative impacts of the global financial crisis and economic downturn. Foreign investors were wary about the rapid spread of the global financial crisis, and opted to move away from Vietnam. Meanwhile, export growth started to decelerate since the major importers of Vietnam's products, such as the United States, Japan, etc., were in deep economic recession.

Accordingly, the Government of Vietnam decided to shift its policies towards stimulating economic activities and ensuring social securities.

Vietnam's Economic Performance in 2008–09

The above developments have had significant impacts on Vietnam's economy in various aspects. The economic performance of Vietnam will be examined in terms of merchandise trade, investment, growth, inflation, balance of payments, and financial system.

Merchandise Trade

Continuing the trend after the WTO accession, Vietnam's comparative advantages seem to be continuously exploited for export acceleration. The value of merchandise exports in 2007, 2008 and 2009 reached US$48.6 billion, US$62.9 billion and US$56.6 billion, respectively. The export growth rate was high in 2008 (29.5 per cent; 21.9 per cent in 2007) due largely to the dramatic surge in world commodity prices. Excluding the effect of rising prices of major products such as rice, crude oil, coal, coffee, rubber, etc., the total value of merchandise exports in 2008 only grew by less than 14 per cent (see Figure 6.2). However, merchandise exports started to fall significantly since the fourth quarter of 2008 due to the impact of global financial crisis which led to a substantial reduction of commodity and oil prices as well as aggregate demand. In fact, the export growth rate in the first three quarters of 2008 reached about 39 per cent, but those for the fourth quarter of 2008 and the first three quarters of 2009 were 6.4 per cent and −14.3 per cent, respectively.

FIGURE 6.2
Export Growth of Major Commodities/
Products (%), 2006–09

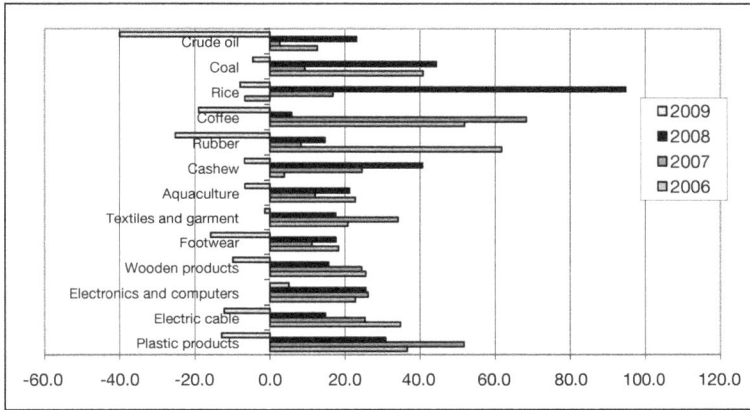

Source: General Statistics Office.

Vietnam's merchandise export began to perform better in the fourth quarter of 2009, thereby restricting the fall in export for 2009 as a whole to 9.7 per cent.

The corresponding changes in Vietnam's merchandise imports were of greater magnitude than those of merchandise export. Total merchandise imports, measured in CIF prices, unless otherwise specified in 2008 reached US$80.4 billion or grew by 28.3 per cent. However, such a growth rate was slower than that in 2007 (39.6 per cent), because of the economic slowdown and the measures for restricting trade deficit since 2007. In 2009, merchandise import even went down to US$68.8 billion, reflecting a decrease by 14.7 per cent. In the first three quarters of 2009, merchandise import even decreased to US$48.3 billion, or by –25.2 per cent. Such a decrease stemmed more largely from the falling prices than the reduction in import volumes. Nonetheless, the trade deficit remained large, and the key trade partners where Vietnam has been experiencing trade deficit are China (US$11.1 billion in 2008 and US$11.3 billion in 2009) and ASEAN (US$9.6 billion in 2008 and US$4.9 billion in 2009).

Investment

In recent years, Vietnam's total investment tended to fall in terms of overall GDP. The investment ratio, measured by total investment over GDP, decreased from 46.5 per cent in 2007 to 43.1 per cent in 2008 and 42.8 per cent in 2009. A salient feature of investment in Vietnam is that the state investment accounts for a large share of total investment. However, the share of state investment declined continuously and drastically from 45.7 per cent in 2006 to 37.2 per cent and 28.5 per cent in 2007 and 2008 respectively, before rising again to 34.8 per cent in 2009 (see Table 6.1). It decreased significantly in 2008 due to the tightening of state investments and stricter domestic credits. Its opposite trend in 2009 was thanks to the implementation of the stimulus package. The increase in real total investment in 2006–07 was due to the expansion of investments from the state budget and by state-owned enterprises (SOEs), while foreign direct investment (FDI) and private sector contributed more significantly to the increased investment in 2008. In 2009, FDI declined both in absolute value and relative to total investment.

Even with unfavourable development in and outside the economy since 2008, Vietnam continued to be a promising

TABLE 6.1
Percentage Distribution of Investment Structure by Ownership, 2006–09

	2006	2007	2008	2009
State sector	45.7	37.2	28.5	34.8
Budget	*24.8*	*20.2*	*16.2*	*21.8*
State credit	*9.1*	*5.7*	*4.1*	*–*
SOEs and others	*11.8*	*11.3*	*8.2*	*–*
Non-State sector	38.1	38.5	40.0	39.5
FDI	16.2	24.3	31.5	25.7
Total	100.0	100.0	100.0	100.0

Source: General Statistics Office.

destination for FDI, reflecting foreign investors' confidence in its growth prospect. In 2008, an estimate of US$64 billion of FDI was registered, and implemented and disbursed FDI already amounted to US$11.5 billion and about US$8.3 billion, respectively (see Figure 6.3). Consequently, the share of FDI in total investment rose drastically from 16.2 per cent in 2006 to 31.5 per cent in 2008 (see Table 6.1). In 2009, however, FDI flows into Vietnam decreased to US$16.3 billion and US$10.0 billion for registered and implemented capital, respectively. Such a decrease also led to the declining share of FDI in total investment to only 25.7 per cent. Traditionally, the major investors in Vietnam were Japan, South Korea, Taiwan, Hong Kong, ASEAN, the United States, EU, China, etc., but in 2009, Vietnam received FDI mostly from the United States, Cayman Islands, Samoa, South Korea, Taiwan, Virgin Islands, Hong Kong, and Singapore, etc.

FIGURE 6.3
FDI In Vietnam, 1998–2009

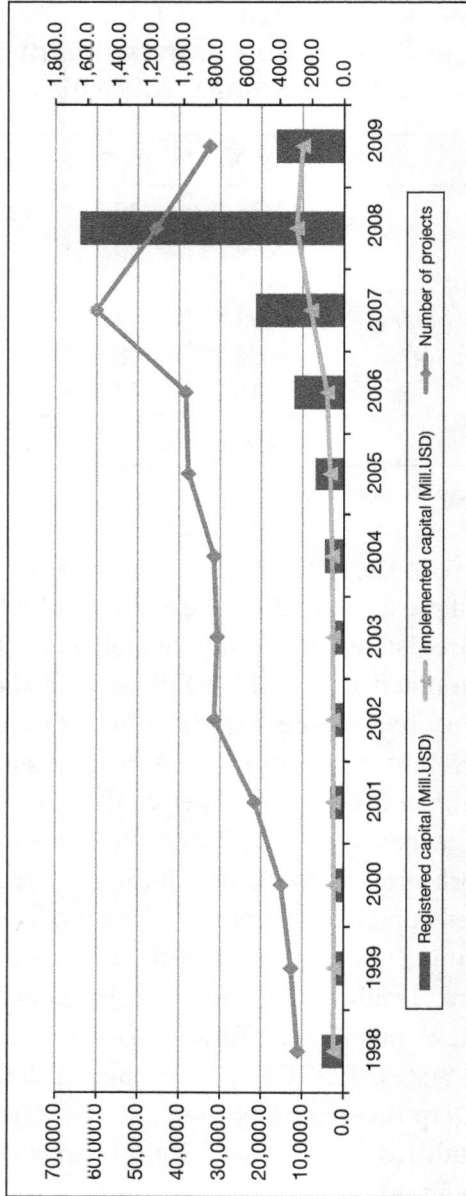

Source: Ministry of Planning and Investment (MPI), Vietnam.

Economic Growth

Notwithstanding the impacts of the global economic recession, Vietnam's economy continued to attain moderate growth, albeit slower than that immediately after the WTO accession. The economic growth rate reached only 6.2 per cent in 2008 and 5.3 per cent in 2009, compared to that of 8.5 per cent in 2007 (see Figure 6.4).

From the supply side, GDP growth continued to be driven by the industry-construction activities. However, the sector experienced a decline in its share from around 41.6 per cent in 2006 to roughly 39.7 per cent in 2008, before a slight recovery to 40.2 per cent in 2009. In 2009, the growth rate of industry — construction sector was 5.5 per cent. This was largely thanks to the growth of mining and construction sectors (7.6 per cent and 11.4 per cent respectively, compared to 2.8 per cent of manufacturing). Meanwhile, the share of agriculture-forestry-aquaculture in GDP has risen from 20.4 per cent in 2006 to 22.1 per cent in 2008, before declining to 20.7 per cent in 2009. The share of overall services sector attained around 38 per cent GDP during 2006–08, whilst increasing to over 39 per cent in 2009.

From another perspective, Vietnam's economic growth relies heavily on foreign savings. Due to the rapid increase in domestic consumption over the years 2007–08, domestic savings as a proportion of GDP experienced continuous falls from 30.6 per cent in 2006 to 29.1 per cent in GDP and 28.8 per cent in 2008. As domestic investment expanded, the domestic savings-investment gap (much more than 10 percentage points) kept widening, and it could hardly be met by overseas capital in sustainable manner.

FIGURE 6.4
Economic Growth in Vietnam, 2006–09

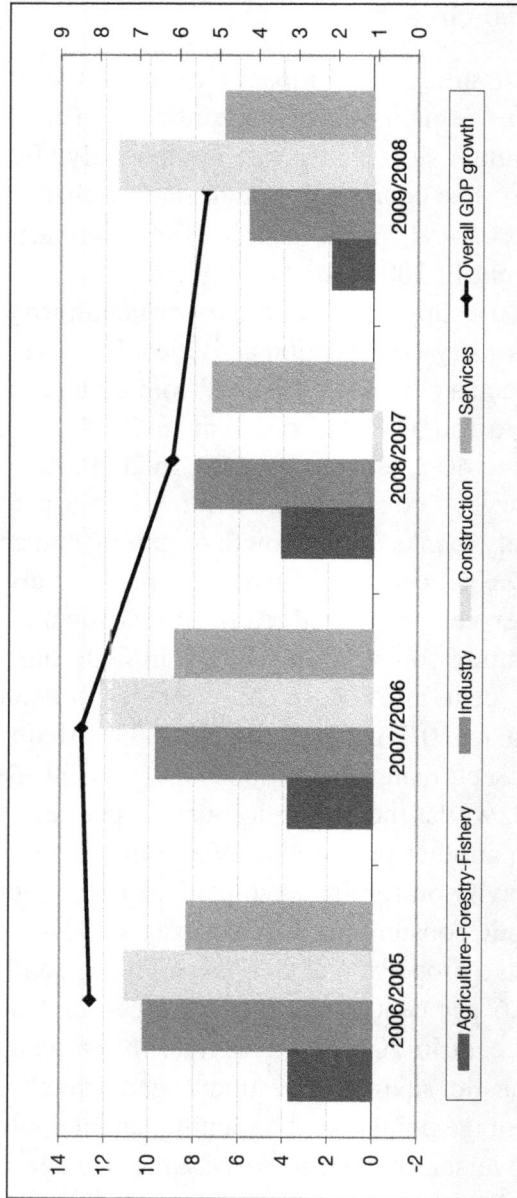

Source: General Statistics Office.

Inflation

From the beginning of 2008, consumer price index based inflation on an y-o-y basis started to rise. The figure reached the peak of 28.3 per cent in August 2008 and even attained an enormous rate of 16.5 per cent after removing the prices of food and foodstuff which account for a large share in the CPI basket (about 43 per cent). The administrative upward adjustment of petroleum price had also some effect on higher inflation (see Figure 6.5).

Vo and Nguyen (2009) have identified several causes of this rapid surge in inflation. First, expansionary macroeconomic policies for many years, whilst facilitating continuous rapid growth over the past period, have contributed to building up dramatic pressures on inflation. This problem was further magnified by the increase in international prices and complicated trade-offs in domestic price stabilization

FIGURE 6.5
Year-on-Year CPI Inflation, 2006–09

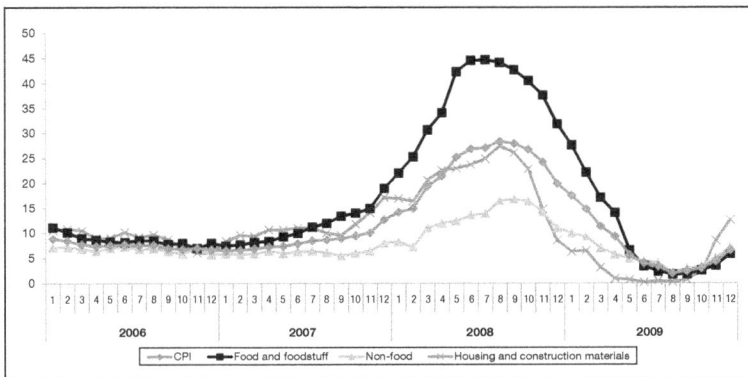

Source: General Statistics Office.

policy. Second, the massive, unprecedented increase in foreign capital inflows in 2007 left policy-makers with enormous perplexity, particularly in formulating policy response. The attempt to control money supply in the second half of 2007 was ineffective (and costly), as it was accompanied by the inadequate sterilization in supplying the domestic currencies for the inflows of foreign exchanges.

Since September 2008, the m-o-m inflation has declined significantly, to –0.19 per cent in October, –0.76 per cent in November and –0.68 per cent in December, leaving the y-o-y inflation rate of 19.9 per cent for 2008 as a whole. This decline continued until March 2009, when y-o-y inflation reached 11.3 per cent while m-o-m inflation was low. The underlying reasons were of both "good luck" (falling international prices of rice and fuels) and "better policy implementation" (the impact of stabilization policies). In subsequent months until September 2009, y-o-y inflation went down further to 2.4 per cent, yet m-o-m inflation tended to hike due to the increases in money supply, salaries/wages and international prices. The m-o-m inflation for the months of April–September 2009 were 0.3 per cent, 0.4 per cent, 0.5 per cent, 0.5 per cent, 0.2 per cent, 0.6 per cent, respectively. During the last quarter of 2009, inflation started to accelerate again: y-o-y inflation rose to over 6.5 per cent in December from just under 3 per cent in October. For 2009 as a whole, the CPI-based inflation rate was reported at just below 6.9 per cent.

Balance of Payment

Vietnam continued to run current account deficit, yet the deficit got larger over time (see Figure 6.6). The deficit was valued at US$10.7 billion (or 11.9 per cent GDP) in 2008 and US$7.7 billion (or 8.3 per cent GDP) in 2009.[1] This result is remarkable, given the fact that the country only incurred a current account deficit of under US$0.2 billion (or 0.3 per cent of GDP) in 2006. The increase in current account deficit was largely due to the surge in trade deficit, to nearly US$12.8 billion (14.2 per cent GDP) in 2008 and US$10.1 billion (or 10.9 per cent GDP) in 2009, from nearly US$2.8 billion (or 4.6 per cent GDP) in 2006. Notably, the trade deficit seemed to be widening even in 2009 when Vietnam suffered from economic difficulties. For the first nine month of 2009, the trade deficit only reached US$6.6 billion, but that in the fourth quarter of 2009 amounted to approximately US$3.5 billion (EIU 2010).

In 2008, the capital account was in large surplus (US$11.2 billion) thanks to the massive inflows of foreign investment. Accordingly, the overall BOP in 2008 reflected

FIGURE 6.6
Vietnam's Balance of Payments, 2007–09

Unit: per cent GDP

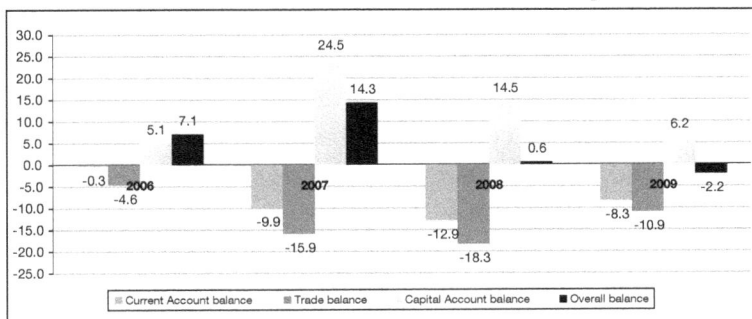

Source: Authors' compilations from various sources.

a minor surplus of only US$0.5 billion. In 2009, however, the inflows of foreign investment was smaller, resulting in a smaller capital account surplus (only US$5.7 billion). As a result, the BOP was in an estimated deficit of approximately US$2 billion.

The rapid increases in inflation and trade deficit, especially in the first half of 2008, have combined to exert high pressures on VND to depreciate. However, since August 2008, the stabilization policy package that Vietnam implemented began to take effect. As a result, trade deficit situation seemed to have been improved, and together with lower inflation, this in turn helped ease the pressure of VND devaluation. As the economy accelerated its growth since the second quarter of 2009, people have raised their demand for imports. This again creates pressures on the VND to further depreciate in recent months.

Financial System

Since 2006–07, the banking sector and the capital and real estate markets in Vietnam have been booming. Such a boom resulted from investors' expectations of profit opportunities once Vietnam opens its services market in line with WTO commitments. Despite the dominance of the state-owned commercial banks (SOCBs) in the banking system, the role of joint-stock commercial banks (JSCBs) has been strengthened, as reflected by their greater shares in total deposits and total credits. The respective share of JSCBs in total credit and total deposits has increased rapidly from 14.5 per cent and 16.7 per cent in 2005 to over 26.5 per cent and 33.1 per cent in 2008 (see Table 6.2). The depth of the financial system has also been improved significantly.

TABLE 6.2
Market Shares of Banks, 2005–08

Unit: per cent

Year	SOCBs		JSCBs		Foreign Banks	
	Credit	Deposits	Credit	Deposits	Credit	Deposits
2005	69.96	73.89	14.51	16.67	9.43	7.9
2006	64.56	69.66	19.31	20.71	9.45	8.1
2007	55.96	59.31	27.74	30.36	9.25	8.78
2008	53.95	57.08	26.51	33.07	11.04	7.12

Source: Nguyen Thi Kim Thanh (2009).

The ratio of total deposits (by households and institutions in credit institutions) over GDP rose from 66.7 per cent in 2005 to 114.0 per cent in 2008, while outstanding loans as percentage of GDP increased from 65.9 per cent in 2005 to 105.0 per cent in 2008 (Nguyen Thi Kim Thanh 2009).

However, some banks experienced serious maturity mismatch. The ratio of long-term loans in total credit seemed to be too high. At the same time, due to uncertainty in the overall macroeconomic situation, the households were more inclined to make short-term deposits. This problem was further complicated by the increase in non-performing loans, particularly those made for purposes of consumption and real estate investment, etc., in the second half of 2008. The proportion of non-performing loans (NPLs) increased from 1.5 per cent by the end of 2007 to about 3.5 per cent by the end of 2008, before declining to about 2.0 per cent in 2009. It should be noted, however, that these figures were based on Vietnam's accounting standard, rather than on one adopted internationally.

Besides, the capacity to manage and control risks remained weak, and failed to catch up with the boom in financial and banking industry. Such a weak capacity at the micro-level constrained the efficiency and prudential management as banking-financial institutions expand the scale and scope of their investment activities. Meanwhile, the monitoring and surveillance system at the macro-level lags far behind the development of the market, while macroeconomic indicators are currently worrisome.

In addition, the banking system appeared to suffer from a lack of liquidity, particularly in the first half of 2008. The declining propensity to save of the households left the banks and other depository institutions in fierce competition to attract deposits. Simultaneously, measures by the State Bank of Vietnam (SBV) to control credits, including some administrative ones to withdraw money from circulation, caused the banks, particularly small JSCBs, to be in a stranded situation, with insufficient funds to meet their lending and investment needs. The situation, nonetheless, has eased significantly since July 2008.

From October 2007 to February 2009, due to fears of macroeconomic instability as well as the contagion effect of the financial crisis, the securities market has gone down, as reflected by the relatively unambiguous downward trend in the VN-Index. Accordingly, the VN-Index fell from around 1,100 in October 2007 to roughly 235 in February 2008, or by approximately 78.7 per cent (see Figure 6.7). Market capitalization decreased from 43 per cent GDP in 2007 to 15 per cent GDP by the end of 2008. In this period, foreign investors were significant net sellers. Since March 2009, however, the market started to recover, reaching over

FIGURE 6.7
VN-Index and Transaction Volume in Vietnam's Securities Market, 2007–09

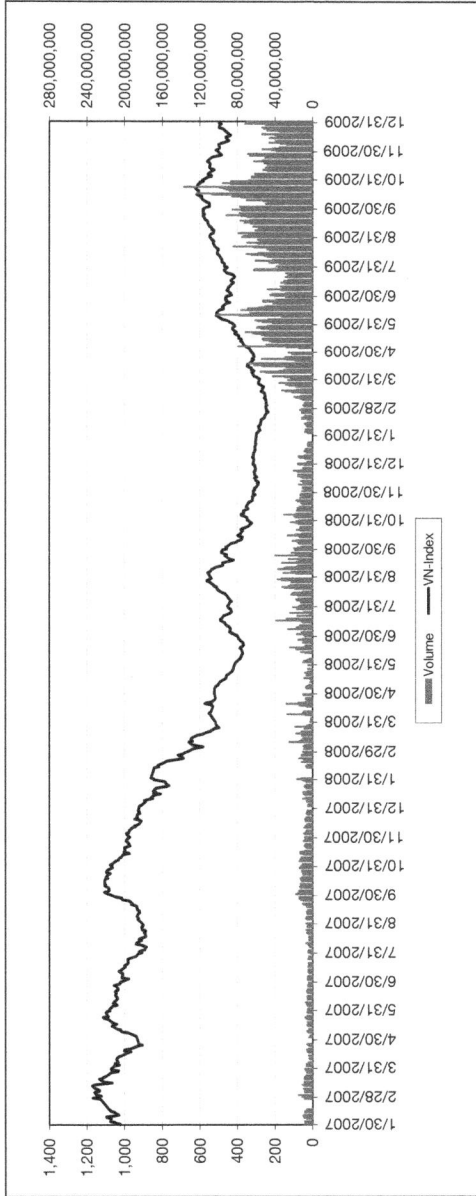

Source: State Securities Commission.

600 in mid-October 2009 as compared to the lowest level of 235 in February 2009. Such a recovery was arguably due to the impacts of the economic stimulus package, better performance of Vietnam's businesses, improved growth prospects after the economic slowdown, and the popularization of margin trading. From late October 2009, however, measures to control credit growth led to a decline in the securities market: the VN-Index has demonstrated a downward trend, and reached just under 500 by the end of 2009.

Policy Response in 2009

To stimulate domestic economic activities, Vietnam has adopted a number of policy changes. On the one hand, the country eased monetary policy. The required reserve ratio (RRR) was reduced significantly from 10 per cent in November 2008 to 3 per cent in March 2009. Meanwhile, the base interest rate was cut down from 13 per cent in October 2008 to 7 per cent in February 2009, and remained unchanged until November 2009 when it was raised to 8 per cent. Similar changes were also in place for refinancing rate and discount rate (see Figure 6.8).

Besides, the exchange rate policy has been implemented in a more flexible manner. The official daily-announced interbank exchange rate was gradually adjusted upward to over 17,000 VND/1 USD in early October 2009. The band for exchange rate transactions, relative to the official rate, was also widened from 2 per cent as at June 2008 to 3 per cent in November 2008 and 5 per cent in March 2009. Despite pledged commitments to maintain stability in exchange rate

FIGURE 6.8
Policy Interest Rates in Vietnam, 2007–09

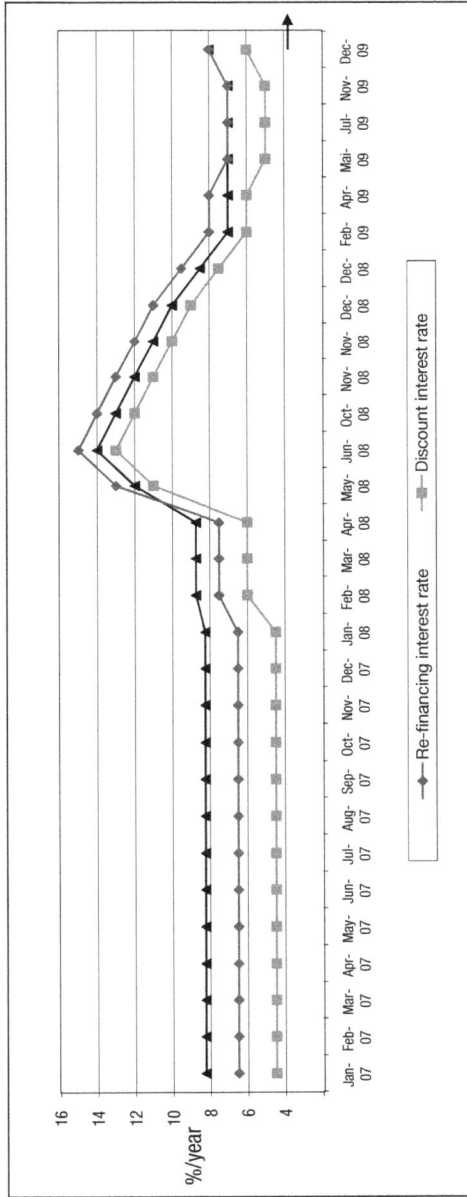

Source: State Bank of Vietnam.

policy, in November 2009, the SBV decided to raise the interbank exchange rate, from 17,034 on 25 November to 17,961 on 26 November. Simultaneously, the trading band was also narrowed to 3 per cent. Although this change appeared reasonable in the context of rapidly growing trade deficit and mounting pressures in the foreign exchange market, it provided a contradiction to previous pledged commitment, and failed to be accompanied by adequate public justification (see Figure 6.9).

Like other countries, Vietnam also implemented a (fiscal) stimulus package. The package was initiated in the Resolution No. 30/2008/NQ-CP in December 2008, and has been realized since February 2009 with the total value of VND 145.6 trillion (or about US$8 billion, or 8.7 per cent GDP). The four main components of the stimulus package are interest rate subsidy for current capital loans, State development investment, exemption — reduction and deferral of taxes, and other expenditures to ensure social safety. The announced and disbursed values of each item are tabulated in Table 6.3. For instance, Vietnam decided to give VND 200,000 for each poor household to help them prepare for the lunar Tet in 2009.

Effect of Policy Response

The above policy measures have produced certain positive impacts on the economy, though it is hardly possible to separate these impacts from others such as recovery of the world and regional economies. Economic growth seemed to accelerate over the quarters of 2009, from 3.1 per cent in the first quarter to 4.5 per cent in the second quarter, 5.8 per cent in the third quarter, and almost 7.8 per cent

TABLE 6.3
Vietnam's Fiscal Stimulus Package in 2009

Unit: billion VND

Stimulus Package	Announcement	Disbursement in 2009 (est.)
1. Interest rate subsidy for current capital loans	17,000	10,000
2. State development investment	90,800	60,800
Various items	*70,800*	*50,800*
Issuance of additional bonds	*20,000*	*10,000*
3. Exemption, reduction, and deferral of taxes	28,000	20,000
4. Other expenditures to ensure social security	9,800	9,800
Total	145,600	100,600
Per cent of total	*100.0*	*69.1*

Source: MPI (2009).

in the fourth quarter. The construction sector appeared to reap the most benefit, as its growth in 2009 (over 11.4 per cent) was higher than that in 2008 (–0.4 per cent). Import growth remained negative, but the pace of reduction was smaller. In fact, import growth was –45.0 per cent for the first quarter, –34.1 per cent for the first half, –25.2 per cent for the first three quarters of 2009, and –14.7 per cent for 2009 as a whole.

In addition, the issues of unemployed/laid-off workers and business bankruptcy became less serious than expected in the early 2009. There were several explanations to this.

First, the stimulus package brought about positive impacts on growth and, accordingly, job creation. Second, Vietnamese firms have undertaken several measures reflecting short-term adjustment to lessen the impact on job losses, such as rotation of workers and reduction of working time, shift, rotational vacation with 70 per cent of basic wage to retain workers. Workers themselves are also less demanding, as they had to choose either to work for fewer hours and remain employed, or to leave firms without any compensation. Third, domestic consumption went up, as proxied by the growth in retail sale of over 10 per cent in real terms. This in turn helped sustain domestic demand for firms' products, thereby increasing derived demand for labours. Finally, the agricultural sector did play an important role as the buffer to absorb the labours laid off by industrial enterprises. Consequently, the issue of unemployment in the context of economic slowdown was mitigated effectively.

With those initial promising signs in economic situation, the projections/forecasts of Vietnam's economic indicators in 2010 now become more optimistic. The official targets for GDP growth and CPI-based inflation in 2010 are 6.5 per cent and no more than 7 per cent, respectively. The World Bank and ADB seem to agree with the official growth target for 2010 while the IMF and UNESCAP produces smaller forecasts than such a target. As for inflation, all project that Vietnam's inflation in 2010 will be well above the target set by the Government of Vietnam.

Despite views of better growth prospects, there remain major concerns about economic development in the subsequent years. The risks of macroeconomic instability seem to be increasing. Inflation tends to hike, particularly as economic growth started to recover. Both the ADB and IMF share the projection that inflation in 2010 will be higher than Vietnam's target (see Table 6.4). Current account deficit is high: the projected figures for 2010 by IMF (as at October 2009), ADB (as at September 2009) and EIU (as at January 2010) are 9.4 per cent GDP, 9.0 per cent GDP, and 12.9 per cent GDP, respectively. In addition, budget deficit is large in 2009, perhaps reaching 9.1 per cent GDP (EIU 2010). This should attract due attention since the ratio of public and public guaranteed debt over GDP in 2008 was already 46 per cent.

On the other hand, Vietnam may face the issue of rising bad debt in 2010. This stems largely from the inability

TABLE 6.4
Some Recent Projections/Forecasts for
Vietnam in 2010

Unit: per cent

	GDP Growth	*Inflation*
Government target	≈ 6.5	≤ 7.0
SBV (Sep): – Scenario 1	6.0–6.5	≤10.0
– Scenario 2	6.2–7.0	7.5–8.5
World Bank (Jan 2010)	6.5	–
ADB (Sep 2009)	6.5	8.5
IMF (Oct 2009)	5.3	11.0
UNESCAP (Dec 2009)	5.7	9.0
CitiGroup (Jan 2010)	6.0	9.4
Goldman Sachs (Dec 2009)	8.2	9.7

Source: Authors' compilations from various sources. Cited in Bui (2010) and Nhat Thinh Trading and Services JSC (2009).

to control money flows for speculation in financial and real estate markets. In fact, even the tasks of compiling investment statistics in these markets cannot be done with strong justification in Vietnam. This prevents market regulators from capturing and analysing the changes in quality of debt and, thus, from undertaking appropriate measures to control bad debt.

The performance of Vietnam economy in 2010, to a very significant extent, depends on how Vietnam could gradually retreat from the excessive state intervention. Monetary policy should be gradually tightened, while more flexibility should be incorporated into the exchange rate policy. In fact, in November 2009, the SBV raised the base interest rate from 7 per cent to 8 per cent, while deciding to control more strictly consumption- and securities-related credits. Both the official exchange rate and band were adjusted, making domestic currency devaluated by more than 10 per cent against the USD within one year. The SBV also set the target of credit growth to be 25 per cent for 2010 (see Figure 6.9). Fiscal policy continues to be important for supporting economic recovery but it should be less expansionary. (The target of fiscal deficit in 2010 is 6.2 per cent of GDP compared to 5 per cent in many years and nearly 7 per cent in 2009.) Besides, monetary and fiscal policies should be better coordinated, to fulfill the economic targets set by the Government. In some cases, the decision and implementation of fiscal policy has reduced significantly the effectiveness of monetary policy.

When and how such a retreat should be implemented needs to be considered with care. In fact, the timing and extent of retreat should be dependent upon domestic and

FIGURE 6.9
Movement of VND/USD Exchange Rate, 2008–09

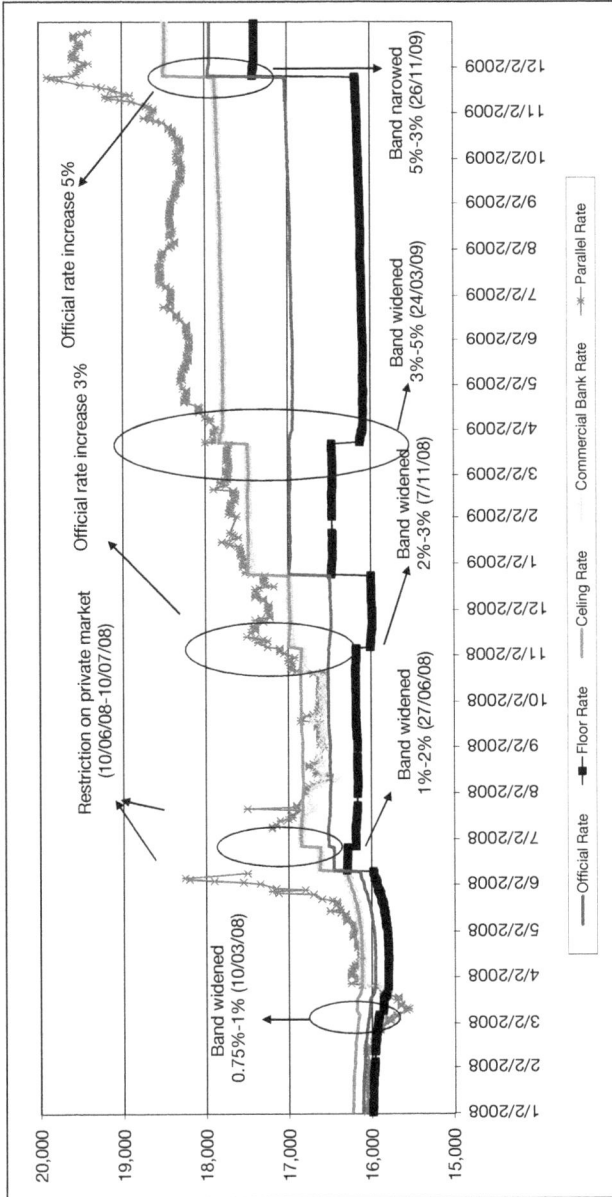

Source: Authors' compilations from various sources.

foreign macroeconomic environment and market response. In a more general framework, Vietnam should continue its domestic reforms and infrastructure development. The focus of reforms should remain on administrative reform, improvement of legal framework for production factor markets and restructuring of state business groups.

Lessons from Macroeconomic Policy Responses

Several lessons can be drawn from the economic developments and associated policy responses in 2009.[2] First, stimulus package needs to be designed with right scale and right target, and be implemented at the right time. Too small a scale will prevent the package from producing desired effects, while too large a scale may lower the efficiency of the package and/or be accompanied by difficulties in retreating from stimulus policy. The stimulus package should also be directed to the right target to ensure that sufficient spillover effects to the rest of the economy can be produced at the minimal costs. For the case of Vietnam, implementation of the stimulus package at the right time is, in addition, critical: the shift in policy direction from maintaining macroeconomic stability to economic stimulus in the fourth quarter of 2008 helped Vietnam overcome the economic slowdown quickly. More specifically, the "dose" of economic stimulus in each period should also be considered carefully. The rapid disbursement of loans with interest rate subsidy and advancement of budget for highly important projects in the early months of 2009 produced spillover effects more quickly to the financial market, increasing fears of speculation and returned macroeconomic instability while possibly constraining the impact of the stimulus package on the real economy.

The transparency and accountability for resource allocation in the fiscal stimulus package remains questionable. A detailed report on various relevant aspects of the package proves to be necessary, but it has not been in place yet. More importantly, during the implementation of the stimulus package, Vietnam failed to undertake adequate assessment of the unwanted effects. For example, the rapid increase in credit and money supply also triggered the boom in the securities market, but such a boom was made possible by the provision of margin trading by securities and financial companies — which were also allowed to make lending with interest rate subsidy of the Government. Accordingly, this sparked the fire for a policy debate on how to implement the stimulus package more effectively.

Second, pledging policy commitments and conforming to those commitments are fundamental to enhancing market confidence. As mentioned above, the SBV decided to make important changes in November 2009 notwithstanding its pledged commitment to keeping the exchange rate stable in various occasions, including the testimony of the Governor to the National Assembly. Understandably, keeping the exchange rate stable is hard considering the widening gap between the official and parallel exchange rates. Yet striving to fulfil the commitments or at least making gradual policy adjustments against the previous commitments may ensure transparency of and market confidence in the policy-making process. From this perspective, the policy changes in November 2009 may create more difficulties to have effective policy adjustment in the longer term, even though it might have produced the gains of beating market expectations in the short-term.

Finally, there is also concern about the possible contradiction between the (necessary) implementation of the short-term "rescue" policy and longer-term structural reforms As an instance, the interest subsidy scheme applies no discriminatory treatment over firms which can produce efficiently and those which cannot; meanwhile, the longer-term structural reforms seek to encourage good businesses while taking bold measures over inefficient ones, even big ones.

Conclusion

The year 2010 is expected to see Vietnam recover from economic slowdown. Economic growth should again accelerate. Yet the lessons over the past couple of years should also make the country weary of the remaining economic challenges as it approaches the year of 2010. On the one hand, it should carefully consider a better balance of growth and inflation targets. Acknowledging the growth-inflation tradeoff, Vietnam needs to analyse the socio-economic context in determining their relative priorities. To this end, the roles of reliable policy analysis and forecast as well as of effective policy formulation and implementation are of crucial importance. On the other hand, coping with the risk of high inflation requires the consistency of monetary and fiscal policies. That is, these policy instruments should be well coordinated to achieve the common target of overall macroeconomic stability. In turn, this necessitates the announcement of credible commitments, i.e. the policy-making process must embody transparency and accountability. The way of adjustment of policy targets should also be improved to enhance, rather than to destroy, the incentives to fulfill them.

While the economy is already on the road to recovery, Vietnam should think carefully about the policy measures to undertake after the global financial crisis. Deeper and wider integration may impose more constraints to policy choices, whilst exposing the country further to external shocks. Consequently, resolving issues associated with macroeconomic management and various social pressures gets more complicated. Promoting high and continuous growth while dealing with macroeconomic instability and social issues thus becomes a multidimensional exercise, involving actions from economic, financial, social, and political stances.

For a longer time horizon, Vietnam should think about its choice of development paradigm. This paradigm should retain the core components of economic growth, underlying institutions (specifically the right interactions between the state-market integration), and policies for efficiency of resource, particularly capital allocation. As Vietnam seeks to promote economic growth and industrialization, it needs to rely on market-friendly institutions and linkages to the world economy. More specifically, the country should strive to establish efficient markets of all types, and develop a system of efficient "hard" and "soft" infrastructure system to better facilitate and encourage economic activities. In addition, the state should be capable of stimulating creativity and preventing macroeconomic, social and environmental risks. Finally, Vietnam should continue to strengthen international linkages, aiming at consolidating its geo-economic position. The key message here is to improve institutional capacity, socio-economic infrastructure, and international linkages to grasp and take full advantage of arising opportunities.

NOTES

1. Source: International Financial Statistics and Economist Intelligence Unit (2010).
2. Vo and Nguyen (2009) also note some policy lessons learnt during the first two years after Vietnam's accession to the WTO.

REFERENCES

Asian Development Bank (ADB). *Asian Development Outlook 2009 Update: Broadening Openness for a Resilient Asia,* 2009.

Bui, Nguyen. "Citigroup: Vietnam's GDP will rise by 6 per cent in 2010" [Citigroup: GDP Việt Nam sẽ tăng trưởng 6per cent trong năm 2010], 2010. Online. Available at <http://bx.businessweek.com/citigroup/view?url=httpper cent3Aper cent2Fper cent2Fwww.baomoi.comper cent2FHomeper cent2FTaiChinhper cent2Fstox.vnper cent2FCitigroup-GDP-Viet-Nam-se-tang-truong-6-trong-nam-2010per cent2F3778954.epi> (accessed 2 March 2010).

Economist Intelligence Unit (EIU). "Vietnam: Country Report for January 2010", 2010.

General Statistics Office (GSO) website. Available at <www.gso.gov.vn>.

International Monetary Fund. *World Economic Outlook 2010: Sustaining the Recovery,* 2009. Online. Available at <http://www.imf.org/external/pubs/ft/weo/2009/02/index.htm> (accessed 2 March 2010).

Ministry of Planning and Investment (MPI). "Report to the Government on Socio-Economic Developments in the First 9 Months of 2009 and Projection for the Whole Year" [Báo cáo cho Chính phủ về tình hình kinh tế — xã hội 9 tháng đầu năm và dự báo cho cả năm]. Mimeographed, 2009.

MPI website. Available at <www.mpi.gov.vn>.

Nguyen, Thi Kim Thanh. "Vietnam's Financial Market: Reform Direction in the Context of International Economic Integration and Financial Crisis". Mimeographed, 2009.

Nhat Thinh Trading and Services JSC. "Goldman Sachs: Vietnam's GDP will rise by 8.2 per cent in 2010" [Goldman Sachs: GDP Việt Nam 2010 tăng 8.2 per cent], 2009. Online. Available at <http://nhatthinh.com/?p=1728&lang=vi> (accessed 2 March 2010).

State Bank of Vietnam (SBV). Annual reports for various years.

United Nations Economic and Social Commission for Asia and the Pacific. *Achieving the Millennium Development Goals in an Era of Global Uncertainty*, 2009. Online. Available at <http://www.mdgasiapacific.org/regional-report-2009-10> (accessed 1 March 2010).

Vo, Tri Thanh and Anh Duong Nguyen. "Vietnam after Two Years of WTO Accession: What Lessons Can Be Learnt". *ASEAN Economic Bulletin* 26, no. 1 (2009): 115–35.

World Bank. *Global Economic Prospects 2010: Crisis, Finance, and Growth*, 2010. Online. Available at <http://web.world bank.org/WBSITE/EXTERNAL/EXTDEC/EXTDECPRO SPECTS/0,,menuPK:476941~pagePK:51084723~piPK: 51084722~theSitePK:476883,00.html> (accessed 2 March 2010).

7

The 2008 Global Economic and Financial Crisis: The Philippine Case

**Ruperto P. Majuca
and Josef T. Yap**

Introduction

The global crisis affected the Philippines through the country's exports (in particular, semiconductor exports) serving as the entry door. Industry (in particular, the manufacturing sector, and to a lesser extent, electricity and gas sector) got hit the most. In the expenditure side, private investments got affected the most, as gross capital formation shrank; private consumption (about 70 per cent of GDP) experienced a temporary slowdown in Q1 of 2009, but rebounded the next quarter. A similar story is mirrored in employment, where the manufacturing employees got affected the most. The impact on domestic employment was felt mostly in terms of the reduction of the rate of new hires and of working hours, more than on retrenchments and lay-offs, except for the manufacturing sector which bore the maximum brunt of the separations. With the possible exception of the stock market, the crisis has had relatively muted impact on the assets markets and the financial sector; likewise, the impact on foreign direct and portfolio investments is not dramatic. Overall, the impact of the crisis on the economy is not as big as that experienced by the advanced industrialized countries, owing to the relatively less open nature of the economy. Green shoots have begun to sprout most likely starting in the second quarter of 2009, but the prospect of recovery was dented somewhat by the two massive storms that devastated the country in September–October 2009. The fiscal and monetary counter-cyclical policy undertaken by the government, although a bit delayed, and the other policy interventions, have helped somewhat to lessen the severity of the crisis and its effects on vulnerable sectors.

Impact on the Macroeconomy

The Entry Door

The spillover effects of the global economic and financial crisis to the Philippine real sector came primarily through the trade channel. Exports contracted an average of 14.3 per cent during the fourth quarter of 2008 to the third quarter of 2009 (see Table 7.1). This is due in large part to the weaker demand for electronics and garments in the international market. Merchandise exports — which accounts for more than 80 per cent of total exports — plummeted by 9.4 per cent, 24.6 per cent, 22.4 per cent, and 14.6 per cent respectively from the fourth quarter of 2008 to the third quarter of 2009. Monthly data also shows that merchandise exports have been

TABLE 7.1
Key Indicators on Philippine Impact of the
Global Economic and Financial Crisis, 2008–09

(in per cent)

Sector	2008				2009		
	1Q	2Q	3Q	4Q	1Q	2Q	3Q
GDP	3.9	4.2	4.6	2.9	0.6	0.8	0.4
Agriculture	2.8	4.9	2.5	2.9	2.1	0.2	1.4
Industry	2.7	4.0	7.6	5.3	−2.5	−1.7	−5.0
Manufacturing	2.4	6.1	5.4	3.4	−7.6	−7.4	−7.8
Construction	−4.3	2.3	20.5	14.5	14.0	14.0	0.9
Electricity Gas & Water	9.5	6.6	9.2	3.8	0.6	−4.9	−6.3
Electricity & Gas	9.8	6.9	9.8	3.8	0.2	−5.5	−7.0
Services	5.2	4.0	3.3	1.3	2.0	2.7	3.8
O. of Dwellings & R. Estate	7.2	7.5	6.7	1.7	0.7	−2.5	−2.3
Real Estate	21.6	22.7	17.4	−0.4	−4.6	−15.8	−13.8
Personal Consumption	5.1	4.1	4.4	5.0	1.3	5.4	3.2
Government Consumption	−0.3	0.0	11.8	2.6	4.5	9.7	8.1
Capital Formation	−1.7	13.6	9.4	−13.1	−15.1	−10.3	−12.1
Fixed Capital	3.0	1.7	7.1	0.1	−7.2	−3.9	−0.9
Construction	−4.1	1.0	14.3	8.2	6.7	8.9	1.7
Public Construction	−10.9	−5.6	23.4	−1.2	11.5	27.7	21.8
Private Construction	−0.2	8.6	9.8	15.4	4.3	−10.1	−9.4
Durable Equipment	9.6	3.7	1.0	−7.9	−18.5	−19.7	−4.2
Changes in Stocks (% capital formation)	6.0	4.1	3.2	−1.3	−2.7	−2.8	−9.2
Exports	−7.7	6.1	3.3	−11.5	−14.7	−18.1	−13.0
Merchandise Exports	−10.9	5.9	4.8	−9.4	−24.6	−22.4	−14.6
Non-Factor Services	5.9	7.3	−4.3	−19.4	21.1	3.0	−4.1
Miscellaneous Services	15.4	19.3	15.7	4.0	56.1	16.7	0.8
Imports	−2.6	0.0	6.7	5.0	−20.6	−2.2	0.1
Merchandise Imports	−3.4	−1.3	5.3	5.8	−22.6	−2.1	1.4
Non-Factor Services	7.7	19.2	28.2	−3.6	1.8	−3.2	−16.1

Note: Unless otherwise indicated, all figures are in per cent, year-on-year, and are based on constant 1985 prices.
Source: National Statistical Coordination Board.

contracting since October 2008, hitting a bottom sometime in the first quarter of 2009, when sales plummeted year-on-year by 41 per cent and 39 per cent, in January and February 2009, respectively (see Figure 7.1). In particular, electronic products (including semiconductors), which comprise about 60 per cent of merchandise exports, consistently contracted since August 2008, as the recession gripped the United States and Japan, the two largest destinations for Philippines exports. This contraction in the electronic products exports also reached the bottom around late 2008 or first quarter of 2009 (when the export revenues of this sector fell 47.6 per cent, 48 per cent, and 45 per cent y-o-y in December 2008, January 2009, and February 2009, respectively) (see Figure 7.1). Garments, the country's second largest export, likewise showed significant contractions due to the crisis. However, garment exports seems to be experiencing a decline even before the crisis, indicating that Philippine competitiveness in garment exports seems to be eroding. The reasons for this long-run trend need to be investigated further.

Meanwhile, imports likewise contracted y-o-y by 20.6 per cent and 2.2 per cent in the first and second quarters of 2009, respectively, given the significant declines in the importation of materials and intermediate goods utilized in the production of export products, as well as the falling oil prices in the global market.

However, business process outsourcing, a component of non-factor services exports, remained a bright spot. National accounts data show that the exports of miscellaneous services including business process outsourcing such as call centres and back office accounting and payroll, after slowing down to a mere 4 per cent y-o-y growth in the fourth quarter of

FIGURE 7.1
Growth Rates of Merchandise Exports and Major Export Products, 2008–09

(in per cent)

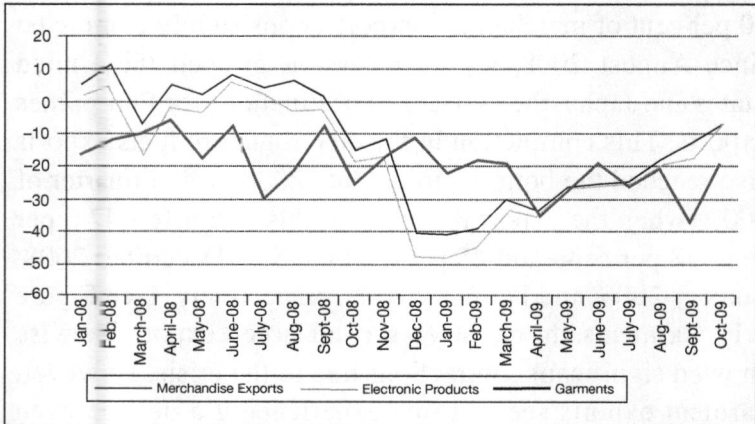

Source: National Statistics Office.

2008, accelerated 56.1 per cent and 16.7 per cent q-o-q in the first and second quarters of 2009, respectively. This pattern however seems to have reversed in third quarter of 2009, where the account registered a meagre 0.8 per cent y-o-y growth.[1] The business process outsourcing currently comprises about 2 to 3 per cent of the gross domestic product (GDP). Overall, total exports of non-factor services (about 8 per cent of GDP) declined 19.4 per cent in the fourth quarter of 2008, bounced back to 21.1 per cent and 3 per cent growth rates in the first and second quarters of 2009, respectively, and then declined again in the third quarter of 2009.

Production Side

As exports plummeted, the industry sector got affected the most on the production side (see Table 7.1). In particular, the manufacturing sector, which contracted by an average of 7.6 per cent, 7.4 per cent, and 7.8 per cent during the first three quarters of 2009, was the hardest hit. In the manufacturing sector, the subsectors that suffered the most from the crisis were leather and leather products, footwear wearing apparel, furniture and fixtures, petroleum and coal products, metal industries and manufacture of machineries (see Table 7.2).

With the closure of some firms particularly in the manufacturing sector, the Manila Electric Company (Meralco) saw its sales to industrial customers drop. Sales associated with electrical machinery (including those of semiconductor firms) account for 25.3 per cent of Meralco sales.[2] Overall, Meralco saw its sales dip during the height of the crisis. Consequently, the electricity and gas subsector reversed its fast growth (average of 8.8 per cent growth) during the first three quarters of 2008 to an average per-quarter contraction of 4.1 per cent during the first three quarters of 2009 (see Table 7.1).

The crisis resulted in an increase in office vacancy rates since the fourth quarter of 2008 (see Figure 7.2) even if landlords already have been cutting office rents since third quarter of 2008 (see Figure 7.3). After consecutive double-digit quarterly y-o-y growth, the real estate sector registered declines starting the fourth quarter of 2008. Also, noticeable is the fall in the office capital values (see Figure 7.4) as well as the decline in the prime three-bedroom

TABLE 7.2
Manufacturing Subsectors Showing Largest
GVA Declines, 2008–09

(in per cent)

Sector	2008		2009		
	Q3	Q4	Q1	Q2	Q3
Tobacco	42.7	20.1	−11.6	0.9	0.8
Textile	−22.4	−14.6	−12.7	−15.3	−14.1
Footwear wearing apparel	7.2	−1.9	−24.4	−20.6	−22.1
Furniture and fixtures	−6.1	−14.8	−26.9	−20.3	−18.9
Leather and leather products	4.7	3.2	−54.0	−46.7	−40.9
Products of petroleum and coal	0.9	9.6	−29.0	−15.8	−19.6
Basic metal industries	0.1	−1.0	−22.4	−21.1	−13.6
Metal industries	7.0	3.3	−24.9	−16.5	−7.3
Machinery, except electrical	11.4	1.9	−22.1	−24.2	−10.9
Electrical machinery	−7.4	−8.0	−18.6	−2.8	−7.9
GVA in Manufacturing	5.4	3.4	−7.6	−7.4	−7.8

Source: National Statistical Coordination Board.

rents (see Figure 7.5) and capital-values (see Figure 7.6). As vacancies rise and more available office space glut the market, not only did office rents and property values decline, office space construction was minimal as well, particularly in the Makati business district. Consistent with these trends, private sector investments in non-residential assets decreased, which caused private construction's gross value added (GVA) to decelerate to 4.3 per cent growth in the first quarter of 2009 (from 15.4 per cent growth in the fourth quarter of 2008), followed by a contraction of 10.1 per cent and 9.4 per cent in the second and third quarters of 2009, respectively.

FIGURE 7.2
Real Estate Indicators: Makati CBD Office
Vacancy Rates, 2007–09

(in per cent)

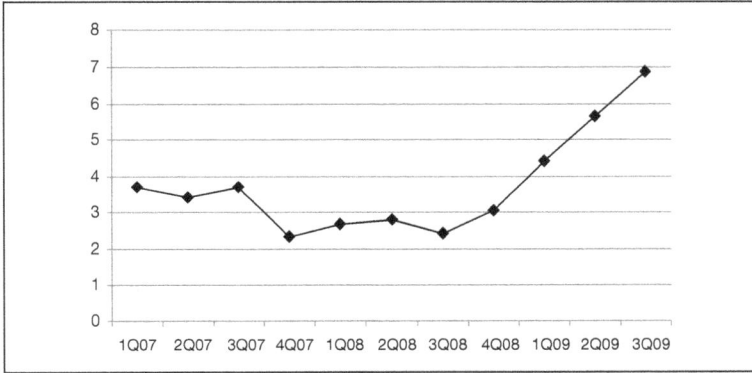

Source: *The Knowledge Report* (Property Market Overview), Colliers International, the Philippines.

FIGURE 7.3
Real Estate Indicators: Makati CBD Office
Rents, 2007–09

(in peso/sq. m./month)

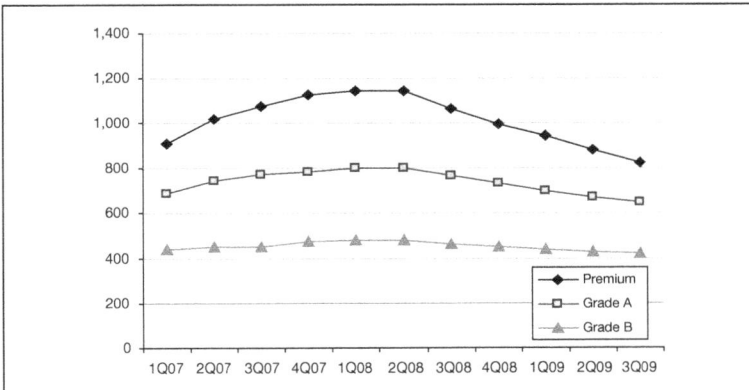

Source: Same as Figure 7.2.

FIGURE 7.4
Real Estate Indicators: Makati CBD Office
Capital Values, 2007–09

(in peso/sq. m.)

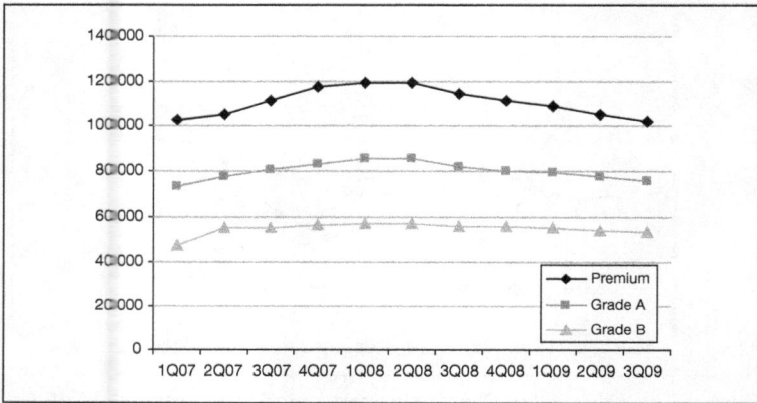

Source: Same as Figure 7.2.

FIGURE 7.5
Real Estate Indicators: Makati CBD Prime
3-Bedroom Rents, 2007–09

(in peso/sq. m./month)

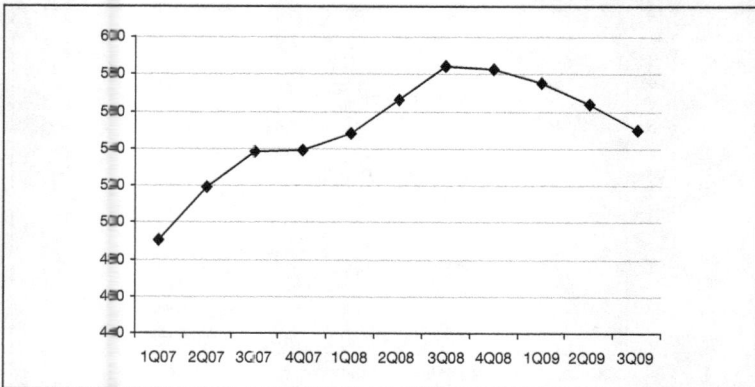

Source: Same as Figure 7.2.

FIGURE 7.6
Real Estate Indicators: Makati CBD Prime
3-Bedroom Capital Values, 2007–09

(in peso/sq. m.)

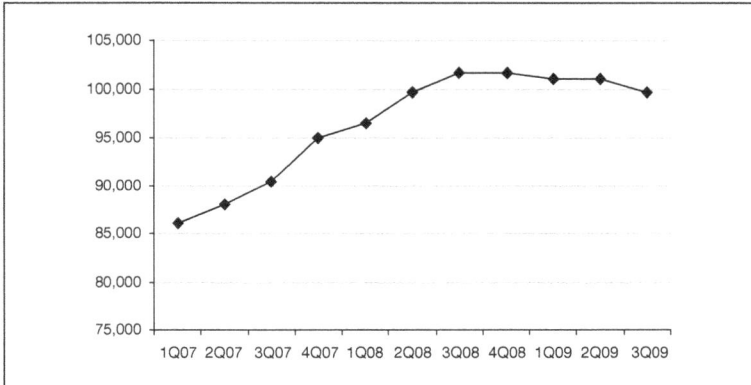

Source: *The Knowledge Report* (Property Market Overview), Colliers International, the Philippines.

Expenditure Side

In the expenditure side, as industry took a hit, firms started cutting back on their investments, as evidenced by the large declines in the capital formation, in particular, in durable equipment investments. Durable equipment investments declined 7.9 per cent, 18.5 per cent, 19.7 per cent, and 4.2 per cent in the fourth quarter of 2008, and the first three quarters of 2009 respectively. Disaggregated data (not shown) reveal a wide-scale contraction across all types of durable equipment investments. Likewise, during the same quarters, firms destocked their inventories by an amount equal to 1.3 per cent, 2.7 per cent, 2.8 per cent, and 9.2 per cent of the gross capital formation. These developments brought down capital formation overall by 13.1 per cent, 15.1 per cent, 10.3 per cent, and 12.1 per cent during the same quarters.

Overall Impact on the National Accounts

The downward shift in aggregate demand, uncertain economic environment, and some precautionary saving motives arising from the slowdown in the growth of the dollar value of the remittances have, to some extent, contributed to the noticeable slowdown in private consumption in the first quarter of 2009. As will be mentioned, although remittances have slowed down in dollar terms, the peso equivalent did not slow down as much, since the peso depreciated in the meantime. This slowdown in private consumption, combined with the drastic drop in exports, resulted in the 7.6 per cent average contraction of the manufacturing sector, which comprises about 22 per cent of real GDP. During the first three quarters of 2009, inventory decumulation and large contractions in durable equipment investments dragged down real GDP, although high inflation in the middle part of 2008 had also contributed to the slowdown of the economy in 2008 (see Table 7.3) (see Yap et al. 2009). However, unlike other Southeast Asian economies, the Philippines is not as reliant on exports, with export-to-GDP ratio as little over 30 per cent; thus, it was relatively less affected by the crisis compared to its neighbours. The Philippines did not experience a recession since seasonally-adjusted real GDP was negative in the first quarter of 2009, but was positive in the second quarter of 2009 (see Figure 7.7), only a slowdown in growth, the worst of which occurred in early 2009.

TABLE 7.3
Inflation Rates, 2007–09

Month	2007		2008		2009	
	Headline Inflation	*Core Inflation*	*Headline Inflation*	*Core Inflation*	*Headline Inflation*	*Core Inflation*
	2.8	2.8	9.3	6.2	3.4	4.1
January	3.9	3.9	4.9	3.4	7.1	6.9
February	2.6	3	5.4	4	7.3	6.4
March	2.2	2.6	6.4	4.8	6.4	5.6
April	2.3	2.6	8.3	5.9	4.8	5
May	2.4	2.6	9.5	6.2	3.3	4.4
June	2.3	2.5	11.4	6.6	1.5	3.9
July	2.6	3	12.3	6.3	0.2	3.6
August	2.4	2.9	12.4	7	0.1	2.9
September	2.7	2.7	11.8	7.5	0.7	2.8
October	2.7	2.4	11.2	7.8	1.6	2.7
November	3.2	2.3	9.9	7.9	2.8	2.7
December	3.9	2.6	8	7.3	4.4	3.2

Sources: National Statistics Office and Bangko Sentral ng Pilipinas.

Impact on Employment

Domestic Employment

Looking at the unemployment rate trends alone may mask the true impact of the crisis on domestic employment. Official data reports only a marginal overall increase in unemployment rates in the country, from 6.8 per cent in October 2008 to 7.1 per cent in October 2009. This gives the impression that the global crisis has had a minimal effect on domestic employment. This may be misleading because the main impact of the crisis on Philippine domestic employment came more from the reduction of working hours/days

FIGURE 7.7
Quarter-on-Quarter GDP and Seasonally-Adjusted GDP Growth Rates

(in per cent)

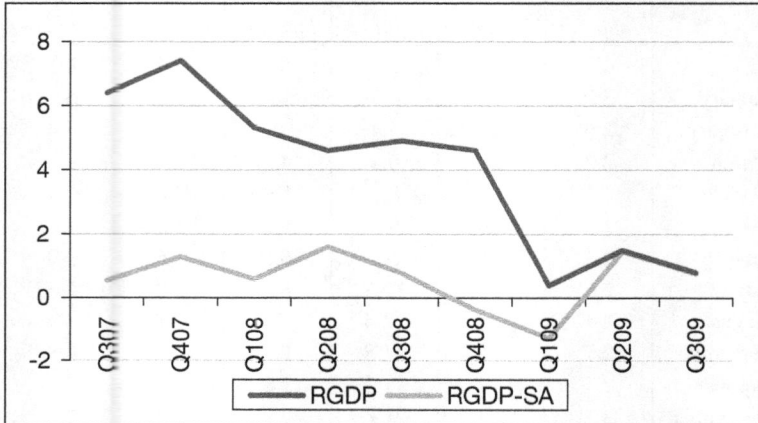

Notes: RGDP = constant 1985 prices GDP quarter-on-quarter growth rates

RGDPSA = quarter-on-quarter growth rates of seasonally-adjusted (constant 1985 prices) GDP

Source: National Statistical Coordination Board.

instead of the firms permanently laying off workers, under the so-called "flexible work arrangements" encouraged by the government, as well as in the reduced hiring rates. The data do not indicate the difficult adjustment process in the labour market.

An examination of the disaggregated employment statistic details shows this. Tables 7.4 (a) and 7.4 (b) indicate that the rate of new hiring decreased from 12.2 per cent in the first quarter of 2008 to 9.3 per cent in the first quarter of 2009, a reduction of almost 3 per cent in the new hiring

TABLE 7.4 (a)
Labour Turnover Rates in Large Enterprises in Metro Manila by Industry, 2008

(in per cent)

Major Industry Group	Accession Rate					Separation Rate				
	1st Qtr	2nd Qtr	3rd Qtr	4th Qtr	Average	1st Qtr	2nd Qtr	3rd Qtr	4th Qtr	Average
All Industries	12.23	10.56	11.05	9.14	10.75	7.46	8.57	9.00	8.45	8.37
Agriculture, Fishing and Forestry	4.23	4.47	6.2	2.14	4.26	4.12	2.34	4.05	3.68	3.55
Agriculture, Hunting and Forestry	3.39	5.78	8.67	2.54	5.1	2.37	1.88	5.41	4.22	3.47
Fishing	4.74	2.54	1.99	1.31	2.65	5.2	3.03	1.74	1.93	2.98
Industry	9.67	7.54	9.29	8.95	8.86	6.7	8.49	10.44	12.46	9.52
Mining and Quarrying	14.98	9.97	11.2	7.47	10.91	1.92	16.81	11.35	15.82	11.48
Manufacturing	6.32	3.87	8.45	10.68	7.33	2.46	3.87	8.82	10.58	6.43
Electricity, Gas and Water Supply	1.87	2.13	3.44	1.08	2.13	8.92	1.26	1.41	0.92	3.13
Construction	20.08	18.93	12.41	5.74	14.29	19.24	22.05	16.39	19.9	19.4
Service	13.46	11.64	11.65	9.29	11.51	7.85	8.66	8.6	7.22	8.08
Wholesale and Retail Trade	10.82	13.51	12.18	12.61	12.28	9.1	11.9	12.72	13.93	11.91
Hotels and Restaurants	14.24	15.83	22.64	12.62	16.33	11.86	11.44	40.98	8.31	18.15
Transport, Storage and Communications	5.59	5.31	5.61	3.31	4.96	3.34	4.23	3.58	3.41	3.64
Financial Intermediation	4.96	6.02	5.01	4.98	5.24	3.27	4.15	3.3	2.54	3.32
Real Estate, Renting and Business Services	23.69	14.62	14.86	10.94	16.03	11.02	9.96	8.64	7.56	9.3
Private Education	1.66	7.34	7.34	3.78	5.03	2.74	16.09	2.34	3.19	6.09
Health and Social Work	4.86	6.68	7.06	4.96	5.89	4.92	5.28	4.95	3.76	4.73
Other Community, Social and Personal Service Activities	9.38	10.74	10.88	8.13	9.78	10.15	9.95	8.16	8.29	9.14

Source: Bureau of Labor and Employment Statistics.

TABLE 7.4 (b)
Labour Turnover Rates in Large Enterprises in Metro Manila by Industry, 2009

(in per cent)

Sector	1st Quarter			2nd Quarter			3rd Quarter		
	Accession Rate	Separation Rate	Per Cent Difference	Accession Rate	Separation Rate	Per Cent Difference	Accession Rate	Separation Rate	Per Cent Difference
All Sectoral Groups	**9.29**	**9.02**	**0.27**	**9.74**	**7.53**	**2.21**	**9.99**	**9.62**	**0.37**
Agriculture, Fishery and Forestry	**3.64**	**1.57**	**2.07**	**3.21**	**4.53**	**(1.32)**	**7.35**	**5.87**	**1.48**
Agriculture, Hunting and Forestry	3.22	2.09	1.13	2.76	3.13	(0.37)	9.96	7.31	2.65
Fishing	4.04	1.07	2.97	3.57	5.64	(2.07)	5.07	4.62	0.45
Industry	**13.41**	**10.02**	**3.39**	**14.67**	**10.80**	**3.87**	**13.93**	**14.85**	**(0.92)**
Mining and Quarrying	17.00	14.63	2.37	19.31	12.23	7.08	15.98	14.46	1.52
Manufacturing	9.82	11.2	-1.38	12.73	10.49	2.24	12.32	12.22	0.10
Electricity, Gas and Water Supply	3.05	3.57	-0.53	3.70	2.05	1.65	2.32	1.73	0.58
Construction	23.16	8.19	14.98	21.88	13.55	8.33	21.10	25.60	(4.50)
Services	**8.13**	**8.8**	**-0.67**	**8.33**	**6.58**	**1.75**	**8.89**	**8.16**	**0.72**
Wholesale and Retail Trade	16.69	16.38	0.31	10.26	9.65	0.61	9.74	1.39	2.52
Hotels and Restaurants	9.09	5.76	3.33	10.66	8.68	1.98	8.99	6.22	2.76
Transport, Storage and Communications	3.26	4.88	-1.63	3.63	3.42	0.21	4.29	3.62	0.67
Financial Intermediation	2.9	3.25	-0.36	3.62	2.85	0.78	2.60	2.78	(0.17)
Real Estate, Renting and Business Activities	7.82	9.61	-1.79	10.76	7.92	2.84	11.79	11.16	0.63
Private Education Services	1.00	1.28	-0.28	10.40	5.97	4.42	2.57	1.69	0.88
Health and Social Works (Private)	4.95	3.74	1.21	4.45	5.17	(0.72)	5.50	3.95	1.55
Other Community, Social and Personal Service Activities	12.25	11.61	0.64	15.23	6.96	8.28	15.09	13.02	2.06

Source: Bureau of Labor and Employment Statistics.

rate. The decline in the rate of hiring continued in the second and third quarters of 2009. Meanwhile, compared to their year-ago levels, separation rates increased by 1.6 per cent in the first quarter of 2009, decreased a bit by 1.0 per cent in the second quarter of 2009, and increased marginally by 0.8 per cent in the third quarter of 2009. That is, the overall impact of the crisis was felt more on the rate of hiring than on the separation rate.

If the effects of the hiring and separation rates are combined, labour turnover rates deteriorated by 4.5 percentage points in the first quarter of 2009, showed a marginal improvement in the second quarter, and deteriorated again by 1.7 percentage points in the third quarter. The manufacturing sector, which bore the brunt of the crisis, registered the highest spikes in separation rates with a dramatic increase of 8.7 per cent during the height of the crisis in the first quarter of 2009, and an increase of 6.6 per cent and 3.4 per cent in the second and third quarters of 2009, respectively. The rate of new hires in the manufacturing sector likewise increased during the first three quarters of 2009: 5.9 per cent, 8.9 per cent and 3.9 per cent, respectively. However, the spikes in the separation rates were larger than the increase in the new hires rates, resulting in the overall deterioration of the labour turnover rates in this sector: changes of –5.2 per cent, 2.2 per cent, and 0.5 per cent in the turnover rates for the first, second and third quarters of 2009, respectively. More importantly, is the issue: what kind of new jobs were created?

A look into the breakdown of employment into "full-time" employment defined as working more than forty hours per week and "part-time" employment during the relevant periods would help shed light on the issue of quality of employment. The proportion of part-time workers to those who are employed and at work increased from an average of 35.5 per cent in 2008 to 37 per cent in January 2009, and, according to preliminary data, this accelerated further to 42 per cent in the second quarter of 2009 (see Table 7.5). However, preliminary data also indicate that this stabilized at 34.5 per cent in July 2009. In contrast, the proportion of full-time workers to those who are employed and at work decreased from an average of 64.5 per cent in 2008 to 63 per cent in the first quarter of 2009, and decelerated further to a mere 58 per cent in the second quarter of 2009. This however appears to have stabilized back up to 65.5 per cent in third quarter of 2009. In absolute terms, this meant that there were around 1.6 million full-time jobs lost from January 2008 to April 2009, and about 2.5 million part-time jobs were created during the same period.

As mentioned earlier, the impact of the crisis was more of a reduction in working hours and subsequent increase in underemployment. Overall, the reduction in the hiring rate was felt most in the first quarter of 2009, while the deterioration in the quality of jobs, as evidenced by the reduced working hours, peaked in the second quarter of 2009, the same quarter where the increase in the separation rate in the manufacturing sector was the highest. The export processing zones and CALABARZON region just south of Metro Manila, where the export and industrial zones are located, were affected the most in terms of employment;[3] while Region III (north of Manila) and Region VII (which includes Cebu City), home to clusters of industrial and manufacturing firms, likewise saw substantial displacement of workers (International Labor Office 2009). Nevertheless,

TABLE 7.5
Employed Persons by Number of Hours Worked, 2007–09

Number of Hours Worked	2007	2008					2009		
		Ave	Jan	Apr	Jul	Oct	Jan	Apr	Jul[p]
Total Employed Workers	33,560	34,089	33,693	33,535	34,593	34,533	34,262	34,993	35,509
At Work	33,098	33,593	33,283	32,702	34,253	34,133	33,687	34,155	35,160
Worked Less than 40 Hours	12,254	11,938	11,877	11,954	11,709	12,211	12,453	14,331	12,115
As Per Cent of those 'At Work'	*37.0*	*35.5*	*35.7*	*36.6*	*34.2*	*35.8*	*37.0*	*42.0*	*34.5*
Less than 20 Hours	4,321	4,212	4,325	4,288	3,942	4,292	4,577	5,115	4,354
20–29 Hours	3,951	3,780	3,764	3,775	3,778	3,801	3,922	4,725	3,792
30–39 Hours	3,982	3,947	3,788	3,891	3,989	4,118	3,953	4,492	3,969
Worked 40 Hours and Over	20,844	21,655	21,407	20,748	22,544	21,922	21,234	19,823	23,044
As Per Cent of those 'At Work'	*63.0*	*64.5*	*64.3*	*63.4*	*65.8*	*64.2*	*63.0*	*58.0*	*65.5*
40–48 Hours	13,243	13,831	13,754	12,991	14,385	14,195	13,483	12,645	14,442
49 and Over	7,601	7,824	7,653	7,757	8,159	7,727	7,750	7,178	8,602
With a Job, Not at Work	462	496	410	833	340	400	575	839	350
Mean Hours of Work	41.4	41.8	41.6	41.6	42.5	41.6	41.3	39.8	42.5

Note: P = preliminary
Source: Bureau of Labor and Employment Statistics.

as of July 2009, full-time employment seems to have returned to its level in 2008. Hence, at the macroeconomic level, the employment impact of the crisis can be described as mild. However, there was indeed a difficult adjustment process during this period.

Overseas Employment

Remittances from overseas Filipino workers play an important role in the Philippine economy. In 2008, for example, total remittances reached $16.4 billion, or around 10 per cent of GDP. Data on remittances shows that monthly remittances slowed down to an average of 3.5 per cent y-o-y growth for the period fourth quarter of 2008 to second quarter of 2009, compared to an average of 14.6 per cent growth during same period the previous year. The data on the y-o-y growth rates of cumulative remittances reveal a similar pattern of slowdown of remittances during the crisis period (see Table 7.6). Decomposed into land-based vs. sea-based workers' remittances, there seems to be a bit of a dip in the sea-based remittances (about 80 per cent of the remittances) in the fourth quarter of 2008, while land-based remittances seem to show a bit of a dip in the first quarter of 2009 (see Figure 7.8). Also, survey data reveal that 39 per cent of households with an overseas Filipino worker (OFW) had an OFW who returned during the past six months, of which 16 per cent was due to retrenchments/lay-offs. Nine per cent of households with OFWs likewise reported wage reductions for during November 2008–April 2009. In short, the global crisis resulted in slowdown (but not the reversal) of the flow of dollar remittances into the country. When translated into peso terms, however, since the currency has

TABLE 7.6
Overseas Filipinos' Remittances, 2007–09

		In US$ Million				In Million
Month		Levels		Growth Rates Yr-on-Yr		Peso Equivalent
		Monthly	Cumulative	Monthly	Cumulative	Monthly
2007	Jan	1,099.40	19.9	19.9	19.9	53,771.65
	Feb	1,085.50	2,184.90	25.4	22.6	52,516.49
	Mar	1,304.80	3,489.70	26.4	24	63,308.90
	Apr	1,191.50	4,681.30	32.6	26.1	56,977.53
	May	1,237.10	5,918.40	8.4	21.9	57,908.65
	Jun	1,115.80	7,034.20	1	18	51,505.33
	Jul	1,096.60	8,130.70	4.6	16	50,037.86
	Aug	1,206.90	9,337.70	10.6	15.3	55,601.88
	Sept	1,139.80	10,477.50	12.4	15	52,578.97
	Oct	1,388.50	11,866.00	17.1	15.2	61,621.63
	Nov	1,187.00	13,053.00	3.8	14.1	51,302.14
	Dec	1,397.00	14,449.90	5.9	13.2	58,310.78
2008	Jan	1,264.00	1,264.00	15	15	51,748.16
	Feb	1,258.60	2,522.70	15.9	15.5	51,187.26
	Mar	1,427.80	3,950.50	9.4	13.2	58,896.75
	Apr	1,410.20	5,360.70	18.4	14.5	58,974.56
	May	1,429.80	6,790.50	15.6	14.7	61,338.42
	Jun	1,450.80	8,241.40	30	17.2	64,241.42
	Jul	1,366.80	9,608.20	24.6	18.2	61,451.33
	Aug	1,332.00	10,940.20	10.4	17.2	59,780.16
	Sept	1,332.90	12,273.10	16.9	17.1	62,233.10
	Oct	1,434.70	13,707.80	3.3	15.5	68,908.64
	Nov	1,311.30	15,019.10	10.5	15.1	64,502.85
	Dec	1,407.70	16,426.90	0.8	13.7	67,696.29
2009ᵖ	Jan	1,265.50	1,265.50	0.1	0.1	59,744.26
	Feb	1,320.00	2,585.50	4.9	2.5	62,805.60
	Mar	1,471.50	4,057.00	3.1	2.7	71,308.89
	Apr	1,441.70	5,498.80	2.2	2.6	69,518.77
	May	1,482.20	6,980.90	3.7	2.8	70,434.14
	Jun	1,498.70	8,479.70	3.3	2.9	71,802.72
	Jul	1,494.00	9,973.70	9.3	3.8	71,936.10
	Aug	1,369.10	11,342.80	2.8	3.7	65,935.86
	Sept	1,446.92	12,789.72	8.6	4.2	69,654.58
	Oct	1,531.29	14,321.01	6.7	4.5	71,741.12

Note: p = preliminary
Source: Bangko Sentral ng Pilipinas; monthly average peso-per-dollar exchange rate was used to generate the peso equivalent.

FIGURE 7.8
Overseas Filipino Remittance, 2008–09

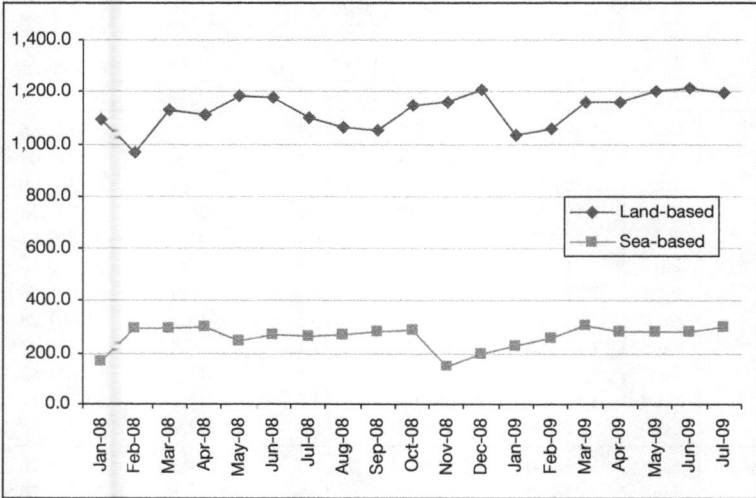

Source: Bangko Sentral ng Pilipinas.

depreciated in the meantime, the peso value of the monthly
remittances did not really slow down, it grew on average
17.5 per cent y-o-y during the comparable period, fourth
quarter of 2008 to second quarter of 2009.

Impact on Investment Flows, Asset Markets and the Financial Sector

Direct and Portfolio Investments

Reflecting the recessionary and uncertain conditions of the
global economy, direct investments registered a net outflow
of $14 million in the first quarter of 2009, a reversal of the
$225 million net inflow from the same period a year ago. This

TABLE 7.7
Philippine Capital and Financial Accounts, 2007–09

(in million US$)

	2007	2008	1Q2007	2Q2007	3Q2007	4Q2007	1Q2008	2Q2008	3Q2008	4Q2008	1Q2009	2Q2009	3Q2009
Capital and Financial Account	**2,889**	**−1,914**	**958**	**−391**	**3,103**	**−143**	**455**	**436**	**472**	**−3,261**	**−1,188**	**−704**	**147**
Capital Account	24	53	15	−21	18	12	21	9	18	5	17	19	33
Credit: Receipts	108	114	28	29	30	21	33	24	32	25	31	36	48
Debit: Payments	84	61	13	50	12	9	12	15	14	20	14	17	15
Financial Account	2,865	−1,967	943	−370	3,085	−155	434	427	454	−3,266	−1,205	−723	114
Direct Investment	−514	1,283	1,498	−2,796	434	244	225	309	480	130	−14	783	249
Debit: Assets, Residents' Investments Abroad	3,442	237	122	3,276	91	47	−6	77	103	85	52	71	128
Credit: Liabilities, Non-Residents' Investments in the Phil.	2,928	1,520	1,620	480	525	291	219	386	583	215	38	854	377
Porfolio Investments	4,382	−2,584	608	1,688	1,668	659	1,001	−1,583	−1,093	−2,124	−109	424	1,234
Debit: Assets, Residents' Investments Abroad	−813	−1,000	1,104	−542	−735	−661	−1,049	−950	1,241	139	42	−110	307
Credit: Liab., Non-Residents' Investments in the Phil.	3,569	−3,584	1,712	1,146	933	−2	−48	−2,533	148	−1,985	−67	314	1,541

Source: Bangko Sentral ng Pilipinas.

was due largely to the 83 per cent contraction of the non-residents' investments from the $266 million level posted from the same period last year. However, direct investments rebounded in the second quarter of 2009, with a net inflow of $785 million, a more than 250 per cent increase from the inflow of the same period a year ago. Fuelled by improving investor sentiment over economic conditions worldwide, equity capital investments totalled $948 million (a more than four-fold jump from the year-ago levels) and reinvestment of earnings amounted to $48 million. In the third quarter of 2009, preliminary data show direct investment registering a positive flow of $114 million, although only 25 per cent of the same figure from year-ago levels.

Similarly, portfolio investments posted a net outflow of $109 million in the first quarter of 2009, a dramatic turnaround from the $1 billion net inflow recorded in the same period of 2008. Actually, portfolio investments have registered large negative outflows since the second quarter of 2008, posting net outflows of $1.6 billion, $1.1 billion, and $2.1 billion in the second, third and fourth quarters of 2008, respectively. By second quarter of 2009, however, portfolio investments experienced a reversal to a net inflow of $424 million. Preliminary data likewise show that the trend was sustained in the third quarter of 2009, as portfolio net inflows reached $1.2 billion, a turnaround of more than $2 billion compared to the same period last year (see Table 7.7).

Asset Markets

Consistent with the developments in the direct and portfolio investments, data from the Philippine stock market also show that stock market index dropped 48 per cent from a high of

3,653 in the fourth quarter of 2007 to its bottom of 1,894.5 in the first quarter of 2009 (see Figure 7.9). The index has been increasing since then, although as of third quarter of 2009, it was still lower than the index in October 2007.

Moreover, the global financial turmoil resulted in a liquidity squeeze and an increase in the price of risk. Data from JP Morgan EMBIG (see Table 7.8) show that the risk premium demanded by investors to buy Philippine foreign currency bond over U.S. Treasuries increased rapidly from 207 basis points at the end of March 2008 to its peak of 546 basis points at the end of December 2008. The Philippine peso likewise exhibited volatility; after appreciating 24 per cent from March 2005 to March 2008, it depreciated by 15 per cent from March 2008 to March 2009. The peso, however, like the Philippine stock market, is among the least affected by the crisis compared to its East Asian neighbours.

FIGURE 7.9
Philippine Stock Exchange Index, 2007–09

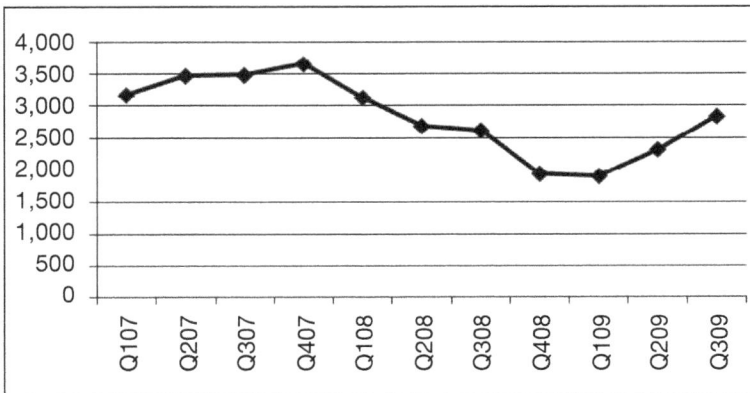

Source: Philippine Stock Exchange.

TABLE 7.8
EMBIG, Basis Points over U.S. Treasuries
(end-of-period), 2007–09

Mar07	Jun07	Sep07	Dec07	Mar08	Jun08	Sep08	Dec08	Mar09
167	155	184	172	207	303	324	546	432

Sources: JP Morgan and Bloomberg.

The Banking Sector[4]

Crucial prudential indicators show the relative health of the banking systems in terms of capital adequacy, profitability, and liquidity cushions (see Tables 7.9 and 7.10). Loan-to-deposit ratios have been rather conservative and many banks report high ratios of short-term assets to liabilities. The ratio of non-performing loans (NPLs) to total loans has continued to decline through 2008 although there was a slight uptick in the early part of 2009. Meanwhile, the key measure of capital adequacy has been sustained at relatively high levels although it has been declining during the past three years.

In 2008, most banks continued to report relatively high rates of return on assets and equity, and did not experience increases in impaired assets. This performance reflects the insignificant exposure of Philippine banks to the toxic structured mortgage products that were extensively sold globally. Given largely domestically-focused business and relatively strong economic activities in 2007, profitability of Philippine banks has generally remained high in 2008.

Undoubtedly, the Philippine financial sector remains vulnerable to further shocks that emanate from global

TABLE 7.9
Non-Performing Loans (% of Commercial Bank Loans), 2004–09

Economy	2000–04 Average	2004	2005	2006	2007	2008[1]	2009[2]
China, People's Rep. of	21.0	13.2	8.6	7.1	6.2	2.5	2.0
Hong Kong, China[3]	4.0	1.6	1.4	1.1	0.9	1.2	1.5
Indonesia	10.2	4.5	7.6	6.1	4.1	3.2	3.6
Korea, Republic of	3.1	2.0	1.3	0.9	0.7	1.2	1.5
Malaysia[3]	8.9	6.8	5.6	4.8	3.2	2.2	2.2
Philippines[3]	14.8	12.7	8.5	5.7	4.4	3.5	3.7
Singapore	5.3	5.0	3.8	2.8	1.5	1.4	–
Taipei, China	5.2	2.8	2.2	2.1	1.8	1.5	–
Thailand[3]	13.5	10.9	8.3	7.5	7.3	5.3	5.5

Notes: – = not available
    1. Data for Singapore as of September 2008.
    2. Data for Malaysia as of May 2009; for the Philippines as of April 2009; for People's Republic of China, Hong Kong, Republic of Korea, and Thailand as of March 2009; and for Indonesia as of January 2009.
    3. Reported non-performing loans are gross classified loans of retail banks.
Source: ADB, Asia Bond Monitor, November 2009.

financial centres. However, there has been no meltdown yet similar to the events of 1997. The resilience stems from more prudent policies and a more conservative approach by the banking system.[5] It would be difficult to establish which factor has been more important. Nevertheless, policies implemented in the aftermath of the 1997 crisis did play a role in limiting the impact of the 2008 global liquidity crunch. The *Bangko Sentral ng Pilipinas (BSP)*, however, must remain vigilant and implement measures to maintain stability of the financial sectors.

TABLE 7.10
Risk-Weighted Capital Adequacy Ratios
(% of Risk-Weighted Assets), 2000–09

Economy	2000–04 Average	2004	2005	2006	2007	2008[1]	2009[2]
China, People's Rep. of	-2.3[3]	-4.7	2.5	4.9	8.4	8.2	–
Hong Kong, China	16.1	15.4	14.8	14.9	13.4	14.7	15.6
Indonesia	18.7	19.4	19.3	21.3	19.3	16.8	17.8
Korea, Republic of	10.7	11.3	12.4	12.3	12.0	12.7	13.4
Malaysia	13.4	14.3	13.6	13.1	12.8	12.2	13.7
Philippines	17.0	18.7	17.7	18.5	15.9	15.7	–
Singapore	17.7	16.2	15.8	15.4	13.5	14.3	–
Taipei, China	10.5	10.7	10.3	10.1	10.6	10.8	–
Thailand	13.2	13.0	14.2	14.5	15.4	14.1	15.2

Notes: – = not available
 1. Data for Singapore as of September 2008 and for People's Republic of China as of March 2008.
 2. Data for Malaysia as of May 2009; for Thailand as of April 2009; for Hong Kong, China and Republic of Korea as of March 2009; and for Indonesia as of January 2009.
 3. Average of 2000 and 2002–04 figures. Figure for 2000 is ratio for state commercial banks.
Source: ADB, Asia Bond Monitor, November 2009.

Impacts on Households and Communities[6]

The economic downturn discussed previously has likely negative social impacts. It would be important to analyse these impacts at the level of individuals, households and communities in order to design countervailing measures and monitor their effectiveness. Unfortunately, while monthly or quarterly data on economic output and prices are available, data on social indicators have lower frequency and in certain cases are irregular. For example, assessing the impact of the crisis on poverty in the Philippines based on official data would not yet be possible since the latest official poverty statistics were obtained in 2006 and the next set would be available only late 2010 when the results of the 2009 Family Income and Expenditure Survey are made available. Thus, to assess the social impacts of the crisis, data collected by local government units using the community based monitoring system (CBMS) will be used.

As part of research efforts to monitor and mitigate the impacts of the global financial and economic crisis, the CBMS Network has launched an initiative to conduct household surveys in selected areas in ten countries that are implementing CBMS in Asia and Africa. Information from these poverty observatories or sentinel sites has been collected over several years thus providing a benchmark for assessing the effects of the crisis. Data collected from March 2009 would then provide information not just on the impacts of the crisis but would also show which individuals, households and communities are able to recover faster.

In the Philippines, there are thirteen sentinel sites all over the country. This section shows the results for ten barangays in the Philippines. They have been classified into Urban NCR (or national capital region), Urban outside NCR and rural areas. The combined sample consists of 3,499 households representing a population of 15,161 persons. The breakdown is shown in Table 7.11. The survey was conducted between March and July of 2009 and the reference period was November 2008 to April 2009.

The more significant transmission channel of the crisis based on the survey appears to be through overseas and

TABLE 7.11

Number of Households and Population by Barangay, 2009

Barangay	Municipality/City	Province	Households		Population	
			No.	%	No.	%
Urban NCR			856	24.5	2,941	19.4
192	Pasay City	NCR-4	856	24.5	2,941	19.4
Urban Outside NCR			1,738	49.7	7,729	51.0
Gumamela	Labo	Camarines Norte	432	12.3	2,060	13.6
Villa Angeles	Orion	Bataan	354	10.1	1,401	9.2
Poblacion III	Santo Tomas	Batangas	466	13.3	2,086	13.8
Magbangon	Cabucgayan	Biliran	259	7.4	1,230	8.1
Masikap	Puerto Princesa City	Palawan	227	6.5	952	6.3
Rural			905	25.9	4,491	29.6
Ando	Borongan	Eastern Samar	174	5.0	892	5.9
San Miguel	Llorente	Eastern Samar	269	7.7	1,372	9.0
Salvacion	Puerto Princesa City	Palawan	237	6.8	1,084	7.1
San Vicente	Santa Elena	Camarines Norte	225	6.4	1,143	7.5
Total			3,499	100.0	15,161	100.0

domestic employment. Impact on domestic employment was examined by looking at changes among self-employed through their entrepreneurial activities and wage and salaried workers.

Overseas Employment

Out of the sample of 3,499 households, 450 or 12.8 per cent had a member who is an OFW (see Table 7.12). 201 of the 450 households, or 44.7 per cent, had an OFW who returned during the period between November 2008 and April 2009. However, only 25 these returnees — which is 5.6 per cent of 450 — indicated retrenchment or lay-off as the reason for returning home. Another way to look at this is that 5.6 per cent of households which rely on OFW remittances saw this source of income disappear as a result of the crisis.

Meanwhile, 9.5 per cent of the households with an OFW, indicated that he/she experienced wage reduction during the period November 2008–April 2009. 8.9 per cent of the households who received remittances during the past six months experienced reduction in amount of remittances received during the same period.

The effects through overseas remittances seem to be mild. As discussed earlier in the macroeconomic section, deployment of OFWs and remittances from OFWs continue to grow. This has mitigated the impact of the crisis. Information on geographical distribution of the overseas workers may offer some possible explanations. A majority of OFWs are based in the Middle East. The said regions are weathering the global crisis relatively better than industrialized countries

TABLE 7.12
Outcome Indicators, OFW-related, 2009

Indicator	Magnitude	Proportion
HH with OFW	450	12.8
HH with returning OFW	201	44.7
HH with returning OFW who was retrenched or laid off from work	25	5.6
HH with OFW who experienced wage reduction	43	9.5
HH who received remittances during the past six months	353	78.4
HH who experienced a decline in the amount of remittances received	40	8.9
HH who experienced a decline in the frequency of receipt of remittances	32	7.1

Source: CBMS Survey 2009.

and therefore not experiencing widespread retrenchment of foreign workers. Many overseas workers either work as a service and sales worker or is classified in the category "trades and related worker". Some of the jobs of overseas workers include housekeepers and related workers, cooks, waiters, waitresses and bartenders, child-care workers, institution- or home-based personal care workers, security guards, and shop or market salespersons (under the services and sales worker classification), carpenters, motor vehicle mechanic, electricians, bakers, and pastry cooks (under the trades and related worker classification). Demand for these kinds of workers remains strong despite the global crisis.

The Department of Labor and Employment and Philippine Overseas Employment Administration acknowledge that some markets, particularly the United States, have cut job orders due to the global crisis but they also insist that labour markets elsewhere remain relatively strong.

Domestic Employment: Entrepreneurial Activities

The study also tried to determine how households were affected through local employment by looking at those who are involved in entrepreneurial activities and those who are wage earners and salaried workers. Out of the population of 15,161, 10,394 are fifteen years or over. 54.8 per cent of the latter or 5,701 persons are considered part of the labour force, 88.5 per cent of whom were employed during the reference period. This translates to unemployment rate of 11.5 per cent. About 62.5 per cent of employed individuals are male while the rest are female (see Table 7.13).

TABLE 7.13
Labour Force Statistics, 2009

Statistics	*Total Number*	*Proportion*	*Male*		*Female*	
			No.	*%*	*No.*	*%*
Population 15 years and over	10,394		5,123	49.3	5,271	50.7
Labour force	5,701	54.8	3,508	61.5	2,193	38.5
Employed	5,046	88.5	3,155	62.5	1,891	37.5
Unemployed	655	11.5	353	53.9	302	46.1

Source: CBMS Survey 2009.

Only relatively few households engaged in a new business during the period (see Table 7.14). Results showed that a mere 2.1 per cent or 75 of the households surveyed actually engaged in new entrepreneurial activity during the six-month period covered by the study. 1,817 of the 3,499 households surveyed — which is 51.9 per cent — engaged in an entrepreneurial activity. Only 19, which is 1 per cent of 1,817, closed their business during the survey period. Meanwhile, 125 or 6.9 per cent of the 1,817 experienced a decline in their monthly income from the business. These

TABLE 7.14
Outcome Indicators: Entrepreneurial
Activities, 2009

Indicator	Magnitude	Proportion
HHs engaged in new entrepreneurial activity	75	2.1
HHs engaged in an entrepreneurial activity	1,817	51.9
HHs which closed a business	19	1.0
HHs with significant change in the monthly income from the business	158	8.7
Increase	33	20.9
Decrease	125	79.1
HHs with significant change in the no. of employed persons in the business	6	0.3
Increase	3	50
Decrease	3	50

Source: CBMS Survey 2009.

results confirm the minimal effect of the crisis in the selected sites in terms of households' engagement in a business or entrepreneurial activity.

Domestic Employment

The global crisis could have potentially affected local employment given the reduction in exports. Unemployment rate, using the data from NSO, went up and employment in the manufacturing sector declined. Labour turnover rate for the first quarter of 2009 in the Philippines is posted at 0.27 per cent indicating that the separation rate (lay-offs) is just slightly lower than accession rate (hirings).

During the period November 2008 to April 2009, 92 households reported job loss of at least one of their members

TABLE 7.15
Outcome Indicators, Wage Earners and
Salaried Workers, 2009

Indicator	Magnitude	Proportion
HH with member who lost job	92	2.6
Members who lost their job	109	2.2
HH with member who experienced wage reduction	74	2.1
HH with member who experienced a reduction in the number of working hours	65	1.9
HH with member who experienced reduction in employment benefits	8	0.2

Source: CBMS Survey 2009.

representing 2.6 per cent of all households surveyed (see Table 7.15). This translates to a total of 109 persons who lost their job during the period.

Policy Responses

Macroeconomic Responses

In 27 January 2009, the Philippine Government launched a P330 billion fiscal stimulus programme dubbed the "Economic Resiliency Plan", with the following components: community-level infrastructure and social welfare (about half of the budget), large infrastructure projects (30 per cent; off-budget, part of the funds will be provided by social security and government financial institutions), and tax cuts to individuals and businesses, and additional social security benefits (about 20 per cent; off-budget, to be taken from the gap between contributions and claims/benefits). The plan focuses on quick-disbursing, high job-generation impact type of projects such as construction, repair, or rehabilitation of irrigation systems, and rural roads.

The Philippine Central Bank cut policy rates six times with total cuts of 200 basis points starting December 2008 until July 2009 to 6.0 per cent for the repurchase facility (overnight lending rate) and 4.0 per cent for the reverse repurchase facility (overnight borrowing rate); it maintained the rates steady since then. It had also cut the reserve requirements by 2 percentage points and took other steps to hold up liquidity.

Other government programmes intended to help the vulnerable sectors were also implemented. Examples of these include the 50 per cent reduction of wharfage fees for exporters, the implementation of "flexible work arrangements" (to counter lay-offs), rapid assistance to laid-off OFWs and workers in the export and economics zones, and the expansion of the social protection programme such as the conditional cash transfers programme as evidenced by the increase in the budgetary allocation for "Social Security, Welfare, and Employment" (see Table 7.16).

As a result of such fiscal stimulus package and the increased rate of fund utilization by government agencies, the public construction component of capital formation (expenditure side) rose 27.7 per cent and 22.2 per cent in the second and third quarters of 2009, respectively, which counteracted the decline in private construction. Likewise, the increased government spending resulted in an increase of 9.7 per cent of government consumption in the second quarter of 2009 from 0 per cent growth last year.

However, the required government expenditure to address the impact of the crisis, as well as poor tax collection has caused the budget deficit to balloon to PHP 266.1 billion (3.6 per cent of 2008 GDP) as of October 2009, more than the full-year deficit ceiling of PHP 250 billion. The tax to GDP ratio has stalled in the range of 12–13 per cent of GDP compared to 14 per cent in 2008 and a peak of 17 per cent in 1997. While there are policy changes that can explain the reversal in the tax to GDP ratio,[7] the Philippines remains one of the countries with a relatively low tax effort in East Asia. It is clear that the institutional changes required to significantly improve tax effort have yet to be implemented. In particular, the deterioration of the tax collection efficiency of the Bureau of Internal Revenue needs to be addressed (see

TABLE 7.16
Expenditure Programme by Social Service Sectors, FY 2008–10

(in million pesos)

Sector	Levels			Share to GDP		
	FY 2008	FY 2009	FY 2010, Proposed	2008	2009*	2010*
GDP (Nominal)	1,314,613	1,426,002	1,541,000	7,423,213	7,794,832	8,337,439
TOTAL	13.8	8.5	8.1	17.7	18.3	18.5
SOCIAL SERVICES	368,342	452,222	479,936	4.96	5.80	5.76
Education, Culture and Manpower Development	186,620	222,291	235,210	2.51	2.85	2.82
Health	18,641	38,442	37,897	0.25	0.49	0.45
Social Security, Welfare and Employment	70,300	90,212	100,988	0.95	1.16	1.21
Housing and Community Development	9,418	5,334	5,368	0.13	0.07	0.06
Land Distribution	4,167	1,279		0.06	0.02	–
Other Social Services	1,226	2,168	2,126	0.02	0.03	0.03
Subsidy to LGUs	77,970	92,496	98,347	1.05	1.19	1.18

Note: *<http://www.dbm.gov.ph/BESF09/A.1.pdf> (high assumption).
Source: Department of Budget and Management.

Manasan 2008, who estimated that, relative to 2004, the tax leakage increased by 0.8 per cent, 0.2 per cent, and 0.5 per cent of GDP, in 2005, 2006, and 2007 respectively).

Assessment of the Government's Response to the Crisis

The monetary and fiscal responses to the crisis, as well as the other government actions aimed at alleviating the impact of the crisis, have helped somewhat to lessen the depth of the crisis in the Philippines and help alleviate its effects on the vulnerable sectors. However, the authors are of the opinion that the fiscal and monetary responses came later than optimal. As early as the beginning of 2008 or by the middle of 2008, at the latest, it was painfully clear that the U.S. economy would experience a recession (e.g., in February 2008, Greenspan said the chance of U.S. recession is 50 per cent or higher;[8] more than 70 per cent of economists surveyed in March 2008 believed the U.S. economy is in a recession;[9] on 1 December 2008, NBER official declared U.S. economy in recession since December 2007) and that the tremors would be felt in the Philippine shores. In the Philippine local setting, the following is the timeline of the impact of the crisis and the release of available data to policy-makers:

1. January 2008: the Philippine stock index dropped 9.81 per cent m-o-m; and has been dropping until January 2009, predicting a downturn of economic activity ahead;[10]
2. August 2008: electronic products exports contracted 6.5 per cent and have been contracting since;

3. 12 August 2008: the data was released with the information that the third quarter leading economic indicators fell, suggesting a deceleration of the economy;

4. September 2008: inflation rate's trajectory went down;

5. October 2008: total merchandise exports contracted 14.9 per cent, and have been contracting since; also industrial production (both volume and value) growth dropped (both m-o-m and y-o-y) and has been dropping since;

6. 4 November 2008: data released — fourth quarter leading indicator dropped further, suggesting continued weakening of economic activity;

7. November 2008: capacity utilization fell and has been dropping since;

8. 18 December 2008: the central bank finally cut policy rates;

9. 27 January 2009: the government unveiled its fiscal stimulus plan; and

10. January or first quarter of 2009: probably bottom of the crisis.

Given the available data (both domestic and international), and the well-known time lags for policy to gain traction (particularly fiscal policy),[11] the authors believe that the fiscal and monetary authorities should have acted earlier. Thus, the authors believe that the central bank acted a little late, and that the fiscal authorities were even more delayed in reacting to the crisis.

Recovery, Prospects, and Uncertainties

Various data sources point to the conclusion that the Philippine economy has probably bottomed sometime in the first quarter of 2009, and that by second quarter of 2009, the Philippines is already in a slow and fragile recovery period. Year-on-year, real GDP growth inched up from 0.6 per cent in the first quarter of 2009 to 0.8 per cent in the second quarter of 2009. Likewise, seasonally-adjusted GDP grew 1.5 per cent and 0.8 per cent in the second and third quarters of 2009, respectively, after a 1.3 per cent decline in the first quarter of 2009, suggesting that the economy may have turned the corner after the first quarter of 2009. Data on capacity utilization and industrial production similarly point to a bottom in first quarter of 2009. Capacity utilization dropped from 82.2 per cent in July 2008 to the bottom of 78.1 per cent in January 2009, and has steadily increased 78.5 per cent in February 2009, 80.7 per cent in March 2009, etc. to 82.3 per cent in October 2009 (see Figure 7.10). Data on the growth (both y-o-y and m-o-m) of the volume and value of industrial production appear to point in the same direction: that the bottom had occurred in early 2009, and that production has gradually improved since then (see Figure 7.11).

Moreover, data on exports point in the same direction — a bottom in the first quarter of 2009. Finally, EMBIG data similarly show a peak of the risk premium in first quarter of 2009, and a downward trend since.

Philippine recovery, however, as these various data sources indicate, is still gaining traction and will probably be gradual. Furthermore, recovery has been recently dented

FIGURE 7.10
Capacity Utilization, 2008–09

(in per cent)

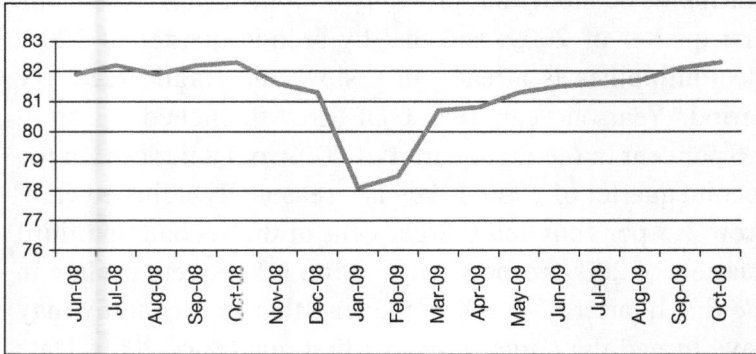

Source: National Statistics Office.

by the two major storms that had struck the country in September–October 2009. Due to climate change, two consecutive severe storms struck the country in September and October 2009. Tropical storm *Ondoy* (international name, "Ketsana") brought 455 millimetres of rainfall for twenty-four hours, almost one-and-a-half times the average rainfall for the entire month of September for 1993–2008, causing massive flooding in Metro Manila and adjacent provinces. After *Ondoy's* unprecented destruction came typhoon *Pepeng* (international name, "Parma"), who wreaked havoc in Northern Luzon. Ondoy and Pepeng devastated mostly the northern part of the archipelago, particularly Luzon, and Regions VI, IX, XII and ARMM, leaving almost a thousand deaths, and billions of pesos of damages to infrastructure and agriculture. These two storms now hold the top two spots for the Philippines' list of tropical cyclones which caused

FIGURE 7.11
Industrial Production, 2008–09

(% change)

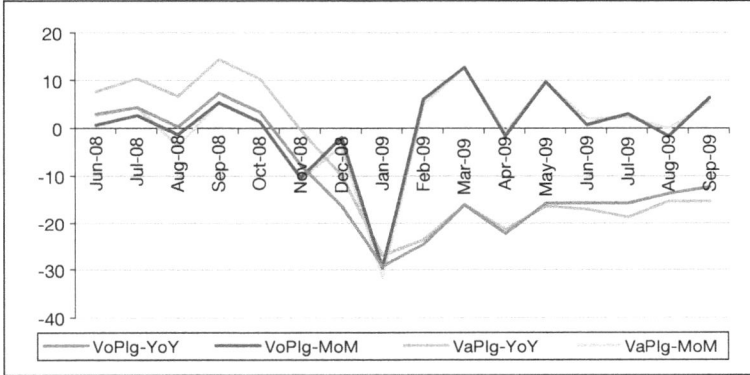

Notes: VoPIg-YoY = volume of production index, growth rate, year-on-
year
VoPIg-MoM = volume of production index, growth rate, month-
on-month
VaPIg-YoY = value of production index, growth rate, year-on-
year
VaPIg-MoM = value of production index, growth rate, month-
on-month
Source: National Statistics Office.

the greatest damage. With an estimated combined damage of PHP 38.3 billion, these two storms were estimated to have shred 0.2 and 0.6, respectively, of nominal third and fourth quarters GDP (Virola 2009).

It does not appear, however, that the Philippine recovery will be V-shaped, but neither do the data indicate that it will be W-shaped. If we have to make an analogy, the pattern of the recovery will either be U-shaped or resemble that of a checkmark — that is, a sharp drop in economic activity during the crisis period, followed by a steady, yet gradual incline up. Furthermore, the authors expect that Philippine recovery will depend on the global recovery, particularly its major export partners such as the United States and Japan and countries with many OFWs such as North America and the Middle East. The upcoming spending for the May 2010 elections, along with improving consumer and business confidence, and international situation, should increase the chances that the recovery will be sustained. However, the lingering effects of the twin-storms could slow the recovery down somewhat. This fragile and slow nature of the recovery, both in the local and global economy, the damage brought about the two typhoons, and the lack of elbow room to conduct further fiscal policy, should be considered in the monetary authority's conduct of an exit strategy.

NOTES

1. This data on miscellaneous services exports need to be disaggregated further to see the impact of the crisis on the BPO industry. On the production side, GVA in Business Services, which includes BPOs shows the following quarterly y-o-y growth:

	2008				2009		
	Q1	*Q2*	*Q3*	*Q4*	*Q1*	*Q2*	*Q3*
GVA in Business Services	8.4	12.1	16.9	5.8	5.4	–0.6	1.2

Again, this underscores the importance of disaggregating how much of this is GVA of the BPO industry. Industry reports however reveal that most BPO firms feel the effect of the crisis on the industry was moderate or minor, with some forecasting for the industry to grow by about 20 per cent for 2009. <http://www.bpap.org/bpap/publications/BPAPJune09%20for%20website%20no%20ads.pdf>; see also <http://pdf.ph/downloads/PDF%202009/Growth%20&%20Investment%20Climate/2nd%20Batch/CRC%20Paper%20-%20IT-BPO%20-%20Prof.%20Rodolfo.pdf>.

2. <http://www.philstar.com/article.aspx?articleid=500000>.

3. Some survey evidence reveal that the semiconductor and electronics industries, which is relatively low value-added and labour-intensive, experienced reduction of production shifts (from three to one) and work week (by up to two days, at times), dismissal of temporary workers, and for contractual workers, a pay reduction of as much as 64 per cent during the height of the crisis (or a pay equivalent of 44 per cent lower than a full-time minimum wage worker) (World Bank 2009).

4. Taken from Yap et al., 2009.

5. A case of "once burned, twice shy".

6. Largely based on Celia Reyes, Alellie Sobreviñas, and Jeremy de Jesus, "The Impact of the Global Financial Crisis on Poverty in the Philippines", paper presented at the 6th CBMS Philippines National Conference, Manila Diamond Hotel, 8–10 December 2009.

7. Among the measures with an adverse impact on revenue collection are the lowering of corporate income tax from 35 to 30 per cent, the higher personal exemptions for individual taxpayers and income tax exemption for minimum wage earners, the tax incentives granted to investors in Personal Equity Retirement Accounts, the tourism incentives under the National Tourism Policy Act, and the imposition of franchise tax on power transmission in lieu of all national and local taxes.

8. <http://money.cnn.com/2008/02/15/news/economy/greenspan/index.htm>.

9. <http://online.wsj.com/article/SB120534519452630845. html>.
10. Cf. Paul Samuelson famously quipped that the stock market "has predicted nine out of the last five recessions".
11. The first author's preliminary estimates using vector autoregressions and structural vector autoregressions, as well as dynamic stochastic general equilibrium-based approaches to tracing the monetary transmission mechanism, for example, reveal that the maximum impact of monetary policy occurs six to ten quarters following the interest rate change (see also Pobre 2003: maximum impact of monetary policy occurs in about eight quarters), similar to the evidence for other countries (e.g., the United States, Korea).

REFERENCES

Asian Development Bank. *Asian Development Outlook 2009 Update*, September 2009. Available at <http://www.adb. org/Documents/Books/ADO/2009/Update/default.asp>.

International Labor Office. "Responses to the Global Economic Crisis: Philippines", September 2009.

Manasan, Rosario. "Are Recent Gains in BIR Tax Effort Sustainable?" *PIDS Policy Notes 2008–07*. Philippines: Philippine Institute for Development Studies, Makati City, 2008. <http://dirp4.pids.gov.ph/ ris/pn/pidspn0807.pdf>.

Pobre, Mervin. "An Analysis of the Monetary Transmission Mechanism in East Asia". *Philippine Journal of Development* 30 (2003): 2.

Virola, Romulo. "Statistically Speaking: The Devastation of *Ondoy* and *Pepeng*", 2009. <http://www.nscb.gov.ph/head lines/StatsSpeak/2009/110909_rav_mrsr_typhoons.asp>.

World Bank. *Philippine Quarterly Update: Towards an Inclusive Recovery*, November 2009. <http://siteresources.

worldbank.org/INTPHILIPPINES/Resources/ PHLQuarterly November2009FINAL.pdf>.

Yap, Josef, Celia Reyes, and Janet Cuenca. "Impact of the Global Financial and Economic Crisis on the Philippines". *PIDS Discussion Paper Series No. 2009–10.* Philippines: Philippine Institute for Development Studies, Makati City, 2009.

8
The Impact of Global Financial Crisis on the Indonesian Economy

Muhammad Chatib Basri

Introduction

After more than four years of economic boom, global growth was slowing markedly in the second half of 2008. Economic growth in emerging and developing economies was also slowing down as global trade slows and financial conditions tighten. The contraction occurred in major developed economies, with the United States and Europe projected to plunge into negative growths around –2.9 per cent and –4.3 per cent respectively in 2009.

Initially there was an ongoing prevailing presumption about "decoupling" wherein the Asian economic growth is considered relatively detached or not fully connected to the economic growth of developed countries like the United States and Europe. Thus, the impact of the global slowdown was considered limited to the Asian economies. Nevertheless, we are one of those who are doubtful as regards this decoupling argument. The data shows that similar downturns took place in emerging markets, in which the economic growth of this group of countries is forecasted to fall from 6 per cent in 2008 to 1.5 per cent in 2009.

We argue that the Asian economies have actually been able to grow because the existing integration among production networks in Asian countries is extremely strong. Intra-industrial trade in East Asia has made the effects on Asia still relatively limited. Many countries in Southeast Asia, including Indonesia for example, are exporting raw materials and intermediary goods to China, Korea and Japan, which are the production network centres. Therefore, the effects on the Indonesian economy, at least up until the second quarter of 2008, were relatively limited. However, it should not be forgotten that the end-buyers of goods coming from production countries in Asian countries are the developed countries, including the United States and Europe. Because of this, if the United States and Europe weaken, then it is unavoidable that the effects will be transmitted to Asian countries. Furthermore, because Asian countries are integrated in terms of production networks, these effects occurred even more quickly than before.

The impact on Indonesian economic growth had occurred through the trade channel. The signs began to appear as early as the fourth quarter of 2008. The downturn of export growth was reflected in the sluggish growth of the Indonesian economy. Even so, the Indonesian economic growth as a whole still managed to reach 6.1 per cent, and this growth was considered the highest in Asia, following China and India. The reason behind Indonesia's relatively good performance was due to the fact Indonesia's economy is relatively insulated from the weakening global economic situation. Indonesia's total export share of the GDP amounted to 29 per cent. This figure was much smaller compared to other countries such as Singapore (234 per cent), Taiwan (74 per cent), Korea (45 per cent).

Nevertheless, faring well with the improvement of the global economics, the Indonesian economic growth of the third quarter of 2009 reached 3.9 per cent (q-o-q) compared to the second quarter of 2009 which grew by 2.3 per cent. This indicates that the economic growth begun to accelerate in the third quarter of 2009. Cumulatively, Indonesia's economic growth for the first nine months of 2009, compared to the same period of 2008 showed an increase of 4.2 per cent. These figures are higher compared to the estimates made by a number of research institutes and observers.

The relatively good performances of the Indonesian economy lead us to the question of why the impact of the global crisis on the Indonesian economy was relatively limited so far. Was it because of the structure of its trade? How effective were the fiscal and monetary policies in mitigating the impact on the Indonesian economy?

This chapter will try to eludicate these questions. In addition it will also discuss the policies that have been issued by the government and Bank Indonesia in terms of anticipating the global financial crisis.

Impact on the Indonesian Economy

Financial Sector

The financial crisis initially begun in the U.S. sub-prime mortgage markets, however, it has precipitated a wider global repricing of risk that was exacerbated by the disclosure of higher than expected losses suffered by financial institutions. The large need of the U.S. banking sector to recapitalize their capital had caused a drying up of liquidity in the international foreign exchange markets. This has caused a big problem for emerging markets especially those that rely on the market, because they suddenly face a condition of shortage of foreign exchange liquidity. The financial crisis has affected emerging markets through a general loss of market confidence and associated repricing of risk that has contributed to a shortage of liquidity in international money markets. As a consequence, emerging markets face increasing difficulties in accessing external financing, which is reflected in increasing yields on international bond issuances due to loss of investors' appetite to emerging markets financial products in general. In Indonesia and other emerging markets, the impact of the financial crisis showed itself in the depreciation of the currency and the decrease of the stock markets' value.

The Indonesia stock exchange composite index was around 2,700 points in February 2008. However, the fallouts from the bankruptcy of Lehman, the takeover of Merrill Lynch, and concerns over AIG had affected emerging markets significantly. The turbulence in the global financial markets in September and October 2008 brought down the Indonesia Stock Market (IDX) Index almost 50 per cent from early September to November 2008. In February 2009, the IDX composite has fallen to 1,285, its level in March 2006 (Basri and Siregar 2009).

As argued by Basri and Siregar (2009) the massive sell-outs of assets by foreign investors in the Indonesian capital market in the last quarter of 2008, had given more pressure on the rupiah depreciation. The rupiah lost 28 per cent of its value against the U.S. dollar between October and November 2008, accompanied by a significant rise in its volatility. Depreciation pressure persisted in February and March 2009, with rupiah fluctuating in the range of Rp 11,500–12,000 per U.S. dollar, a substantially higher than its average level of around Rp 9,050 per U.S. dollar in February 2008.

As for credit growth, Basri and Siregar (2009) indicate that banking credit growth at the end of 2008 did still occur, even though it had already started to slow down. Furthermore, in 2009, there was a sharp decline in credit growth, which dropped from 32 per cent down to only 10 per cent.

One important factor to take into consideration is the issue of confidence. Basri and Siregar (2009) indicates that confidence among banks had declined as well. The size of interbank borrowing and lending declined by 59.3 per cent to Rp 83 8 trillion in December 2008 from Rp 206.0 trillion in December 2007 (Gunawan et al. 2009). In addition, the sharp competition between banks had pushed them to raise deposit rate to the higher level. One month deposit account interest rates at several commercial banks had even reached 16 per cent since December 2008. This was clearly far higher compared to the prevailing maximum guarantee rate of 9 75 per cent set by the deposit insurance company (LPS). Special high interest rates were provided by several banks for fresh and large deposits (usually of around Rp 1 billion) (Basri and Siregar 2009). This indicates that the banking industry has to give high interest rates so that major customers do not withdraw their funds on deposit from banks. This was in connection with the policy taken by the government and Bank Indonesia to only provide deposit insurance up to a level of Rp 2 billion. That was in spite of the fact that other countries such as Singapore and Malaysia provided full insurance. With this difference in insurance provision, there was pressure for arbitrage to be carried out on deposit accounts in Indonesia to Singapore, Malaysia or other countries that provided full insurance. In addition, there were also flights to quality, i.e. depositors moving their funds to large banks and state banks (although not to foreign banks like in the 1997/98 crisis), thus deepening the problem of liquidity imbalance and segmentation in the banking system. The description above helps us to understand that the Indonesian financial sector was under pressure due to the global financial crisis.

Collapse of Indonesia's Exports

The weakness of global economic growth had already had an effect in terms of reducing demand for Indonesian exports. In addition, the decline in global demand had already created a weakness in demand for primary and additional exports, and as a result of this the prices of commodities and mining products also decreased.

This decline occurred due to two reasons, firstly, it was due to the fall in commodity prices, and secondly it was due to the collapse of demand to the global slowdown. The Indonesian exports were seen to experience a sharp decline, especially in the agriculture, oil and gas, and mineral sectors. Papanek, Basri and Schydlowsky (2009) indicate that there

TABLE 8.1
Exports at Current and Constant Prices, 1975–2009
Commodities in US$ billion and per cent

	a. Current Price Annual Per Cent Change						b. Constant Price Annual Per Cent Change At 1980–2008 Average Prices						At 1908–09 Prices
	75–85	85–90	90–96	96–08	04–08	I'08–I'09	75–85	85–90	90–96	96–08	04–08	I'08–I'09	I'08–I'09
TOTAL EXPORTS	10.1	6.4	11.8	8.9	17.8	–31.8	0.7	7.3	9.1	5.1	5.4	–19.5	–16.2
Non-oil/gas total	12.6	19.4	17.6	9.2	18.0	–25.3	0.8	11.7	13.9	7.6	7.2	–20.5	–17.3
Labour-intensive manufactures*	61.8	44.6	17.1	3.2	7.1	–13.8	49.5	31.9	17.1	3.9	3.1	–13.6	–13.2
Commodity-based exports	9.6	2.6	7.5	9.9	21.7	–38.3	0.2	4.5	5.0	3.4	5.5	–22.8	–16.0

	c. Increase in $ billion in Current Prices						d. Increase in $ billion at Constant Prices = Change in Quantity Weighted by Price/Unit Value At 1980–2008 Average Prices						At 2008–09 Prices
	75–85	85–90	90–96	96–08	04–08	I'08–I'09	75–85	85–90	90–96	96–08	04–08	I'08–I'09	I'08–I'09
TOTAL EXPORTS	11.5	6.8	24.1	87.6	65.8	–10.7	1.6	9.7	22.4	45.4	19.1	–5.0	–5.0
Non-oil/gas total	4.1	8.4	23.4	70.2	52.3	–6.7	0.7	7.3	20.5	52.7	21.8	–4.7	–4.4
Labour-intensive manufactures	0.6	3.2	6.0	4.5	3.4	–0.5	0.8	2.4	4.9	4.7	1.5	–0.4	–0.5
Commodity-based exports	10.6	2.4	10.9	64.8	52.2	–9.2	0.5	5.3	9.3	18.0	10.4	–3.4	–3.4

Note: *Includes: textiles, garments, footwear, furniture
Source: Papanek, Basri and Schydlowsky (2009).

was an extremely sharp decline in exports, particularly in current price, in the first half of 2009 compared to the same period in the previous year. Table 8.1 suggests that the decline in exports was mostly driven by price (current prices) rather than volume (contant prices).

It is worth noting, that this sharp decline in exports was not only experienced by Indonesia. Similar decline happened in many countries such as China, Singapore, Malaysia and Thailand. If seem from the magnitude in the contraction of exports that occurred, the effect of the global financial crisis towards the Indonesian economy was in fact relatively the same (see Figure 8.1). Then, it is interesting to discuss why the impact on the Indonesian economy was relatively

FIGURE 8.1
Growth of Export (y-o-y), 2008–09

(in per cent)

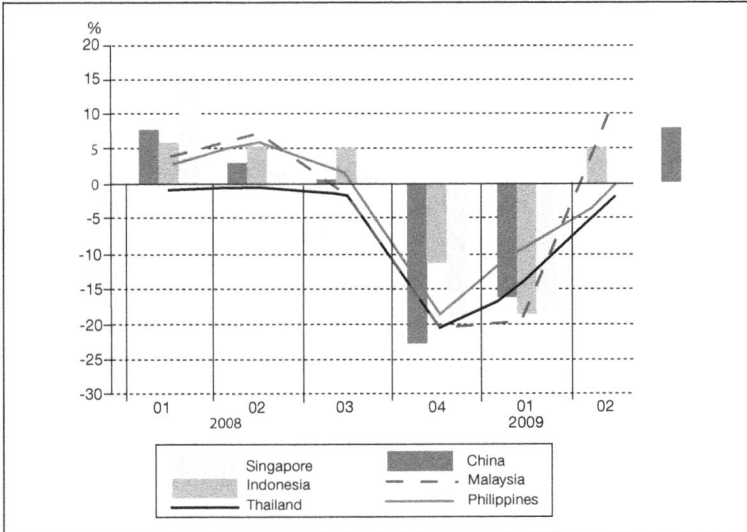

limited compared to other countries in the region. The author considers that the effect on the Indonesian economy was limited because the structure of exports within the Indonesian economy is relatively small compared to countries such as Singapore, Thailand and Malaysia. In addition, Indonesia was left behind in production networks (Ando and Kimura 2007). As a result, the effects of the global crisis against the Indonesian economy also became limited. In fact this was not something that had been planned. Indonesia certainly only wished for a large portion of the large exports within the economy. But several obstacles from the supply side (Soesastro and Basri 2005; Basri and Patunru 2008) had already made Indonesia become less competitive and its growth of exports relatively limited.

The Domestic Economy

Many economists believe recessions in the U.S., German, and French economies have moved into the recovery phase. The IMF recently revised upward its growth forecast for OECD countries to 2.5 per cent from 2 per cent. Recent trade data, at least among East Asian economies, indicates signs of positive growth in trade. Faring well with the improvement of the global economics, the Indonesian export growth continued to improve. Futhermore, the economic growth of the third quarter of 2009 reached 3.9 per cent (q-o-q). This was obviously higher than the second quarter 2009 of 2.3 per cent (q-o-q). This indicates that the economic growth begun to accelerate in the third quarter of 2009 (see Figure 8.2). The y-o-y GDP growth recorded 4.2 per cent in the third quarter of 2009. Cumulatively, Indonesia's economic growth for the first three quarters of 2009, compared to the same period of 2008 showed an increase of 4.2 per cent (see Figure 8.3). These figures are higher compared to the estimates made by a number of research institutes, observers and business people.

The GDP data shows that Indonesia's domestic demand has been quite resilient. Economic growth continues to depend heavily on private consumption (accounted for 65 per cent of GDP) and government expenditure. The strong growth in private consumption was driven by non-food products. Several leading indicators, including cement and motor vehicle sales, reflect the ability of durable goods to boost the economy. Growth rates of other non-food items have also generally accelerated since mid-2001, owing to increases in consumer credit and wages and a decline in the prices of some goods. A recovery in consumer confidence and the inflation hedging activities of consumers may also have prompted the surge in durable goods consumption. Private consumption expanded by 4.7 per cent in the third quarter of 2009 and contributed 2.7 per cent out of 4.2 per cent growth in real GDP in that quarter (see Figures 8.4 and 8.5). Growth in government spending also started picking up since the third quarter of 2008 in response to government fiscal stimulus and spending acceleration. Private investment spending (Gross Fixed Capital Formation (GFCF)) was also expanding rapidly throughout 2008. But growth in private investment spending has weaken considerably in the first and second quarters of 2009 as the global financial meltdown affected credit line for investment and pushed up the price of risk. However, GFCF started to pick up in the third quarter of 2009. Overall, Indonesian economy remains cruising at

Muhammad Chatib Basri

FIGURE 8.2
GDP Growth (q-o-q)

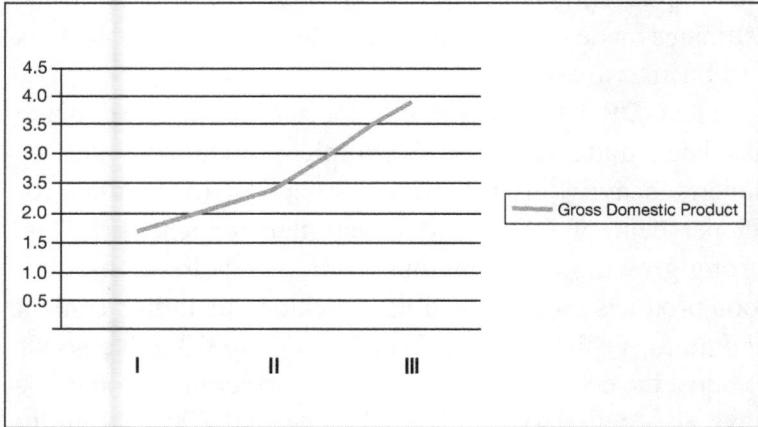

Source: Indonesia Census Bureau (BPS).

FIGURE 8.3
GDP Growth (1Q–3Q 2009)

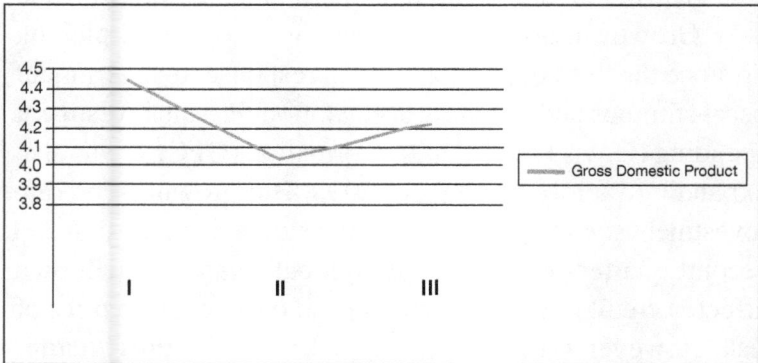

Source: Indonesia Census Bureau (BPS).

FIGURE 8.4
Private Consumption Growth (q-o-q)

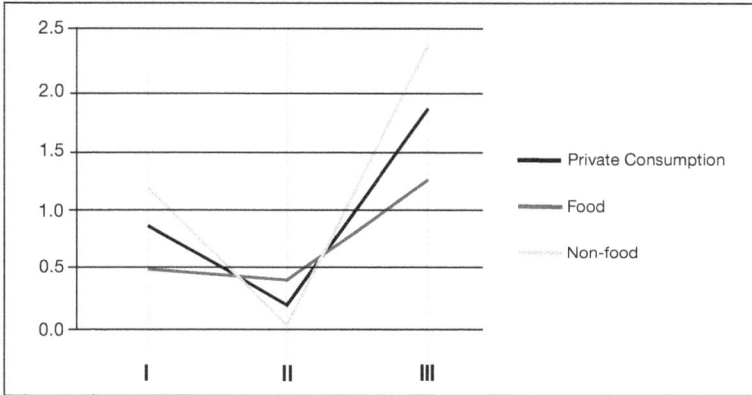

Source: Indonesia Census Bureau (BPS).

FIGURE 8.5
Investment Growth (1Q–3Q 2009)

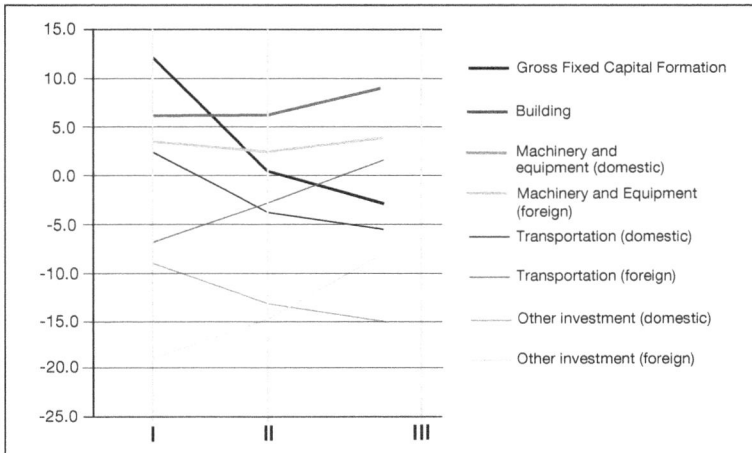

Source: Indonesia Census Bureau (BPS).

4.2 per cent growth rate in the third quarter using domestic demand engine while export engine suffers a malfunction.

From the production side, the three sectors which reached the highest growth (y-to-y) were Electricity, Gas and Water 18.2 per cent, Transportation and Communication 5.1 per cent and Agricultural Sector 2.7 per cent. These growths showed improvements in the three sectors in the second quarter. The three sectors were the non-tradable sectors. This is consistent that in the global crises the sectors much affected were the tradable sectors.

This was also a sign of how the non-tradable sector managed to relatively ride over the global economic waves. If we look into the source of growth, it could be seen that the contribution from the tradable sector was only 1.2 per cent from the total economic growth of 4.2 per cent. Meaning the contribution of the whole tradable sector towards the entire economic growth was merely less than 30 per cent. These data indicates that the source of economic growth was contributed more by the growth of the non-tradable sector such as Electricity, Gas and Water which reached a growth of 18.2 per cent, Construction Sector, Trade, Hotel and Restaurant, Transportation and Communication, and Financial, Ownership and Business Services, as well as Services Sector.

These data also suggests that the Indonesian economic growth was still dominated by the non-tradable sector. In a situation wherein the external situation is still in turmoil and undergoing problems, the big portion and the non-traded sector actually could provide cushion to lessen the impact of the ongoing global financial crises. The important lesson from this crisis is the impact of the global crisis was relatively limited due to the strong domestic demand.

Macroeconomic Progress

The macroeconomic progress continued with low inflation rate of 2.8 per cent in 2009, declining interest rate, rupiah continued to appreciate against the dollar and surging stock prices. Factors underpinning the rupiah's strength include the increase in net capital inflows created by a relatively high discrepancy between the rate of Bank Indonesia Certificate and international interest rates, the high returns of mutual funds, and global sentiment due to the depreciation of the dollar against most currencies. The strengthening of the rupiah and Indonesia's stable macroeconomic conditions has given Bank Indonesia room to lower the interest rate. Despite the relatively low BI rate, lending rates remained high. As a result, the impact of declining interest rates to the real sector has yet to emerge to any significant extent. The banking sector remains reluctant to provide lending to the real sector, where risk remains high due to uncertainties from the global crisis and some unsettling issues on the investment climate, such as labour policies, the costs of doing business and smuggling.

Difference Between 1998 and 2008 Crises

The 1998 crisis experience has been quite traumatic for all of us in Asia, and particularly in Indonesia. The important question is what made the 2008 crisis different from the

1998? By answering this question, then we can learn why Indonesian economic performance was relatively good during the 2008 crisis. We argue that there are several differences between the 1998 and the 2008 crisis (see Table 8.2).

Firstly, the origin of the crisis. In 1998, the initial debate in the country centred on the link between currency depreciation and economic fundamentals. One view suggests that Indonesia's economy was basically sound as it had been before, while others argue that Indonesia's economy was fundamentally poor or far worse than reported by the government or other bodies such as the World Bank (Soesastro and Basri 1998). Aswicahyono and Hill (2002) point out that there is no clear link between the Krugman "myth" and the current crisis. They argue that the crisis in 1997–98 had mainly to do with financial markets, exchange rates, the problem of short-term debt, capital mobility and political disturbances. We have to admit that there was a fundamental problem in the Indonesian economy in 1998, especially in the financial sector. Thus, when the financial crisis hit Thailand, the impact on the Indonesian economy was very dreadful. Thus, the 1998 crisis was home ground but not home alone. In contrast, the 2008 crisis was almost entirely external or to be more precise it was triggered by the sub-prime crisis in the United States.

Secondly, the condition of the financial sector. As pointed out by Soesastro and Basri (1998), Stiglitz and Greenwald (2003), and Fane and Macleod (2004) many banks in Indonesia were very weak. They had made bad loans. In the case of Indonesia, there was a lending boom. The loan-to-deposit ratio was more than 100 per cent in 1997, whereas the ratio of non-performing loan (NPL) to total credit was

TABLE 8.2
Policy Responses in 1998 and 2008

The 1998 Crisis	*The 2008 Crisis*
1. Monetary policy: extremely strict. Bank of Indonesia increased interest rate levels to very high levels. Deposit account interest rates reached 60 per cent in the peak crisis period. As regards liquidity, the government implemented a liquidity squeeze.	1. Monetary policy: Bank Indonesia interest rate was reduced by 300 basis points from 9.5 per cent to 6.5 per cent. Liquidity was relaxed.
2. Fiscal policy: to being with these was a budget surplus, then this was revised by permitting a large budget deficit.	2. Fiscal policy: the stimulus was implemented, the budget deficit enlargened, taxes reduced.
3. Banking health: Prudential banking regulations were extremely weak. NPLs reached 27 per cent. LDR became more than 100 per cent.	3. Banking health: Prudential banking regulations were relatively tight. NPL less than 4 per cent, LDR 77 per cent, CAR around 17 per cent.
4. Response towards banking: closure of sixteen banks, which then led to rushes.	4. Response towards banking: deposit insurance increased from Rp 100 million to Rp 2 billion per account.
5. Policies focused towards structural reform by carrying out economic liberalizations, getting rid of monopolies and licencing.	5. Safeguarded relatively open trade regime.
6. Exchange rate regime: managed floating. Economic players were not used to exchange rate risk changes and did not carry out hedging.	6. Exchange rate regime: flexible. Economic players start to become used to exchange rate risk changes.

around 27 per cent in September 1997. On the contrary, the financial situation is relatively healthier than ten years ago, the NPL was less than 4 per cent in 2008.

In addition, unlike ten years ago economic agents now have learnt how to diversify their risk. Before the Bank Indonesia abandoned the managed floating system in 1997, there was no point to hedge their asset because the Indonesian rupiah constantly depreciated by 5 per cent every year. But now the game is completely different. The economic agents have diversified their portfolio and hedged their asset. Thus, if there is a sudden reversal of capital inflows, the impact will be relatively small compared to ten years ago.

Thirdly, the policy responses. As argued by Stiglitz and Greenwald (2003), as the economy goes into a deep recession due to contractionary devaluation, many firms go into distress. The central bank responded to the crisis by raising the interest rate to a very high level. As argued by Stiglitz and Greenwald, this policy increased the probability of default and thereby increased the probability of capital outflow. In contrast, in 2008 Bank Indonesia responded to the crisis by lowering the interest rate and ensuring there was enough liquidity in the financial system. Bank Indonesia has cut the rate from 9.5 per cent in November 2008 to 6.5 per cent by the end of 2009. As a result, the probability of default was relatively low in 2008, making the impact on non-performing loans of the banking sector also relatively small.

Fourthly, the political situation. The political crisis and change of government in 1998 made the economic crisis far worse compared to 2008. The bad economic situation had already caused the political crisis and supported the change of government, and on the other hand the dynamic of the political change had already made the economic crisis worse. One factor that was different between the political situations in 1998 and 2008 was the level of confidence in the government. From the beginning, the crisis of the level of confidence in the Soeharto government had reached its lowest point. Because of this there was much pressure to carry out political reform as well as calls for democracy (Bresnan 2005; Schwarz 1999; Aswicahyono and Hill 2002).

Indonesia's experience during the Asian financial crisis in 1998 suggests that the disruption and instability in the financial sector could lead to severe crisis of confidence. At that time, Indonesia suffered from bank runs due to loss of confidence. Indonesia's experience shows that the cost of allowing such situation to happen was very much higher than the cost of preventing a loss of confidence. Based on this, Indonesia strongly supports immediate efforts to restore confidence in the financial sector.

Key areas for action include:
1. *Ensuring the existence of liquidity in the system.* The Government of Indonesia (GOI) and Bank Indonesia (BI) have taken measures to ensure liquidity.
2. *Maintaining confidence in the banking sector by providing guarantees.* The GOI and BI have increased the ceiling for the guarantee on deposits from Rp 100 million to Rp 2 billion per account. Such a move to provide guarantee needs to be coordinated internationally to avoid capital migration that could further destabilize the global financial system.
3. *Mitigating the impact of the financial crisis to the poorest segment of society* by providing social safety net.

4. *Supporting the move already taken by the United States and Europe to inject capital to the banking sector.*
5. *Other necessary steps to ensure the unlocking of the credit crunch, including for trade financing which is already beginning to affect trade flows.*
6. *Lowering the interest rate.* Unlike in 1998, Bank Indonesia responded to the crisis by lowering the interest rate. The 50 basis point cut announced in the second week of January 2009, and two more 50 basis point reductions in the first week of February and March 2009 were steps in the right direction. Bank Indonesia has cut the rate from 9.5 per cent in November 2008 to 6.5 per cent by the end of 2009. Nevertheless, as argued by Basri and Siregar (2009), despite Bank Indonesia's low interest policy, the banking sector continued to face high borrowing costs due to the agency cost problem. Banks remained unwilling to lend to each other until early 2009. Although the effectiveness of monetary policy has been limited to boost the economy, at least the low interest rate policy succeeded to reduce the probability of default of the companies, which helped to minimize the impact of the financial crisis on the real economy.
7. *Counter-cyclical policy through fiscal expansion.* In a situation where monetary transmissions are not yet fully effective because of agency cost problems, then, like it or not, the role of fiscal policies must be more dominant. This is what will in fact support consumption. The Minister for Finance has unveiled a stimulus package for 2009, worth around Rp 73.3 trillion (or around US$6.4 billion), to boost the economy amid the threat of economic downturn. The package is broken

down into three major categories, namely income tax cuts, waives of tax and import duties, and subsidies and government expenditure. In line with Keynes (1936), aiming to stimulate more spending by the household and corporate, around 60 per cent of the Indonesian fiscal stimulus has been allocated to cover cuts in income taxes. To minimize the effects of the global financial crisis, the government cuts individual income tax from 35 per cent to 30 per cent as well as corporate income tax from 30 per cent to 28 per cent. Recognizing the high dependency of the local industries (both on tradable and non-tradable sectors) on imports, as discussed earlier, around Rp 2.5 trillion would finance waives of import duties for raw materials and capital goods. This is part of over Rp 13 trillion package on tax and duties, about 18 per cent of total stimulus package, to predominantly support businesses. To help reduce the operation cost of businesses, the stimulus package also covers diesel and electricity subsidy. Last but not least, close to Rp 12.2 trillion will be allocated to support infrastructure and rural sector development. In view of the measures above, the government has committed to raise its fiscal deficit to 2.6 per cent of GDP in 2009. Nevertheless, there are a number of shortcomings in the implementation of the expansionary measures to achieve the much needed targets. It is important to note that the forecasted deficit of 2.6 per cent of GDP is partly driven by the decline in the revenue (especially tax and non-tax revenues). Only about 1.2 per cent of GDP can be considered as the real expansionary. Two main constraints limit the fiscal space for a much-higher stimulus. Furthermore, it is of interest to note that central government expenditure so far has always been far below the government target. In 2008 the budget deficit was targeted around 2.1 per cent of GDP, however, the out-turn of budget deficit was only 0.1 per cent. This seems to be caused by administrative hurdles including an introduction of a new budget authorization process as well as tighter anti-corruption measures that were aimed at making tendering process more transparent but resulted in delayed spending (Basri and Patunru 2006). The out-turn of budget in 2009 was only 1.6 per cent. This problem led us to the question of how effective the fiscal stimulus will be, given the inability of the central government to spend their money. Under these particular circumstances, we argue that it is more effective for the central government to focus the fiscal stimulus on income tax cuts and waives of tax. In fact, this is consistent with what the Indonesian Government has done i.e. 60 per cent of its fiscal stimulus has been allocated to cover cuts in income taxes. Our next question is will the tax cut be effective? The U.S. experience shows us that the fiscal stimulus through tax cut was not really effective due to three factors: the access to formal banking credits, the demographic structure and its relative high MPC (Krugman 2008; Modigliani and Brumberg 1955). Thus, instead of increasing their spending, the households in the United States responded to the tax cut by increasing their savings. We argue, however, that fiscal stimulus through tax cut to some extent can be more effective in Indonesia for three reasons: first, unlike in the United States, the household group in Indonesia holds less saving and has a limited access to formal banking credits. Hence, spending behaviours of this group are likely to be influenced more by *current* income, instead of *permanent* income (Modigliani and Brumberg 1955). Second, given the stage of development, it is more likely that the marginal propensity to consume in Indonesia is higher than in the United States. Third, as pointed out by Modigliani and Brumberg (1955) consumption behaviour may vary by stage of life. Based on this theory, consumption may be relatively high in the society which is dominated by young population compared to that with aging population. However, this argument has to be juxtaposed against the fact that the impact of fiscal stimulus on the economy may not be as large as we thought because some of the tax cut is focused on the individual income tax at the highest tax bracket, as well as corporate income tax. While it is true that by raising the non-taxable income threshold from Rp 13.2 million per year (Rp 1.1 million per month) to Rp 15.84 million per year (Rp 1.32 million per month) may induce consumption for the low income people, the number of people who have tax file numbers is relatively small.

Importance of Domestic Demand

The importance of domestic demand in insulating growth from global recession is not unique for Indonesia. We find that at least in Asia, countries that maintained or even increased their share of domestic demand in GDP were relatively in a better position to withstand the global economic downturn (see Figure 8.6). Indonesia increased its share of domestic demand in GDP to 97 per cent in 2007 from 88 per cent in 2000 and experienced a 0.22 percentage point decline in GDP growth in 2008. Bangladesh and Malaysia are examples where domestic demand had slightly declined but still could prevent their GDP from declining further. Meanwhile, India and Vietnam, both have become important exporting economies, increased their share of domestic demand and experienced relatively lower decline in GDP growth compare to other economies. The most extreme case is Singapore whose exports was 234 per cent of GDP and experienced 6.6 percentage point decline in its GDP growth in 2008.

FIGURE 8.6
Domestic Demand and Resilience from Global Crisis

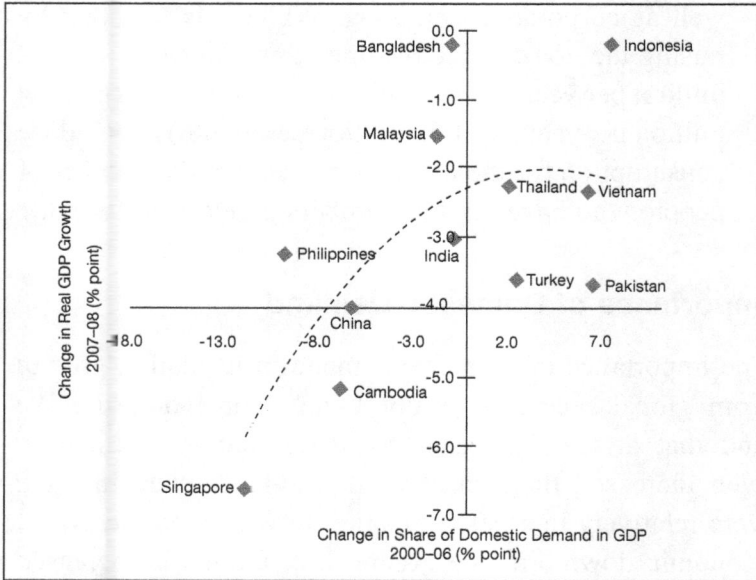

Sources: EIU, Basri and Rahardja (2009).

We now turn to investigate the impact of a shock in domestic demand *vis-à-vis* a shock in exports to path of GDP movement. What we would like to know is whether domestic demand has the capacity to sustain GDP growth as exports.

We estimate a vector autoregressive (VAR) model consisting of growth of GDP, exports, and domestic demand using quarterly data from 2000 until second quarter of 2009. The sample size is relatively short for a typical time series exercise. But extending the data to include series in 1990s could posses another problem because Indonesian census bureau (BPS) changed the base year for GDP in 1993 and later in 2000. Nominal GDP figures in series with previous base year tend to be lower than nominal GDP figures in the new base year. To date, there has not been any systematic attempt to backcast the quarterly GDP series to the early 1990s with 2000 base year. As exogenous variables, we included dummy variables that capture internal shocks such as election and reduction in oil subsidies, and external shocks such as U.S. recession in 2001 and global financial crisis in 2008 and 2009. Despite the relatively short sample, we choose VAR because its simplicity and ability to exploit the inter-relationship between those variables through feedback process (see Appendix for VAR estimation results). We also use VAR not for investigating certain parameters but for gauging the impact of shocks on the evolution path of GDP.

The regression result reveals several interesting findings. First, the statistics shows that both domestic demand and exports have noticeable impact on evolution of GDP. Separate likelihood ratio tests reject both null hypotheses that lags in exports and lags in domestic demand have no impact on subsequent sequences of GDP. Secondly, the impulse response function (IRF) of GDP i.e., sequence of impact multiplier from an exogenous shock on GDP, due to shock in exports accelerates faster in the beginning but then converges with the IRF of GDP due to domestic demand (see Figure 8.7). We use generalized impulse as introduced by Pesaran and Shin (1998) in order to ensure the result is invariant from ordering of endogenous variables in VAR. This result confirms our prior presumption that domestic demand already has the lifting power to take GDP off. Thirdly, the result from variance decomposition also suggests that shock from export explain movement in GDP more than shock on domestic demand (see Figure 8.8). This is also rather interesting because it suggests that export shock causes more variation in GDP movement compared to domestic demand shock. In sum, these exercises suggest that both exports and domestic demand are important in lifting GDP level but the former could have a stronger impact on the variation of GDP movement.

It is interesting to note that, on the contrary to most analysts, we believe trade had a significant role in propelling Indonesia's economic growth up until the global crisis. The role of exports in driving growth has been quite significant, and this explained why the economic growth declined from 6.4 per cent in the first half of 2008 to around 4 per cent in 2009. Nevertheless, since the share of export in the Indonesian economy was relatively small compared to most Asian countries, the impact of the decline of export to the Indonesian economy due the global financial crisis was relatively limited compared to other countries.

FIGURE 8.7
Impulse Response Function of GDP due to
Exports and Domestic Demand Shocks

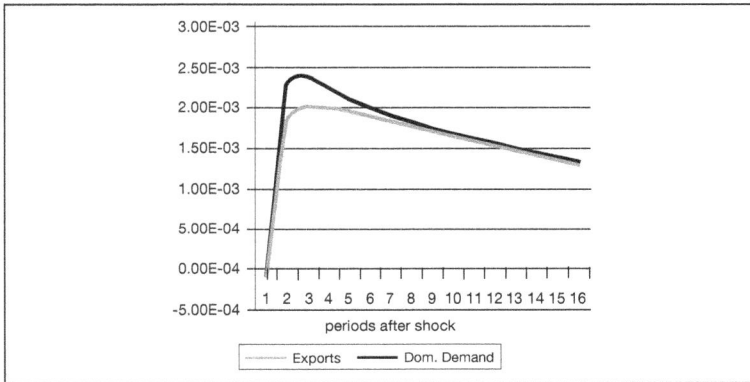

Source: Basri and Rahardja (2009).

FIGURE 8.8
Variance Decomposition of GDP due to Exports
and Domestic Demand Shocks

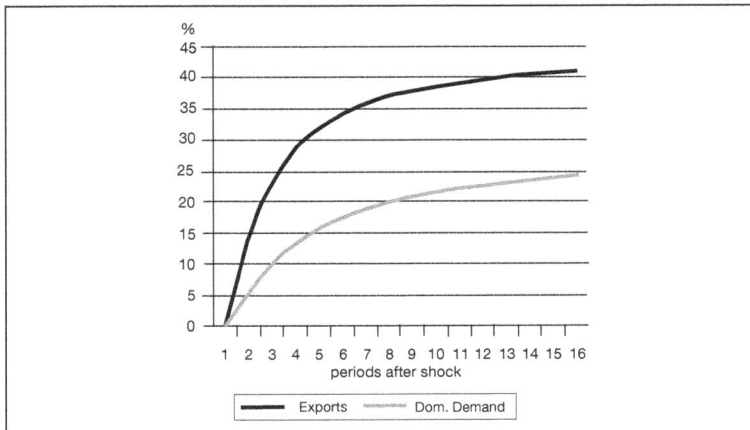

Source: Basri and Rahardja (2009).

Lesson Learnt and the Way Ahead

As had been discussed previously, one of the most important lessons from the global financial crises was to safeguard the balance between export orientation and domestic economy. The role of domestic economy, whether one likes it or not, is most important to secure economic stability and to boost economic growth. Global financial crises underscores the importance of securing some "structure" for the economy in the midst of globalization. Crisis had pointed out to us that there should be some conscious efforts to develop and secure some minimal amount of "structure" in domestic economy, if we do not want the economy to be so dependent on external shock. Indonesia's relatively small export share has already saved Indonesia from the global financial crisis.

On the other hand, this chapter indicates that exports are a source of Indonesia's economic growth. Exports have a large effect in supporting economic growth, albeit less stable compared to domestic demand. Because of this, a strategy safeguarding a balance between domestic economy and global orientation, such as becoming a part of a production network, promoting export oriented growth must become a part of the development strategy of the national economy. The implication is that there has to be a balance between business integrated with the Indonesian economy and the global economy with efforts to integrate the Indonesian economy internally.

This lead us to the question if Indonesia needs to adopt a policy of inward looking, focusing only on domestic demand, and becoming protectionist? We certainly do not believe that turning inward and becoming protectionist will serve the best interest of the country because openness has its share in accelerating Indonesia's development in the last three decades. But we do believe that it is time to pay more attention in boosting domestic demand and removing bottlenecks that prevent it from accelerating. In fact, we found many similarities on issues confronting growth in domestic demand with issues undermining Indonesia's competitiveness in the global economy.

We argue that we should focus our attention on the policy which can support both domestic market and export. Basri and Rahardja (2009) point out the importance of logistics in supporting both export and domestic markets. One of the most neglected features when conducting economic analysis on Indonesia is the fact that it is an island country. In an archipelago country such as this, the role of transaction cost, especially logistics cost are relatively higher compared to the continental countries. The reason is simple, transport cost, inventory cost, as well as inter-island shipping requirements are higher, making transaction costs higher, and in turn will cause production costs to increase. The distance between economic activities will obviously impact trade pattern. Some studies show that the logistic costs in Indonesia is relatively high (LPEM-FEUI 2005; Patunru et al. 2007).

In such condition, for a number of regions in Indonesia, logistics may be the key that will unlock the door to prosperity. In order that "trade logistics" — the capacity to integrate domestic economy and also to connect domestic economy with international markets through the transportation of goods — represents a very important factor in the economic growth potential of a country. With background such as those, we are of the opinion that Indonesia should give its first priority to the development of physical infrastructure that could integrate the domestic economy. This is most important for a country such as Indonesia. On top of those in line with the development of physical infrastructure, Indonesia must ensure that domestic "soft" infrastructure included the improvement of bureaucracy, the simplifying of investment permit process, the lowering of the cost of doing business, the certainty of the law, and the simplification of regulations must be carried out to facilitate economic activities to proceed faster.

Appendix

Estimating Vector Autoregression (VAR)

We estimate the following VAR system consisting of three variables with the following standard representation:

$$x_t = a_{10} + \sum_{j=1}^{p} \alpha_{1t} x_{it-j} + \sum_{j=1}^{p} \beta_{1t} dd_{it-j} + \sum_{j=1}^{p} Y_{1t} y_{it-j}$$

$$\sum_{j=1}^{p} \alpha_{1t} x_{it-j} + \sum_{j=1}^{p} \beta_{2t} dd_{it-j} + \sum_{j=1}^{p} Y_{2t} y_i$$

$$\sum_{j=1}^{p} \alpha_{2t} x_{it-j} + \sum_{j=1}^{p} \beta_{3t} dd_{it-j} + \sum_{j=1}^{p} Y_{3t} y_{it-}$$

Where x, dd, y, are quarterly logs of exports, domestic demand, and non-oil GDP, respectively. All of those series are seasonally adjusted before differencing. Z is a variable containing contemporaneous shocks such as removal of oil subsidies, global economic crisis, and *Ied'l Fitri* period. We assign Z equals to 1 for a negative shock and zero otherwise. Instead of differencing those series, we control common trend to preserve other co-movement relationship between those variables.

Given the length of sample, we decide whether it is possible to cut down the lags from 4 periods to 2 and then 2 periods to 1 using Likelihood Ratio Test. The final result is the following table (t-statistics are given in parentheses).

Explanatory variables:	*xt*	*ddt*	*yt*
xt-1	0.846	−0.029	0.056
	(7.790)	−(1.300)	(3.570)
ddt-1	0.823	0.603	0.194
	(1.310)	(4.730)	(2.170)
yt-1	0.219	0.610	0.277
	(0.220)	(3.050)	(1.960)
Constant	−11.288	−2.326	6.009
	−(0.945)	(0.956)	(3.510)
Z	−0.153	0.002	−0.008
	−(4.762)	(0.340)	(1.834)
TREND	−0.010	−0.003	0.007
	−(0.798)	−(1.201)	(3.771)
No. of obs		37	
Adj. R-squared	0.973	0.997	0.999
F-statistic	183.56	1,802.50	4,646.30
Log likelihood	74.0	132.9	145.9
Akaike AIC	−3.57	−6.75	−7.45
Schwarz SC	−3.22	−6.40	−7.11
Mean dependent	12.12	12.84	12.87
Log likelihood		353.42	
Akaike information criterion			−17.81
Schwarz criterion			−16.76

To investigate the short-term impact of a shock to all variables, we plot generalized impulse functions that are invariant from VAR ordering (Pesaran and Shin 1998).

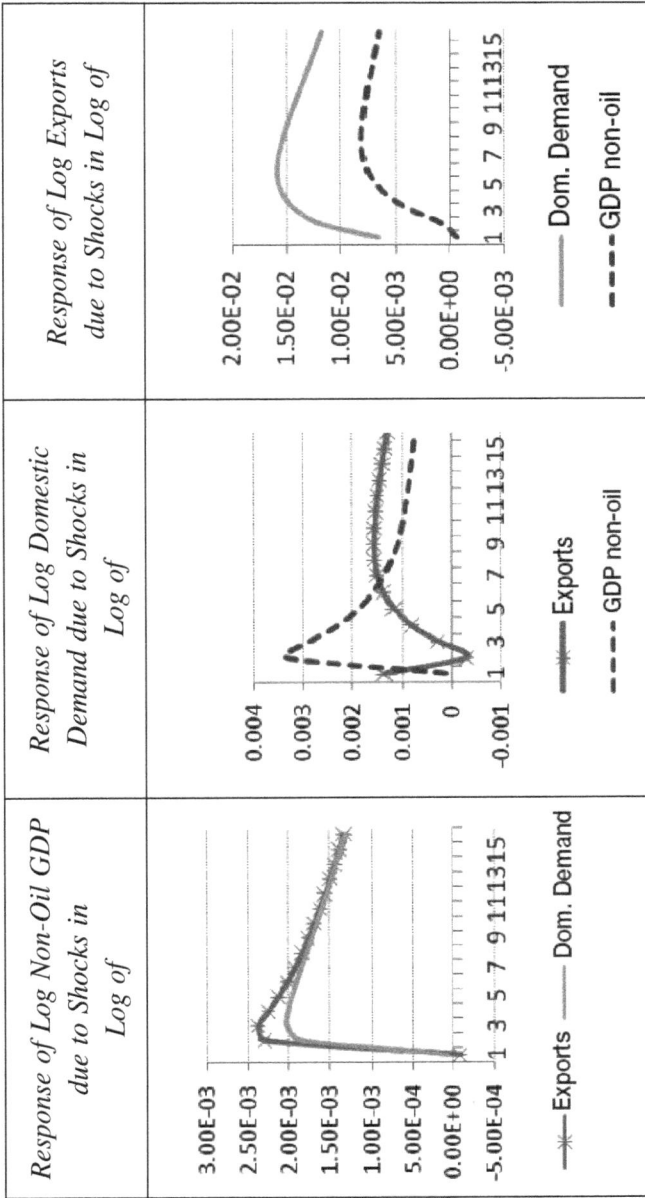

Response of Log Non-Oil GDP due to Shocks in Log of

Response of Log Domestic Demand due to Shocks in Log of

Response of Log Exports due to Shocks in Log of

Likewise, the variance decomposition results are given as follows:

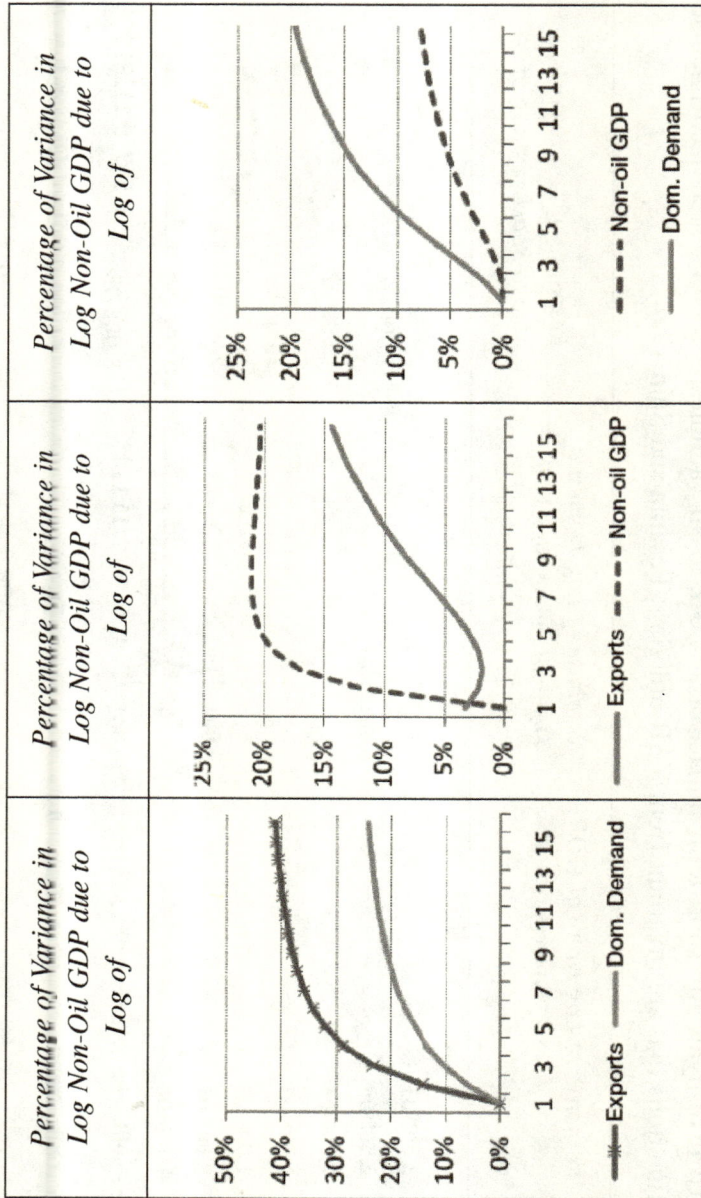

| Percentage of Variance in Log Non-Oil GDP due to Log of | Percentage of Variance in Log Non-Oil GDP due to Log of | Percentage of Variance in Log Non-Oil GDP due to Log of |

REFERENCES

Ando, Mitsuyo and F. Kimura. "Fragmentation in East Asia", 2007. <www.haveman.org/EITI07/ando.pdf>.

Aswicahyono, H and Hal Hill. "'Perspiration' versus 'Inspiration' in Asian Industrialisation: Indonesia before the Crisis". *The Journal of Development Studies* 38, no. 3 (2002): 138–63.

Basri, M. Chatib and Arianto A. Patunru. "Survey of Recent Developments". *Bulletin of Indonesian Economic Studies* 42, no. 3 (2006): 295–319.

———. "Indonesia's Supply Constraints". Background Paper prepared for OECD, 2008.

Basri, M. Chatib and Reza Y. Siregar. "Navigating Policy Responses at the National Level in the Midst of the Global Financial Crisis: The Experience of Indonesia". *Asian Economic Paper* 8, no. 3 (2009): 1–35.

Basri, M. Chatib and Sjamsu Rahardja. "Indonesia Navigating Beyond Recovery: Growth Strategy in an Archipelagic Country". Paper prepared for the OECD conference, Paris, 24 September 2009.

Bresnan, John. *Indonesia: The Great Transition*. New York: Rowman & Littlefield Publishers Inc., 2005.

Fane, George and Ross Macleod. "Banking Collapse and Restructuring in Indonesia, 1997–2001". Mimeographed. Economics Division RSPAS, Australian National University, 2004.

Gunawan, Anton H., Helmi Arman, and Anton Hendranata. "Indonesia 2009 Economic Outlook: Slowing, Not Falling". PT Bank Danamon Indonesia, Tbk., Jakarta, 7 January 2009.

IMF. "Global Economic Prospect and Economic Challenges". Unpublished report, 2009.

Keynes, John Maynard. *The General Theory of Employment, Interest and Money*. London: Macmillan, 1936.

Krugman, Paul. "Fiscal Stimulus". *New York Times*, 21 January 2003.

LPEM-FEUI. "Inefficiency in the Logistics of Export Industries: The Case of Indonesia". Report in collaboration with Japan Bank for International Cooperation (JBIC), Jakarta, 2005.

Modigliani, F. and R. Brumberg. "Utility Analysis and the Consumption Function: An Interpretation of Cross-section Data". In *Post Keynesian Economics*, edited by K. Kurihara. London: George Allen and Unwin, 1955.

Papanek, Gustav, M. Chatib Basri, and Daniel Schydlowsky. "The Impact of World Recession on Indonesia and Appropriate Policy Response: Some Lessons for Asia". Paper prepared for Asian Development Bank Report, 2009.

Patunru, A.A., N. Nurridzki, and Rivayani. "Port Competition in Indonesia". Paper prepared for Asian Development Bank Institute, 2007. Also as "Port Competitiveness: A Case Study of Semarang and Surabaya, Indonesia". In *Infrastructure's Role in Lowering Asia's Trade Costs: Building for Trade*, edited by D. Brooks and D. Hummels. Cheltenham: Edward Elgar, forthcoming.

Pesaran, Hashem H. and Yongcheol Shin. "Generalized Impulse Response Analysis in Linear Multivariate Models". *Economic Letters* 58 (1998): 17–29.

Schwarz, Adam. *A Nation in Waiting*. Sydney: Allen & Unwin, 1999.

Soesastro, H. and M.C. Basri. "Survey of Recent Developments". *Bulletin of Indonesian Economic Studies* 34, no. 1 (1998): 3–54.

———. "Political Economy of Trade Policy in Indonesia". *Asean Economic Bulletin* 22, no. 1 (2005): 3–18.

Stiglitz, J. and Bruce Greenwald. *Towards New Paradigm in Monetary Economics*. Cambridge: Cambridge University Press, 2003.

Index